Ancient Egyptian Myths and Legends

The Presentation of Ani to Osiris

From the Papyrus of Ani

Reproduced from the Facsimile by Permission of the Director of the British Museum

(page 324)

Ancient Egyptian Myths and Legends

by

LEWIS SPENCE

DOVER PUBLICATIONS, INC.
New York

This Dover edition, first published in 1990, is an unabridged republication of the work originally published in 1915 by George G. Harrap & Company, London, under the title *Myths & Legends of Ancient Egypt.* Those illustrations originally in color are reproduced here in black and white. The order and position of many of the illustrations have been altered.

Manufactured in the United States of America
Dover Publications, Inc., 31 East 2nd Street, Mineola, N.Y. 11501

Library of Congress Cataloging-in-Publication Data

Spence, Lewis, 1874–1955.
[Myths & legends of ancient Egypt]
Ancient Egyptian myths and legends / by Lewis Spence.
p. cm.
Reprint. Originally published: Myths & legends of ancient Egypt. London : G. Harrap, 1915.
Includes index.
ISBN 0-486-26525-0
1. Mythology, Egyptian. I. Title.
BL2441.S7 1990
299′.31—dc20 90-41240
CIP

PREFACE

IN this volume the religious history of ancient Egypt has been reviewed in the light of the science of modern mythology. Few Egyptologists are well informed regarding the basic laws of that science, and much misapprehension regarding the character and attributes of many of the deities worshipped in the Nile Valley in times past has thereby resulted. The statement that Egyptian religious ideas cannot be collated with barbarian and savage conceptions simply because they are Egyptian and therefore 'classic' and inviolate will no longer remain unquestioned among that section of the public accustomed to think for itself, and such pronouncements as that the animal gods of Egypt have no connexion with totemic origins will shortly assume their proper perspective.

In advancing ideas so iconoclastic—which all will remember were adumbrated by the late Mr. Andrew Lang and strongly buttressed by Sir James Frazer—it is essential that I should at the outset protect myself against any charges of lack of acquaintance with the science of Egyptology. Such a work as this, which attempts to further recent views concerning a well-worn subject, must by the very circumstances of its effort be cast and written in popular style. That such a treatment is sufficient to prejudice it in the eyes of a certain type of critic I am well aware. A long series of handbooks and articles had prepared critics for my work in this series upon Mexican and Peruvian myth, and it was generally admitted that I spoke upon these subjects out of the authority of long experience.

I find it necessary to state, then, that the study of Egyptian hieroglyphs is not new to me. For several years I laboured at these assiduously, studying the languages, Semitic and African, including Coptic, which are cognate with the Egyptian. In the study of hieroglyphic systems I was attracted toward the wonderful system of writing which prevailed among the Maya of Central America, and through it to the consideration of Mexican archæology in general. My grounding in the Egyptian language has also stood me in good stead, and if for reasons connected with the necessity for popular presentation my pages are not littered with hieroglyphs, I can lay claim to such a knowledge of Egyptian linguistic origins as can control any derivations here attempted—which, however, have not been ventured upon without the countenance of other and higher authorities. If I have differed from Egyptologists of standing in matters mythological, I have been sedulously careful not to attempt the impertinence of contradicting them in matters linguistic.

Their lifelong acquaintance with original texts gives them, of course, authority to which I gladly bow, but I feel, on the other hand, that my own close studies of mythological problems, which are as vital to the interests of the science as its linguistic and archæological sides, entitle me to advance my personal views upon such, even when these are opposed to those of authorities whose reputation in the field of Egyptology stands deservedly high.

Students of myth and Egyptology, as well as the general reader drawn to the subjects by the glamour of the mystic atmosphere which, let us hope, will ever surround them, will find that I have not hesitated to attack hypotheses concerning the character and attributes of certain deities the mythological type of which may have been regarded by many as ultimately fixed. This applies especially to my attempted reconstruction of the natures of Osiris, Isis, Thoth, and several other divinities. My remarks, too, upon totemism in Egypt may engender opposition, though I believe that the rank of the authorities I can call to my aid will succeed in disarming criticism of my arguments.

No one can rightly comprehend the trend and currents of Egyptian faith who does not possess some acquaintance with Egyptian history, manners, and customs. I have therefore provided brief synopses of these, as well as some account of Egyptian archæology. To Mr. W. G. Blaikie Murdoch, whose works and influence on modern art are well known to its more serious students, I am obliged for the greatest possible assistance and guidance in the section dealing with the art of ancient Egypt. To my assistants, Miss Mavie Jack and Miss Katherine Nixey, I am much beholden for the collection and arrangement of valuable material and for many suggestions.

L. S.

The Egyptian Symbol for the Soul (page 5)
In the British Museum

CONTENTS

LIST OF ILLUSTRATIONS

LIST OF ILLUSTRATIONS

CHAPTER I: INTRODUCTORY

THE group of beliefs which constituted what for convenience' sake is called the Egyptian religion in an existence of some thousands of years passed through nearly every phase known to the student of comparative mythology. If the theologians of ancient Egypt found it impossible to form a pantheon of deities with any hope of consistency, assigning to each god or goddess his or her proper position in the divine galaxy as ruling over a definite sphere, cosmic or psychical, it may be asked in what manner the modern mythologist is better equipped to reduce to order elements so recondite and difficult of elucidation as the mythic shapes of the divinities worshipped in the Nile Valley. But the answer is ready. The modern science of comparative religion is extending year by year, and its light is slowly but certainly becoming diffused among the dark places of the ancient faiths. By the gleam of this magic lamp, then—more wonderful than any dreamt of by the makers of Eastern fable—let us walk in the gloom of the pyramids, in the cool shadows of ruined temples, aye, through the tortuous labyrinth of the Egyptian mind itself, trusting that by virtue of the light we carry we shall succeed in unravelling to some extent the age-long enigma of this mystic land.

One of the first considerations which occur to us is that among such a concourse of gods as is presented by the Egyptian religion it would have been surprising if confusion had not arisen in the native mind concerning them. This is proved by the texts, which display in many cases much difficulty in defining the exact qualities of certain deities, their grouping and classification. The origin of this haziness is not far to seek.

The deities of the country multiplied at such an astonishing rate that whereas we find the texts of the early dynasties give us the names of some two hundred deities only, the later Theban Recension (or version) of the *Book of the Dead* supplies nearly five hundred, to which remain to be added the names of mythological beings to the number of eight hundred.

Local Gods

Another cause which made for confusion was that in every large town of Upper and Lower Egypt and its neighbourhood religion took what might almost be called a local form. Thus the great gods of the country were known by different names in each nome or province, their ritual was distinctive, and even the legends of their origin and adventures assumed a different shape. Many of the great cities, too, possessed special gods of their own, and to these were often added the attributes of one or more of the greater and more popular forms of godhead. The faith of the city that was the royal residence became the religion *par excellence* of the entire kingdom, its temple became the Mecca of all good Egyptians, and its god was, so long as these conditions obtained, the Jupiter of the Egyptian pantheon. It might have been expected that when Egypt attained a uniformity of culture, art, and nationhood, her religion, as in the case of other peoples, would also become uniform and simplified. But such a consummation was never achieved. Even foreign intercourse failed almost entirely to break down the religious conservatism of priesthood and people. Indeed, the people may be said to have proved themselves more conservative than the priests. Alterations in religious policy, differentiation in legend and hieratic texts emanated from time to time from the various colleges of priests, or from that fount of religion, the sovereign himself; but never was a change made in deference to the popular clamour unless it was a reversion to an older type. Indeed, as the dynasties advance we behold the spectacle of a theological gulf growing betwixt priests and people, the former becoming more idealistic and the latter remaining as true to the outer semblance of things, the symbolic, as of old.

The evolution of religion in ancient Egypt must have taken the same course as among other races, and any hypothesis which attempts to explain it otherwise is almost certainly doomed to non-success. Of late years many works by learned Egyptologists have been published which purport to supply a more or less wide survey of Egyptian mythology and to unravel its deeper significances. The authors of some of these works, however admirable they may be as archæologists or as translators of hieroglyphic texts, are for the most part but poorly equipped to grapple with mythological difficulties. To ensure success in mythological elucidation a special training is necessary, and a prolonged familiarity with the phenomena of early religion in its many and diverse forms is a first essential. In the work of one foreign Egyptologist of standing, for example, a candid confession is made of ignorance regarding mythological processes. He claims to present the "Egyptian religion as it appears to an unprejudiced observer who knows nothing of the modern science of religions." Another Egyptologist of the first rank writes upon the subject of totemism in the most elementary manner, and puts forward the claim that such a system never existed in the Nile valley. But these questions will be dealt with in their proper places.

Beginning with forms of the lower cultus—forms almost certainly of African origin—the older religion of Egypt persisted strongly up to the time of the Hyksos period, after which time the official religion of the country may be found in one or other form of sun-worship. That is to say, all the principal deities of the country were at some time amalgamated or identified with the central idea of a sun-god.

The Egyptian religion of the Middle and Late Kingdoms was as much a thing of philosophic invention as later Greek myth, only, so far as we have the means of judging, it was not nearly so artistic or successful. For, whereas we find numerous allusions in the texts to definite myths, we seldom find in Egyptian literature the myths themselves. Indeed, our chief repository of Egyptian religious tales is the *De Iside et Osiride* of the Greek Plutarch—an uncertain authority. It is presumed that the myths were so well known popularly that to write them down for the use of such a highly religious people as the Egyptians would have been a work of supererogation. The loss to posterity, however, is immeasurable, and, lacking a full chronicle of the deeds of the gods of Egypt, we can only grope through textual and allied matter for scraps of intelligence which, when pieced together, present anything but an appearance of solidity and comprehensiveness.

Animism

It has been admitted that the ancient Egyptians, like other early races, could not have evolved a religion unless by the usual processes of religious growth. Thus we discover, by means of numerous clues more or less strong, that they passed through the phase known as animism, or animatism.[1] This is the belief

[1] Certain forms of belief are now spoken of by some mythologists as 'pre-animistic.' But these are not as yet sufficiently well defined to permit of accurate classification. See Marett, *The Threshold of Religion*.

that practically every object in the universe surrounding man has a soul and a personality such as he himself possesses. Man at an early date of his consciousness formulated the belief in a soul, that mysterious second self which even the most debased races believe in. The phenomena of sleep, the return of consciousness after slumber, and the strange experiences of life and adventures in dreamland while asleep would force early man to the conclusion that he possessed a double or second self, and it was merely an extension of that idea which made him suppose that this secondary personality would continue to exist after death.

But what proof have we that the early dwellers in Egypt passed through this phase ? Besides the belief in a human soul, the animistic condition of mind sees in every natural object a living entity. Thus trees, rivers, winds, and animals all possess the gift of rational thought and speech. How is it possible to prove that the ancient Egyptians believed that such objects possessed conscious souls and individualities of their own ?

First as to the early Egyptian belief that man himself possessed a soul. The Egyptian symbol for the soul (the *ba*) is a man-headed bird. Now the conception of the soul as a bird is a very common one among savages and barbarians of a low order. To uncultured man the bird is always incomprehensible because of its magical power of flight, its appearance in the sky where dwell the gods, and its song, approaching speech. From the bird the savage evolves the idea of the winged spirit or god, the messenger from the heavens. Thus many supernatural beings in all mythological systems are given wings. Many American Indian tribes believe that birds are the visible spirits of the dead. The Powhatans of Virginia believed that birds received the souls of their chiefs at death, and the

Aztecs that the spirits of departed warriors took the shapes of humming-birds and flitted from flower to flower in the sunshine. The Boros of Brazil believe that the soul has the shape of a bird, and passes in that form out of the body in dream.[1] The Bilquila Indians of British Columbia conceive the soul as residing in an egg situated in the nape of the neck. If the shell cracks and the soul flies away the man must perish. A Melanesian magician was accustomed to send out his soul in the form of an eagle to find out what was happening in passing ships. Pliny states that the soul of Aristeas of Proconnesus was seen to issue from his mouth in the shape of a raven. A like belief occurs in countries so far distant from one another as Bohemia and Malaysia.

We see from these parallel examples, then, that the ancient Egyptians were not singular in figuring the soul in bird-shape. This idea partakes of the nature of animistic belief. But other and more concrete examples of this phase of religious activity occur to us. For instance, the objects found in early graves in Egypt, as elsewhere, are sometimes broken with the manifest intention of setting free their 'spirits,' doubtless to join that of their owner. Again, in the myth of Osiris we find that his coffin when at rest in Byblos became entangled in the growth of a tree—an obvious piece of folk-memory crystallizing the race reminiscence of an early form of tree-worship—a branch of animistic belief. In the texts, too, statements frequently occur which can be referred only to an early condition of animism. Thus each door in the other-world was sentient, and would open if correctly adjured. We find in chapter lxxxvi of the Papyrus of Ani the Flame of the Sun addressed as an individual, as is the ferry-boat of Ra in chapter xlii.

[1] K. von den Steinen *Unter den Naturvolker Zentral-Brasiliens* (Berlin, 1894).

"I am the knot of the Aser tree," says the dead man in the same chapter, referring to the tree which wound itself around the coffin of Osiris. All these are animistic references, and could be easily multiplied by a glance through any representative Egyptian manuscript. The practice of magic, too, in later times in the Nile Valley is to some extent merely a survival of animistic belief.

Fetishism and Totemism

Fetishism, too, bulks largely in Egyptian religious conceptions. Many of the gods are represented as carrying the fetishes from which they may have originally been derived. Thus the arrow of Neith is fetishistic (a statement which will afterwards be justified), as are the symbols of Min and other deities.

Fetishism, regarding which I have given a prolonged explanation elsewhere,[1] is a term applied to the use of objects large or small, natural or artificial, regarded as possessing consciousness, volition, and supernatural qualities—in short, a fetish object is the home of a wandering spirit which has taken up residence there. The remnants of fetishism are also to be discerned in the amulets which were worn by every Egyptian, living and dead. All amulets partake of the nature of fetishes, and the remark is often heard that good luck resides in them. That is, just as the savage believes that a powerful agency working for his good dwells in the portable fetish, so the civilized man cannot altogether discredit the idea that the object attached to his watch-chain does not possess some inherent quality of good fortune. Many of these amulets typify divinities, such as the 'buckle' sign which symbolizes the protection of Isis; the sacred eye representative of Horus; and the symbol

[1] See *Myths and Legends oj the North American Indians*, p. 87.

of the parallel fingers might perhaps recall the fetishistic necklaces of fingers found among many savage peoples.

Many Egyptologists deny that totemism entered as a force into the religion of ancient Egypt. Totemism may be defined as the recognition, exploitation, and adjustment of the imaginary mystic relationship of the individual or the tribe to the supernatural powers or spirits which surround them. Whereas the fetish is to some extent the servant of its owner, a spirit lured to dwell in a material object to do the behest of an individual or a community, the totem, whether personal or tribal, is a patron and protector and is often represented in animal or vegetable shape. The basic difference between the individual and tribal totem is still obscure, but for our present purpose it will be sufficient to deal with the latter. The most notable antagonist of the theory that some of the divinities of ancient Egypt are of totemic origin is Dr. E. A. Wallis Budge, the well-known Egyptologist. In his *Gods of the Egyptians* he says: "It now seems to be generally admitted by ethnologists that there are three main causes which have induced men to worship animals, *i.e.* they have worshipped them as animals or as the dwelling-place of gods or as representatives of tribal ancestors. There is no reason whatsoever for doubting that in neolithic times the primitive Egyptians worshipped animals as animals and as nothing more." None of the above statements approaches a definition of totemism. The theory that the totem is a tribal ancestor is now regarded as doubtful. Dr. Budge continues: "The question as to whether the Egyptians worshipped animals as representatives of tribal ancestors or 'totems' is one which has given rise to much discussion, and this is not to be wondered at, for the subject is one of difficulty. We know that many of the standards which represent the nomes of Egypt are distinguished by figures of birds and animals, *e.g.* the hawk, the bull, the hare, etc. But it is not clear whether these are intended to represent 'totems' or not. . . . The animal or bird standing on the top of a nome perch or standard is not intended for a fetish or a representative of a tribal ancestor, but for a creature which was regarded as the deity under whose protection the people of a certain tract of territory were placed, and we may assume that within the limits of that territory it was unlawful to kill or injure such animal or bird." Totems are invariably carried on banners, poles, and shields, and it is unlawful to kill them. He also states that the totemic theory "may explain certain facts connected with the animal-worship of numbers of savage and half-savage tribes in some parts of the world, but it cannot in the writer's opinion be regarded as affording an explanation of the animal-worship of the Egyptians."

Wherefore, it may be asked, was Egypt alone immune from the influence of totemism? Dr. Budge continues, by way of final refutation of the totemic theory, that on nome standards several objects besides animals were worshipped and regarded as gods, or that they became the symbols of the deities which were worshipped in them. Thus on some standards were displayed representations of hills, arrows, fish, and so forth. These objects, Dr. Budge seems to imply, cannot be fetishistic or totemic. Dr. Budge cannot, for example, find the reason why three hills were connected with a god. This does not present a mythological problem of high complexity. In many parts of the world mountain-peaks, separately or in groups, are objects of direct worship. A mountain may be worshipped because it is the abode of a god; for its own sake, as were Olympus, Sinai, and Carmel, which latterly became the high places of deities ; or because they were supposed to be the birthplaces of certain tribes. In old Peru, for example, as we are informed by the Indian writer Salcamayhua, each localized tribe or Ayllu had its own *paccarisca*, or place of origin, many of which were mountains which were addressed by the natives in the formula :

> "Thou art my birthplace,
> Thou art my life-spring,
> Guard me from evil,
> O paccarisca !"

These mountains were, of course, oracular, as those represented on the Egyptian standards would probably be. That they were worshipped as the houses of oracles and for their own sakes, and not as the home of a deity, seems to be proved in that they, rather than such a deity, are represented in the standards.

Neither can Dr. Budge decipher in a mythological sense the symbol of two arrows placed notch to notch with double barbs pointing outward. Arrows of this type are common as fetishes in several parts of the world. Among the Cheyenne Indians of the Plains the set of four sacred 'medicine' arrows constitutes the tribal palladium which they claim to have had from the beginning of the world, and which was annually utilized in tribal ceremonial as lately as 1904. They also had a rite spoken of as 'fixing' the arrows, which was undertaken by priests specially set apart as the guardians of this great fetish.[1]

But there are other and much more apparent proofs of the totemic nature of a number of the Egyptian deities. It is obvious, for example, that the cat-headed Bast, who was worshipped first in the shape of a cat,

[1] See *Handbook oj North American Indians*, article "Cheyenne."

was originally a cat totem. The crocodile was the incarnation of the god Sebek, and dwelt in a lake near Krokodilopolis. Ra and Horus are represented with the heads of hawks, and Thoth with the head of an ibis. Anubis has the head of a jackal. That some of these forms are totemic is not open to doubt. But it was a decadent totemism, in which the more primitive sentiment was focused on particular animals considered as divine, totems which had become full-fledged divinities. The Egyptians carried standards on which were represented their totemic animals precisely as the natives of the Upper Darling engrave their totem on their shields, and as several American tribes in time of war carry sticks surmounted by pieces of bark on which their animal totems are painted. An instance of protection by a totem is alluded to by Diodorus, who states that there was a tale in Egypt that one of the ancient kings had been saved from death by a crocodile. Lastly, in many of the nomes of Egypt certain animals were not eaten by the inhabitants. This is a sure indication of the existence of totemism, for the presence of which in Egypt no better proof could be adduced.

There is no reason to suppose, however, that in later times animals were not worshipped in Egypt for other than totemic reasons. The later worship of animals may have been a relic of totemism, but it is more likely to have been merely symbolic in character. Even when the attendant rites and beliefs of totemism cease to be recognized, the totem animal may retain its bestial form instead of assuming a semi-human one. There is a pony totem worshipped by a certain tribe of North American Indians which is at present in course of evolution into a full-fledged divinity, but which persists in retaining its equine form. Again, the ability of the Egyptian gods to transform themselves into animals by means of magical formulæ[1] is eloquent in many cases of their totemic origin. It has been said that not only individual animals but all the animals of a class were sacred in certain nomes. In these cases, says Wiedemann, "the animals were not honoured as gods, but rather as specially favoured by the gods." But as this is exactly what happens among peoples in the totemic stage, this contention must fall to the ground.

Creation Myths

There are several accounts in existence which deal with the Egyptian conception of the creation of the world and of man. We find a company of eight gods alluded to in the Pyramid Texts as the original makers and moulders of the universe. The god Nu and his consort Nut were deities of the firmament and the rain which proceeds therefrom. Hehu and Hehut appear to personify fire, and Kekui and Kekuit the darkness which brooded over the primeval abyss of water. Kerh and Kerhet also appear to have personified Night or Chaos. Some of these gods have the heads of frogs,[2] others those of serpents, and in this connexion we are reminded of the deities which are alluded to in the story of creation recorded in the *Popol Vuh*, the sacred book of the Kiche Indians of Guatemala, two of whom, Xpiyacoc and Xmucane, are called "the ancient serpents covered with green feathers," male and female. We find in the account of the creation story now under consideration the admixture of the germs of life enveloped in thick darkness, so well known to the student of mythology as symptomatic of creation myths all the world over. A papyrus (*c.* 312 B.C.) preserved in the British Museum contains a series of chapters of a

[1] As do many primitive supernatural beings all over the world.

[2] This is typical of many water-gods in America and Australia. See Lang, *Myth, Ritual, and Religion*, vol. i, p. 43.

magical nature, the object of which is to destroy Apepi, the fiend of darkness, and in it we find two copies of the story of creation which detail the means by which the sun came into being. In one account the god Ra says that he took upon himself the form of Khepera, the deity who was usually credited with the creative faculty. He proceeds to say that he continued to create new things out of those which he had already made, and that they went forth from his mouth. "Heaven," he says, "did not exist and earth had not come into being, and the things of the earth and creeping things had not come into existence in that place, and I raised them from out of Nu from a state of inactivity." This would imply that Khepera moulded life in the universe from the matter supplied from the watery abyss of Nu. "I found no place," says Khepera, "whereon I could stand. I worked a charm upon my own heart. I laid a foundation in Maāt. I made every form. I was one by myself. I had not emitted from myself the god Shu, and I had not spit out from myself the goddess Tefnut. There was no other being who worked with me." The word Maāt signifies law, order, or regularity, and from the allusion to working a charm upon his heart we may take it that Khepera made use of magical skill in the creative process, or it may mean, in Scriptural phraseology, that "he took thought unto himself" to make a world. The god continues that from the foundation of his heart multitudes of things came into being. But the sun, the eye of Nu, was "covered up behind Shu and Tefnut," and it was only after an indefinite period of time that these two beings, the children of Nu, were raised up from out the watery mass and brought their father's eye along with them. In this connexion we find that the sun, as an eye, has a certain affinity with water. Thus Odin pledged his eye to Mimir for a draught from the well of wisdom, and we find that sacred wells famous for the cure of blindness are often connected with legends of saints who sacrificed their own eyesight.[1] The allusion in those legends is probably to the circumstance that the sun as reflected in water has the appearance of an eye. Thus when Shu and Tefnut arose from the waters the eye of Nu followed them. Shu in this case may represent the daylight and Tefnut moisture.

Khepera then wept copiously, and from the tears which he shed sprang men and women. The god then made another eye, which in all probability was the moon. After this he created plants and herbs, reptiles and creeping things, while from Shu and Tefnut came Geb and Nut, Osiris and Isis, Set, Nephthys and Horus at a birth. These make up the company of the great gods at Heliopolis, and this is sufficient to show that the latter part of the story at least was a priestly concoction.

But there was another version, obviously an account of the creation according to the worshippers of Osiris. In the beginning of this Khepera tells us at once that he is Osiris, the cause of primeval matter. This account was merely a frank usurpation of the creation legend for the behoof of the Osirian cult. Osiris in this version states that in the beginning he was entirely alone. From the inert abyss of Nu he raised a god-soul—that is, he gave the primeval abyss a soul of its own. The myth then proceeds word for word in exactly the same manner as that which deals with the creative work of Khepera. But only so far, for we find Nu in a measure identified with Khepera, and Osiris declaring that his eye, the sun, was covered over with large bushes for a long period of years. Men are then

[1] See Gomme, *Ethnology in Folklore.*

made by a process similar to that described in the first legend. From these accounts we find that the ancient Egyptians believed that an eternal deity dwelling in a primeval abyss where he could find no foothold endowed the watery mass beneath him with a soul; that he created the earth by placing a charm upon his heart, otherwise from his own consciousness, and that it served him as a place to stand upon; that he produced the gods Shu and Tefnut, who in turn became the parents of the great company of gods; and that he dispersed the darkness by making the sun and moon out of his eyes. After these acts followed the almost insensible creation of men and women by the process of weeping, and the more sophisticated making of vegetation, reptiles, and stars. In all this we see the survival of a creation myth of a most primitive and barbarous type, which much more resembles the crude imaginings of the Red Man than any concept which might be presumed to have arisen from the consciousness of 'classic' Egypt. But it is from such unpromising material that all religious systems spring, and however strenuous the defence made in order to prove that the Egyptians differed in this respect from other races, that defence is bound in no prolonged time to be battered down by the ruthless artillery of fact.

We have references to other deities in the Pyramid Texts, some of whom appear to be nameless. For example, in the text of Pepi I we find homage rendered to one who has four faces and who brings the storm. This would seem to be a god of wind and rain, whose countenances are set toward the four points of the compass, whence come the four winds. Indeed, the context proves this when it says: "Thou hast taken thy spear which is dear to thee, thy pointed weapon which thrusteth down river-banks with double point like the darts of Ra and a double haft like the claws of the goddess Maftet."

The 'Companies' of the Gods

In the Pyramid Texts we find frequent mention of several groups consisting of nine gods each. One of these companies of gods, or Enneads, was called the Great and another the Little, and the nine gods of Horus are also alluded to. It is not known, however, whether this group is in any way connected with either of the others. We also read in the Pyramid Texts of Teta of a double group of eighteen gods which recur in the text of Pepi I. These eighteen gods may simply be the Great and Little companies of gods taken together. In the texts of Pepi I and Teta, however, we find a third company of nine gods, officially recognized by the priests of Heliopolis, and all three companies are represented by twenty-seven symbols representing the word *neter* (god) placed in a row.

Although these companies of gods are spoken of as containing nine deities, that is owing to their designation of *Pesedt*, which signifies 'nine.' The Little company in reality contains eleven gods, but nine was their original number, and, as Sir Gaston Maspero says, each of them, especially the first and last, could be developed. A local company such as that of Heliopolis might have the god of another nome or district embraced in it in one of two ways; that is, the alien god might replace one of the local gods or be set side by side with him. Again, strange gods could be absorbed in the leader of the *Pesedt*. When a fresh god was admitted into a company all the other deities who were connected with him were also included, but their names were not classed beside those of its original members.

These three companies of gods were fully developed

by the period of the Fifth Dynasty, and there is little doubt that the Egyptian theology owed the formation of this pantheon to the caste of priests ruling at Heliopolis.

To the third *Pesedt* they gave no name. The gods of the first company are Tem, Shu, Tefnut, Qeb, Nut, Osiris, Isis, Set, Nephthys. Occasionally Horus is given as the chief of the company instead of Tem. In the text of Unas we find the names of the gods of the Little company given, but they are for the most part quite unimportant. The third company is rarely mentioned, and the names of its gods are unknown. Earth as well as heaven and the underworld had its quota of deities, and it is considered highly probable that the three companies of gods are referable one to each of these regions. The members of each company varied in different periods and in different cities. But the great local god or goddess was always the head of the company in a given vicinity. As has been said, he might be joined to another deity. At Heliopolis, for example, where the chief local god was Tem, the priests joined to his name that of Ra, and addressed him in prayer as Ra-Tem. Texts of all periods show that the chief local gods of many cities retained their pre-eminence almost to the end. The land of Egypt was divided into provinces called *hesput*, to which the Greeks gave the name of *nome*. In each of these a certain god or group of gods held sway, the variation being caused by racial and other considerations. To the people of each nome their god was the deity *par excellence*, and in early times it is plain that the worship of each province amounted almost to a separate religion. This division of the country must have taken place at an early epoch, and it certainly contributed greatly to the conservation of religious differences. The nome gods certainly date from pre-dynastic times, as is proved by inscriptions antedating the Pyramid Texts. The number of these provinces varied from one period to another, but the average seems to have been between thirty-five and forty. It would serve no purpose to enumerate the gods of the various nomes in this place, as many of them are obscure, but as each deity is dealt with the nome to which he belongs will be mentioned. Several nomes worshipped the same god. For example, Horus was worshipped in not less than six, while in three provinces Khnemu was worshipped, and Hathor in six.

The Egyptian Idea of God

The word by which the Egyptians implied deity and, indeed, supernatural beings of any description was *neter*. The hieroglyphic which represents this idea is described by most Egyptologists as resembling an axe-head let into a long wooden handle. Some archæologists have attempted to show that the figure resembled in outline a roll of yellow cloth, the lower part bound or laced over, the upper part appearing as a flap at the top, probably for unwinding. It has been thought possible that the object represents a fetish—for instance, a bone carefully wound round with cloth, and not the cloth alone.

We are ignorant ot most of the gods worshipped during the first four dynasties, chiefly because of the lack of documentary evidence, although some are known from the inscription called the Palermo Stone, which alludes to several local deities. Some portions of the *Book of the Dead* may have been revised during the First Dynasty, and from this we may argue that the religion of the Egyptians, as revealed in the later texts, closely resembled that in existence during the first three dynasties. It is only when we come to the Fifth and Sixth Dynasties that we discover material for the study of the Egyptian pantheon in the Pyramid Texts of Unas, Teta, Pepi the First, and others. By this period the first phase of Egyptian development appears to have been entered upon. At the same time it is plain that the material afforded by the Pyramid Texts contains stratum upon stratum of religious thought and conception, in all probability bequeathed to the pyramid builders by innumerable generations of men. In these wondrous texts we find crystallized examples of the most primitive and barbarous religious elements —animistic, fetishistic, and totemic. These texts are for the most part funerary and, in consequence, relate chiefly to deities of the underworld.

Deities of the Pyramid Texts

In order to understand this earliest fixed phase of religious thought in Egypt, it is necessary to pass in brief review the deities alluded to in the Pyramid Texts, and for the moment to regard them separately from the rest of the Egyptian pantheon. In doing so we must beware of definitely labelling these conceptions with such names as 'water-god,' 'thunder-god,' 'sun-god,' and so forth. Despite the labours of the last half-century, the science of mythology is yet in its infancy, and workers in its sphere are now beginning to suspect that mere variants or phases of certain deities, which are by no means separate entities, have in many cases been credited with an individual status they do not deserve. The deities of the Greek and Roman pantheons are doubtless good examples of gods whose attributes are finally fixed. Thus one may say of Mars that he is a war-god, and of Pallas Athene that she is a goddess of wisdom, but these were merely the attributes possessed by these deities which were most popular and uppermost in the public consciousness. Recent research has proved that most of the Greek and Roman deities are traceable to earlier forms, some of which possess a variety of attributes, others of which are more simple in form than the later conception which is developed from them. Again, many deities which exhibit some particular tendency are necessarily connected with other natural forms. Thus many rain gods or goddesses are connected with thunder and lightning. Possession of the lightning arrow frequently implies a connexion with hunting or war. All moon-gods are deities of moisture, and preside over birth. Some deities of rain preside also over the winds, thunder and lightning, the chase and war, general culture, and so forth. A sun-god, as lord of the vault of heaven, can preside over all the meteorological manifestations thereof. He is god of growth, of wealth, because gold possesses the yellow colour of his beams, of travelling, because he walks the heavens, and he rules countless other departments of existence. From polytheism may evolve in time a condition of monotheism, in which one god holds complete sway over mankind—that is, one deity may become so popular, or the priestly caste connected with him so powerful, that all other cults languish as his spreads and grows. But, on the other hand, polytheism, or the multiplicity of deities, may well spring from an early monotheism,[1] itself the child of a successful fetish or totem, for the attributes of a great single god may, in the hands of a people still partially in the animistic stage, become so infused with individuality as to appear entirely separate entities. In dealing, then, with the

[1] See Lang, *The Making of Religion* and *The New Mythology*, for hypothesis of a monotheism prior to animistic belief.

gods alluded to in the Pyramid Texts, several of which are obviously derivative, we must recollect that although in a manner it is necessary to affix to them some more or less definite description, it will be well to bear in mind the substance of this paragraph.

We are not at present finally considering the natures or characteristics of the deities mentioned in the Pyramid Texts, but merely affording such a brief outline of them as will give the reader some idea of Egyptian religion in general during the early dynasties.

The goddess Net, or Neith, who is mentioned in the Pyramid Texts of Unas, is a figure in which we descry a personification of moisture or rain, because of her possession of the arrow, the symbol of lightning. The hawk-headed Horus, probably originally a hawk totem, is one of the manifestations of the sun-deity, from whom he may have evolved, or with whom he may have been confounded. Khepera, also found in the Unas Texts, is another form of the sun. His possession of the beetle glyph is symbolical of the manner in which the sun rolls over the face of the sky as the Egyptian beetle or scarabæus rolled its eggs over the sand. Khnemu, the ram-headed, whose name signifies 'the moulder' or 'uniter,' was probably the totemic deity of an immigrant race who had achieved godhead, and perhaps monotheism, or at least creatorship, in another sphere, and who had been accepted into Egyptian belief with all his attributes. Sebek, the crocodile-god, Ra and Ptah, two other forms of the sun-god, Nu, the watery mass of heaven, are also alluded to in the Pyramid Texts of Unas and Teta, as is Hathor.

Early Burials

Egyptian religious tenets carefully fostered the idea of the preservation of the human body after death. In the earliest period the burials of the time throw much light on the nature of religious belief. The corpse was buried in such a posture that it would appear to have been doubled up prior to interment. The knees touch the chin, and the hands are disposed in front of the face. The head was turned to the west. In later prehistoric times the body was often closely bound with wrappings which were so tightly drawn as to force all the bones parallel with each other. Later still, a less contracted attitude was adopted, which in turn gave way to a fully extended position. In the late prehistoric period the corpse is found wrapped in linen cloths. It was surrounded with articles provided for its use, nourishment, or defence in the other-world, or perhaps for that of its *ka*, or double-stone vessels containing beer, unguents of various kinds, flint knives and spear-heads, necklaces and other objects of daily use which the deceased had employed during life. Amulets were placed upon the corpse to protect it against evil spirits both in this world and in the life beyond.

In the Old Kingdom, which may be designated the Pyramid Age, we find a new description of burial coming into fashion. Mummification of a simple kind became the vogue. There is good reason to suppose that this custom arose out of the cult of Osiris, the god of the dead, and it powerfully influenced all future Egyptian funerary and theological practice and thought. But between what may be conveniently described as the 'prehistoric' period and that of the Pyramids several other types of tomb had found popularity. The Pharaoh, during the First Dynasty, was buried in a large rectangular building of brick, which had several chambers inaccessible from outside. In one of these the body of the king was laid, and in the others a variety of offerings and utensils were stored. The whole was merely an elaboration of the prehistoric method of sepulture. The exterior of the tomb was broken up by niches in the form of doors, through which it was thought the *ka* of the dead king would be able to leave and re-enter his tomb at will. Round the whole a wall was built, and fresh offerings to the deceased royalty were placed within the niches or alcoves of the tomb from time to time, and over all a mound of earth or brick was probably heaped. The name-stele of the monarch was blazoned in hieroglyphs on a large memorial slab outside, without any allusion to his life, character, or actions. Several of the early royal burial-places contain the graves of women, servants, and dogs. These in true Neolithic fashion had been slaughtered at the grave of the Pharaoh in order that they might accompany him and attend to his comfort and requirements in the new life. Later these sacrifices were discontinued, and instead of a graveside holocaust the images or pictures of wives and dependents were placed in the royal tomb.

The Pyramid

From such a resting-place was gradually evolved the stupendous conception of the pyramid. The pyramid is, in effect, nothing but a vast funeral cairn, a huge grave-mound, on which, instead of stones or pieces of rock, enormous blocks of granite were piled. Often the burial-chamber it contains is nothing than a mere vault, to which access is gained by a narrow passage or gallery, which was carefully blocked up after the royal funeral.

Originally these burial-chambers were quite unadorned, and it was not until the end of the Middle Kingdom that it became usual to inscribe their walls with texts relating to the future life. Thus originated those wonderful Pyramid Texts from which we have learned so much of the lore of ancient Egypt. On the eastern side of the pyramid was built a temple dedicated to the defunct monarch, in which offerings to his manes were duly and punctually made. As he became deified upon death, so his statue in his character of a divinity was placed in an apartment specially prepared for it. The pile of stones proper from which the pyramid was evolved may be traced to the retaining wall of the tomb. By the Third Dynasty this small retaining wall had become roofed over and expanded into a solid mass of brickwork, called by the Arabs a *mastaba*, which was practically a truncated pyramid. This pile of brickwork was later in the same dynasty copied in stone, as at Saqqara, and enlarged by repeated additions and successive coats of masonry. Lastly, the whole received a casing of limestone blocks, and we have such a structure as the pyramid of Medum.

Pyramidal Architecture

The pyramidal form of architecture is peculiar to Egypt, and even there is confined to the period from the Fourth to the Twelfth Dynasty, or before 3000 B.C. The Mexican and Central American teocalli, or stepped temple, has frequently been erroneously compared to the pyramid, but whereas it was a place of worship, the Egyptian form was purely a place of sepulture. A definite design lay behind each of these vast structures. It seems to have occurred to some writers that the pyramids were built haphazard and by dint of brute force. So far from this being the case, they were constructed with extraordinary care, and mathematical computations of considerable complexity are manifest in their design.

The early pyramids were composed of horizontal layers of rough-hewn blocks of stone, held together principally by their own weight, but between the interstices of which mortar was placed. In the later stages of the type the core of the structure was formed chiefly of rubble, of which stone, mud, and mud bricks were the principal constituents. This was faced outwardly with a fine casing of stone, carefully dressed and joined, and the mortuary-chambers showed similar care in construction. These were generally placed below the ground level, and access was gained to them by a gallery opening on the northern side of the pyramid. These are usually blocked once or more by massive monoliths, and were sometimes closed externally by stone doors revolving on a pivot in order that the priests might gain entrance when desired.

The first pyramid has been definitely attributed to Cheops or Khufu, and is situated at Gizeh. The second is credited to Dad-ef-ra, and was built at Abu Roash. Khafra was entombed in the second pyramid of Gizeh, and that known as 'the Upper' at the same place was tenanted by the corpse of Menkaura. The smaller structures at Gizeh near the great and third pyramids were constructed for the families of Khufu and Khafra.

'Lost' Pyramids

Several of the pyramids alluded to in the ancient texts of these buildings have either entirely disappeared, or cannot be identified. Thus the burial-place of Shepseskaf, known by the delightful title of 'the Cool,' is unknown. We can picture the shaven priests stealing into the recesses of its thickly shadowed galleries to shelter from the fierce Egyptian sun. No doubt the *ka* of Shepseskaf found its shade acceptable enough as he played at draughts with his mummy in its inaccessible chambers. It is known that the pyramid of Menkauhor, 'the most divine edifice,' is somewhere at Saqqara, but which of its stately piles can be attributed to him it is impossible to say. So with the pyramid of Assa, who is mentioned in tablets at Saqqara, Karnak, and elsewhere. This was called 'the Beautiful.' Neither can the similarly named 'beautiful rising' of Rameses and the 'firm life' of Neferarkara be satisfactorily placed. It is highly unlikely that these structures can have crumbled into a ruin so complete that no trace whatsoever has been left of them—that is, unless they were built of mud bricks. The brick pyramid of Amenemhat III at Howara, however, still remains, as does that of Senusert III at Dahshur.

So much has been written of late concerning the pyramids that it would be idle to pursue the subject further in a work such as this, which professes to give an account of the mythology of Egypt and an outline only of its polity and arts. There can be little interest for the general reader in mere measurements and records of bulk.

Mummification

Mummification was, as has been said, probably an invention of the Osirian cult. The priests of Osiris taught that the body of man was a sacred thing and not to be abandoned to the beasts of the desert, because from it would spring the effulgent and regenerated envelope of the purified spirit. In prehistoric times some attempt appears to have been made toward preservation, either by drying in the sun or smearing the corpse with a resinous preparation; and as the centuries went by this primitive treatment developed into

The Pyramids at Gizeh

(page 25)

Photo Bonfils

(page 29)

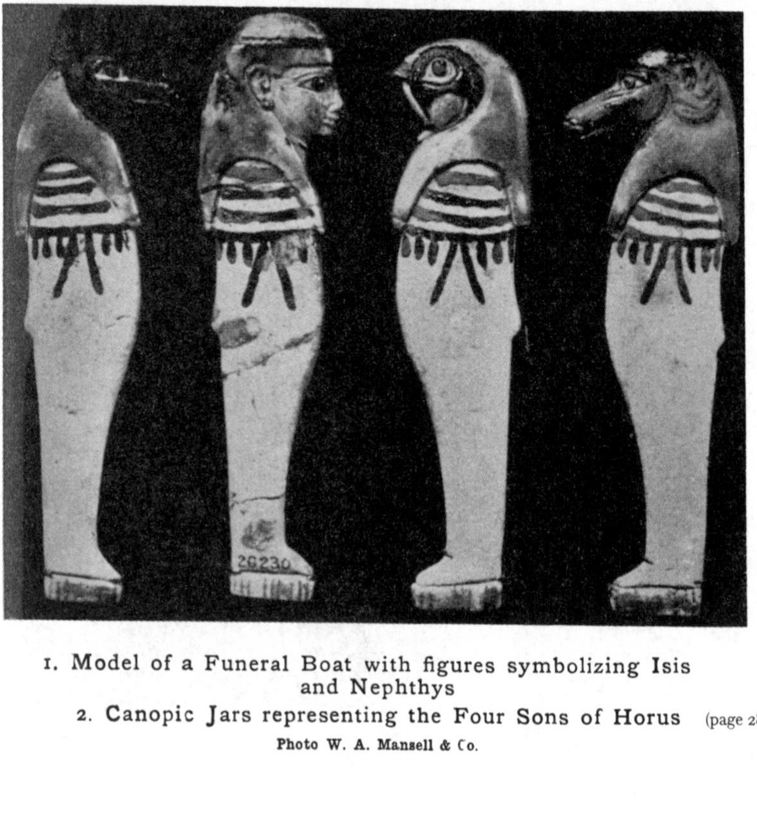

1. Model of a Funeral Boat with figures symbolizing Isis and Nephthys

2. Canopic Jars representing the Four Sons of Horus (page 28)

Photo W. A. Mansell & Co.

the elaborate art of embalming, with all its gloomy, if picturesque, ceremonial. By the time of the Middle Kingdom, as is evidenced by the graves of Beni Hassan, the practice prevailed of removing the internal organs and placing them in a box divided into four compartments inscribed with the names of the four canopic deities who presided over them. In some burials of this date, to avoid the trouble of removing the intestines those responsible for the obsequies simply made up parcels which purported, by written descriptions upon them, to contain the organs in question, believing, doubtless, that the written statement that these bundles contained the heart, lungs, and so forth was magically efficacious, and quite as satisfactory as their real presence within the receptacle.

We do not find the process of mummification reaching any degree of elaboration until the period of the New Kingdom. At first it was confined to the Pharaohs alone, who were identified with Osiris ; but the necessity for a retinue which would attend him in the dark halls of the Tuat prescribed that his courtiers also should be embalmed. The custom was taken up by the wealthy, and filtered down from rank to rank until at length even the corpse of the poorest Egyptian was at least subjected to a process of pickling in a bath of natron. The art reached its height in the Twenty-first Dynasty. At that period the process was costly in the extreme, and a mummification of an elaborate kind cost about £700 in modern currency. When the relations of the deceased consulted the professional embalmers they were shown models of mummies, one of which they selected. The corpse was then placed in the hands of the embalmers. First of all they injected a corrosive into the brain cavity, after which its softened contents were removed through the nostrils by hooked instruments. A mummifier, whose office rendered him almost a pariah, so sacred was the human body considered, made an incision in the corpse with a flint knife, a time-honoured instrument that seems eloquent of prehistoric practice. The intestines and the principal organs were then removed, washed, and steeped in palm wine. The body then underwent a drying process, and, according to the period, was stripped of its flesh, only the skin remaining, or was stuffed with sawdust, skilfully introduced through incisions, so that the natural form was completely restored. The cavity occupied by the organs might otherwise be stuffed with myrrh, cassia, or other spices. When sewn up the corpse was next pickled in a bath of natron for seventy days, and then meticulously bandaged with linen which had been dipped in some adhesive substance. A coffin was built for it which retained the shape of the human form, and which was gaily and elaborately painted with figures of divinities, amulets, symbols, and sometimes burial scenes. The carven countenance of the deceased surmounted this funerary finery, and the short wig, typical of the living Egyptian, glowed in gilded hues or in less costly colour above the conventional death-mask, which in general bore but little resemblance to him.

The canopic jars in which the intestines were placed had lids so carven as to resemble human heads, but subsequent to the Eighteenth Dynasty the heads of the four sons of Horus, the man-headed Mesti, the ape-headed Hapi, the jackal Tuamutef, and the falcon Qebhsennŭf, the 'genii' who guarded the north, south, east, and west, were represented upon their covers. In their respective jars were placed the stomach and larger intestines, the smaller intestines, the lungs and heart, and the liver and gall-bladder. These jars were placed in the tomb beside the mummy, so that upon resurrection it could easily command their contents. It is a striking circumstance that we discover a parallel to these 'genii' among the ancient Maya of Central America, who possessed four deities placed one at each point of the compass to uphold the heavens. Their names were Kan, Muluc, Ix, and Cauac, or, according to other authorities, Hobnil, Kanzicnal, Zaczini, and Hozanek, and it has been stated that the Maya made use of funerary jars called after these, *bacabs*, which held the internal organs of their dead.[1] Strangely enough, the ancient Mexicans also practised a description of mummification, as did the Peruvians.[2]

Funeral Offerings

The tomb furniture of the Egyptians of the higher ranks was elaborate and costly—chairs, jars, weapons, mirrors, sometimes even chariots, and wigs. Beginning with the Middle Kingdom (Eighteenth Dynasty), small statuettes, called *ushabtiu*, were placed in each tomb. These represented various trades, and were supposed to assist or serve the deceased in the otherworld. The walls of the tomb and the sides of the sarcophagus were usually covered with texts from the *Book of the Dead*, or formulæ devoting offerings of loaves, geese, beer, and other provisions to the *ka* of the deceased. The burial ceremony was stately and imposing. Sometimes it chanced that the corpse had to be conveyed by water, and gaily painted boats held the funeral procession ; or else the chain of mourners moved slowly along by the western bank of the Nile. The ceremonial

[1] H. de Charencey, *Le Mythe de Votan*, p. 39. There is but little substantiation for the latter part of this statement, however. The *bacabs* were closely identified with the Maya *chac*, or rain-gods.

[2] See my *Myths of Mexico and Peru*.

at the tomb appears to have been almost of a theatrical character, and symbolized the night journey of Ra-Osiris. The prescribed prayers were recited, and incense was offered up. The kinsmen of the deceased were loud in their lamentations, and were assisted in these by a professional class of mourners who 'keened' loudly and shrilly as the procession slowly approached the *mastaba*, or tomb, in which the mummy was to be laid to rest. It was taken from the coffin when it arrived at the door of its long home, and was placed upright against the wall of the *mastaba* by a priest wearing the mask of the jackal-headed god Anubis. At this point an elaborate ceremony was performed, known as the 'opening of the mouth.' With many magical spells and signs the mouth of the deceased was opened by means of a hook, after which he was supposed to be able to make use of his mouth for the purpose of speaking, eating, or drinking. Special literature had sprung up in connexion with this custom, and was known as *The Book of the Opening of the Mouth*. Elaborate and numerous were the instruments employed in the ceremony: the *pesh-ken*, or hook, made of a pinkish flint, the knife of greyish-green stone, the vases, small stone knives representing the 'metal of the north' and the 'metal of the south,' the unguents and oils, and so on. Interminable was the ceremonial in the case of a person of importance, at least twenty-eight formulæ having to be recited, many of which were accompanied by lustration, purification, and, on the part of the priests who officiated, a change of costume. The coffin containing the mummy was then lowered into the tomb by means of a long rope, and was received by the grave-diggers.

THE KA AND THE BA

The Ka

The dead man was practically at the mercy of the living for subsistence in the otherworld. Unless his kinsmen continued their offerings to him he was indeed in bad case, for his *ka* would starve. This *ka* was his double, and came into the world at the same time as himself. It must be sharply distinguished from the *ba*, or soul, which usually took the form of a bird after the death of its owner, and, indeed, was capable of assuming such shape as it chose if the funeral ceremonies were carried out correctly. Some Egyptologists consider the *ka* to be the special active force which imbues the human being with life, and it may be equivalent to the Hebrew expression 'spirit' as apart from 'soul.' In the book of Genesis we are informed that God breathed the breath of life into man and he lived. In like manner did He lay His arms behind the primeval gods, and forthwith His *ka* went up over them, and they lived. When the man died his *ka* quitted the body, but did not cease to take an interest in it, and on occasion even reanimated it. It was on behalf of the *ka* that Egyptian tombs were so well furnished with food and drink, and the necessities, not to say the luxuries, of existence.

The Ba

The *ba*, as has been mentioned, did not remain with the body, but took wing after death. Among primitive peoples—the aborigines of America, for instance—the soul is frequently regarded as possessing the form and attributes of a bird. The ability of the bird to make passage for itself across the great ocean of air, the incomprehensibility of its gift of flight, the mystery of its song, its connexion with 'heaven,' render it a being at once strange and enviable. Such freedom, argues primitive man, must have the liberated soul, untrammelled by the hindering flesh. So, too, must gods and spirits be winged, and such, he hopes, will be his own condition when he has shaken off the mortal coil and rises on pinions to the heavenly mansions. Thus the Bororos of Brazil believe that the soul possesses the form of a bird. The Bilquila Indians of British Columbia think that the soul dwells in an egg in the nape of the neck, and that upon death this egg is hatched and the enclosed bird takes flight. In Bohemian folk-lore we learn that the soul is popularly conceived as a white bird. The Malays and the Battas of Sumatra also depict the immortal part of man in bird-shape, as do the Javanese and Borneans. Thus we see that the Egyptian concept is paralleled in many a distant land. But nowhere do we find the belief so strong or so persistent over a prolonged period of time as in the valley of the Nile.

No race conferred so much importance and dignity upon the cult of the dead as the Egyptian. It is no exaggeration to say that the life of the Egyptian of the cultured class was one prolonged preparation for death. It is probable, however, that he was, through force of custom and environment, unaware of the circumstance. It is dangerous to indulge in a universal assertion with reference to an entire nation. But if any people ever regarded life as a mere academy of preparation for eternity, it was the mysterious and fascinating race whose vast remains litter the banks of the world's most ancient river, and frown upon the less majestic undertakings of a civilization which has usurped the theatre of their myriad wondrous deeds.

CHAPTER II: EXPLORATION, HISTORY, AND CUSTOMS

The Nile Valley

THE River Nile is the element which creates the special characteristics of Egypt, and differentiates it from other parts of the Sahara Desert. At its annual overflow this river deposits a rich sediment, which makes the fertile plains on either side such a contrast to the brown monotony of the desert. East and west of the Nile valley stretch great wastes, broken here and there by green oases, and the general scenery is too uniform to be interesting, the Delta itself presenting a richly cultivated level plain, interspersed by the lofty dark brown mounds of ancient cities and villages set in groves of palm-trees.

In Upper Egypt the Nile valley is narrow, and is bounded by mountains inconsiderable in height, and which never rise into peaks. Sometimes they approach the river in the form of promontories, and sometimes are divided by the beds of ancient watercourses. These are sufficiently picturesque, but otherwise the landscape is not striking. In colour, however, it is remarkably so. "The bright green of the fields, the reddish brown or dull green of the great river contrasting with the bare yellow rocks seen beneath a brilliant sun and deep blue sky, present views of great beauty."

Racial Origin

The question of the racial origin of the people of ancient Egypt is one of great complexity. In graves and early cultural remains we find traces of several races which at remote periods entered the country, and concerning whom the data are so scanty that it is highly dangerous to generalize about them. According to

Professor Sergi of Rome, the originator of the theory that a great civilizing stock arose at an early period on the southern shores of the Mediterranean, the ancient Egyptian belonged to the eastern branch of this race, along with the Nubians, Abyssinians, Galla, Masai, and Somali. The evidence of language is vague, for in this, as in other instances, it may only be cultural.

Another theory is that which would people the Nile valley in early times with a pygmy race, who were dispossessed and driven out by the immigrant Mediterraneans. The theory that the Mediterranean people entered Egypt directly from their original home does not agree with that which would make a stone-working race populating the country at an early period emanate from Palestine. It would appear from a consideration of the data that these were Mediterraneans who had had long practice in working in stone in a country abounding in that material. These were probably followed by successive immigrations from the east and from Arabia or its neighbourhood, whence came a people cognate with the Babylonians and conversant with their culture, which they had absorbed in a common early home which cannot now be located. These imposed their Semitic vocabulary upon the Hamitic syntax of the people they found in the Nile valley. But although they revolutionized the language, they only partially succeeded in altering the religion, which remained for the most part of the Osirian type, blending later with the Horus hawk-worship of the new-comers. There are not wanting those who think that these immigrants from Arabia were Hamites, who attained to a high civilization in Western Arabia, and, pressed on by Semitic hordes from the north, crossed the Red Sea in vessels and made their first base in Egypt at Berenice. The dynastic Egyptians, according to this view, are Hamitic, and not far removed in physical type from the Galla of to-day, but had, perhaps, some element of the proto-Semitic.[1] They are thought "to have concentrated themselves in the narrow strip of fertility along the banks of the Nile." It would indeed be difficult to discern where else they could have concentrated themselves.

The dynastic history of ancient Egypt extends, at the lowest computation, over a period of more than three thousand years. In view of chronological difficulties, it has been found convenient to adopt the dynastic system of reckoning chosen by Manetho, an Egyptian priest who lived in the third century before Christ. Manetho divided the history of Egypt into thirty-one dynasties, of which some twenty-six comprise the period between Mena's Conquest and the Persian Conquest, while the others cover the period of Persian, Hellenic, and Latin supremacy. With the Persian Conquest, however, came the disintegration of the Egyptian Empire, and at that point purely native history comes to an end.

Though Manetho's dynastic divisions have been adopted by modern Egyptologists, his chronology is not so well received, though it is supported by at least one distinguished authority—Professor Flinders Petrie. The general tendency at the present day is to accept the minimum chronology which is known as that of the Berlin School, which places Mena's Conquest at 3400 B.C. and the Twelfth Dynasty about 2000 B.C., rather than that of Professor Petrie, which would place these events at 5500 B.C. and 3400 B.C. respectively. It is customary to group the various dynasties into three

[1] See Seligmann, *Journal of the Royal Anthropological Institute*, vol. xliii.

periods—the Old Kingdom, comprising Dynasties I to VIII; the Middle Kingdom, Dynasties IX to XVIII; and the New Empire, Dynasties XVIII to XXVI. These divisions, however, do not imply any break in the course of Egyptian history, but are merely used for the sake of convenience. The following Table compares the systems of dating in vogue with students of Egyptian history, according to Professor Petrie and the Berlin School, as represented by Professor Breasted:

	PETRIE (1906) B.C.	BERLIN SCHOOL (1906) B.C.
I	5510	3400
II	5247	
III	4945	2980
IV	4731	2900
V	4454	2750
VI	4206	2625
VII	4003	2475
VIII	3933	
IX	3787	2445
X	3687	
XI	3502	2160
XII	3459	2000
XIII	3246	1788
XIV	2793	
XV	2533	
XVI	2249	
XVII	1731	
XVIII	1580	1580
XIX	1322	1350
XX	1202	1200
XXI	1102	1090
XXII	958	945
XXIII	755	745
XXIV	721	718
XXV	715	712
XXVI	664	663
XXVII	525	525
XXVIII	405	
XXIX	399	
XXX	378	

Egyptian Exploration

Egypt, with its mighty ruins wrapped in silence and mystery, long ago attracted the curiosity of the traveller, for the traditions of a high civilization, of its religion, government, and culture, lingered in the memory of man ; and there, from temple, pyramid, palace, and city, he has sought and gained actual and manifold proofs of the existence of that ancient kingdom. And not only has its own history thus been unveiled to the modern world, but intertwined therewith has been traced that of other nations and powers, among them Persia, Greece, and Rome.

The earliest instance in this country of the collecting of Egyptian antiques is in 1683, when a valuable stele belonging to the Old Kingdom was brought from Saqqara and presented to the Ashmolean Museum at Oxford, while in the eighteenth century some attempt was made at planning and describing Egyptian ruins, and the identification of some of the sites with cities mentioned in classical writings. In 1798 a scientific commission, including artists and archæologists, accompanied Napoleon's military expedition into Egypt, and much valuable work was accomplished by these savants, the record of which fills several volumes of the *Description de l'Egypte*, while the large collection of antiquities gathered by them, including the famous Rosetta Stone, which proved the key to the mystery of the Egyptian hieroglyphic writing, came into British possession in the year 1801. Then, under Mehemet Ali, Egypt was opened to Europeans, and from this time onward great numbers of antiquities were taken from the country and found their way into European collections and museums, especially the British Museum, the Louvre, and those at Leyden, Berlin, and Turin.

The largest collection of Egyptian objects is that at Cairo.

Early Researches

In 1821 came the decipherment of the Rosetta Stone by Champollion, and this added a new zest to exploration and collecting. Champollion himself, together with Rosellini, was sent by the Governments of France and Tuscany on an expedition to Egypt, and much was done in copying stelæ and inscriptions. But the Prussian Government initiated a greater undertaking in 1842, under Lepsius, who extended his researches from Egypt into Nubia as far as Khartoum, and again into Syria and Palestine. This expedition, with its scientific methods, yielded a wonderful harvest of valuable results. The official preservation of the ancient monuments and ruins against exploitation by dealers or destruction by vandals was first undertaken by Mehemet Ali, who appointed Mariette to this onerous post, and under his wise and able direction invaluable work was accomplished. This has been developed under the British suzerainty. The ancient sites are claimed by the Government, and the Service of Antiquities has an annual grant of large dimensions and employs many European and native officials. All provinces are included in its survey, and no excavations may take place without its permission; and this is granted to responsible persons only, and on the terms that half of the antiquities discovered shall become the property of the Egyptian Government, the other half going to the finders. Sir Gaston Maspero, director of the Museum at Cairo, has made many brilliant contributions to Egyptian archæology. As early as 1862 the Scottish archæologist, Rhind, saw the necessity for some definite scientific and comprehensive system of excavation if really valuable results were to be obtained, and lamented the lack of any such methods in his time. In 1883 this system of investigation was inaugurated at Tanis under Professor Flinders Petrie. Everything, large and small, found during the excavation of city, temple, or grave is collected and interpreted, and made to yield its quota of evidence and information. This method gives every object its value. Attention is not concentrated on one department alone, hence nothing is wasted or lost, and knowledge of the arts and crafts, the customs, the literature and religion of ancient Egypt is slowly gathered, and all takes its due place in the pageant of history unfolded before us.

Much of the mystery that hung over Egypt has departed, but the glamour and fascination she exerted in the past are still as great as ever. These are not lessened by our more intimate knowledge of her ancient civilization, but rather increased a hundredfold. The silence of centuries has been broken, the hieroglyphs have told their tale to modern man, who listens with ever-deepening interest to the voice of the Past. The drifting sand of the desert has been cleared away and ancient buildings stand again in the sunlight and yield their secrets veiled for so many centuries. The graves tell over again the unchanging sorrow of death and the world-old longings of man. Apart from the literary remains, papyri and inscriptions, the material results have been immense. The ancient topography of the land has become known by the remains of roads, canals, quarries, and mines. The sites of towns, with the temples, fortifications, and private dwellings, have been comprehensively treated, so that the record is almost complete from the building of the foundation to the decorative designs of the artists. The site of each city, again, is generally that of several belonging to different epochs; the ruins of the older buildings were levelled to an even surface and the newer one begun several feet higher. The artificial mounds thus made are sometimes as much as 80 or 90 feet in height. These foundations did not deter the Egyptian architects from erecting lofty buildings, such as those in Memphis, for in several cities walls exist to-day from 30 to 40 feet in height. To support these they were thickened at the base and the floors vaulted. Amongst the limestone remains of houses are often found fragments of sandstone, granite, and alabaster quarried from some ruined temple, which shows that the Egyptians of those far-away days did exactly the same as their descendants, and despoiled the neglected and ruined monuments.

Town Planning

The plan of a town excavated shows the houses gathered closely around the temple and its square enclosure. This served as fortress and refuge if the town were attacked. The plan was regular in towns that were built in one period, with wide paved streets running at right angles and provided with stone channels to carry off water and drainage. The buildings were arranged in line. In cities that were the product of centuries there was, however, great irregularity—houses heaped in mazes of blind alleys, and dark, narrow streets. There was generally an open space, shaded by sycamores, used two or three times a month as a market-place. The poorer classes were housed in hovels, rarely exceeding 12 or 16 feet in length, and little better than the huts of the fellaheen of to-day. The houses of the middle class, such as shop-keepers, small officials, and foremen, were of a better description, though rather small. They usually contained half a dozen rooms, and some were two or three stories high, while narrow courtyards separated them from the street, though more often the house fronted directly on the road and was built on three sides of a courtyard. That excellent sanitary and hygienic conditions were known in ancient Egypt has been amply proved, for even poorer houses at Kahûn boasted a stone tank, and this luxury was universal except among the very poor. At Tell el Amarna, in the house of a high official of the Eighteenth Dynasty, an elaborate bath and ingenious system of water-supply have been found. The arrangements of the ordinary house were much the same as obtain in the East of to-day, the ground floor including store-rooms, barns, and stables ; the next for living and sleeping ; the roof for sleeping in summer, while here also the women gossiped and cooked. An outside staircase, narrow and very steep, led to the upper rooms. These were oblong in shape, and the door was the only means of ventilation and lighting. For decoration the walls were sometimes whitewashed, or decorated with red and yellow, or painted with domestic scenes.

Palaces and Mansions

The palaces and mansions of the wealthy and great generally stood in the midst of a garden or courtyard planted with trees surrounded with crenellated walls, broken only by a doorway, which often indicated the social importance of the family. At times it was a portico supported on columns and adorned with statues ; at others, a pylon similar to those at the entrance of temples. "The interior," says Maspero, "almost resembled a small town divided into quarters by irregular walls. In some cases the dwelling-house stood at the farther end ; while the granaries, stables, and domestic offices were distributed in different parts of the enclosure." Paintings and plans on walls of tombs, the remains of houses at Tell el Amarna and of the palace of Akhenaten, have supplied the means by which we learn these details. The pictorial plan of a Theban house, half palace, half villa, is thus elucidated by Maspero : "The enclosure is rectangular, surrounded by a crenellated wall. The principal entrance opens upon a road bordered by trees by the side of a canal or branch of the Nile. The garden is symmetrically divided by low stone walls. In the centre is a large trellis supported on four rows of small columns ; to right and left are four pools stocked with ducks and geese, two leafy conservatories, two summer-houses, and avenues of sycamores, date-palms, and dôm-palms. At the back, facing the entrance, is the house, two-storied and of small dimensions, surmounted by a painted cornice." On one of the tombs of Tell el Amarna is to be found a representation of the palace of Aï, who later ascended the throne of Egypt. This is of large size, rectangular in shape, the facade wider than the sides. The staircases running to the terraced roof lead into two small chambers at each corner of the back wall. The dwelling-house itself is contained within this outer building, and was sacred to the family and its head, and only intimate friends had the right of entrance. The remains of the ruined palace of Akhenaten at Tell el Amarna also follows much the same plan, with the addition of a pavilion for the queen's use, containing a large hall 51 feet by 21 feet. In this palace was another immense hall, its dimensions being 423 feet by 234 feet. It contained 542 mud pillars, 52 inches square. It communicated with five smaller halls. "The pillars were whitened, and the ceilings were painted with vine-leaves and bunches of grapes on a yellow ground." Many of the mansions and houses afford some beautiful specimens of the decorative art of those days. Remains of the domestic architecture of the Old Kingdom are not numerous, but the general plan seems to have been much the same as in the later periods. The small antiquities discovered, such as utensils, clothes, weapons, amulets, and other articles which have been found in great numbers, fill in the picture of the domestic life of ancient Egypt ; while temple and fortress and monument tell of the religion, the warfare, and the enterprise in that distant epoch.

These excavations cover a large area. Upper, Middle, and Lower Egypt and Nubia have been extensively explored, likewise the Sinai Peninsula and Syria, with its numerous tablets of conquest. In Nubia, states an authority, owing to the poverty of the country and its scanty population, the proportion of monuments surviving is infinitely greater than in Egypt. Many temples, tombs, quarries, forts, grottos, and pyramids have been found in a good state of preservation. In Upper Egypt are to be found the great pyramids and the necropolis of Memphis, with various smaller pyramids to the south, and it also boasts of the stupendous ruins of Thebes on both sides of the river, the tombs and quarries of Assuan, and the temples of Philæ, though these by no means exhaust the list of sites which have been excavated, while it is well known that many still hold mysteries as yet untouched.

Life and Law in Ancient Egypt

The existence of Egypt as a native monarchy stretched over such an extended period that it is extremely difficult to generalize concerning the method of its government or the life of its people. At the same time no civilization with a record of thousands of years behind it exhibits less change either in political or domestic affairs. It is certain that once an agricultural mode of life was accepted by the Egyptians they quickly contracted those manners and customs which they retained up to the period of foreign invasion ; and so far as the lower classes are concerned, there can be little doubt that the stream of daily life flowed on from century to century placid and unaltered. The science of folklore has of late years proved to us how little alteration the passage of time brings to the life and thought of a people whose environment is such that outward forces are seldom brought to bear upon them. Especially was this the case with the inhabitants of the Nile valley, who for many centuries were sheltered by geographical and other peculiarities from the inroads of other civilized races, and who by the time that foreign invaders mingled with them had attained such a settled course of existence, and were so powerfully influenced by tradition, as to be practically immune from the effects of racial intermixture. It must also be borne in mind that such invaders as Egypt knew would not bring their womankind with them, and that their marriage to Egyptian women would have the effect in a generation or two of completely absorbing them into the native population, so that the racial standard remained practically unaltered. Again, their numbers would be relatively small compared with the population of Egypt. The environment of the Nile valley is exceptionally well suited to the continuance of type, as is evidenced by the persistence of form in its domestic and other animals. Time and again have foreign sheep, goats, asses, and so forth been introduced into it, with the result that shortly afterward they became absorbed into the prevailing Egyptian type of their kind, with scarcely any modification. The horse and the camel were comparatively late importations into Egypt, and the tardy introduction of the former is eloquent of the isolated character of the country.

The feudal system was general throughout ancient Egypt, and the Pharaoh was chiefly employed in keeping his greater subjects in check. These modelled their principalities upon the central power, and even such as had no claim to royal blood kept up establishments of considerable magnitude. Officials swarmed in the Nile valley, and it does not seem that they were actuated by a very high standard of political morality, or, at least in practice, they fell short of it. Members of the royal family were generally granted high office, and this meant that the country was in effect administered by an hereditary bureaucracy. A chancellor or vizier was directly responsible to the monarch for the condition of the country—its business, finance, and legal administration.

Commerce

We know but little concerning the commercial affairs of ancient Egypt. In all probability open-air markets were held. Currency was unknown until the era of the Persian invasion, and until then rings of gold, silver, and bronze were employed in exchange. Barter, however, prevailed universally. Corn was, of course, the staple produce of Egypt, and seems to have been exported to some extent to other countries, as were papyrus rolls and linen; but practically all silver and copper had to be imported, as had precious woods, the pelts of rare animals, ivory, spices and incense, and stone for the manufacture of rare vessels. Many of these supplies reached Egypt in the shape of tribute, but records are extant of expeditions sent out by the king for the purpose of obtaining foreign rarities. A great deal of Egyptian trade was in the hands of foreigners. The Phœnicians evidently opened up communication with Egypt as early as the Third Dynasty. In later times an extensive trade was carried on with Greece, and Psammetichus I (*c.* 570 B.C.) founded the town of Naucratis as the centre of Greek trade in Egypt.

Agriculture

Agriculture was the backbone of Egyptian wealth; the nature of the soil—rich, black mud, deposited by the Nile, which also served to irrigate it—rendered the practice of farming peculiarly simple. The intense heat, too, assisted the speedy growth of grain. Cultivation was possible almost all the year round, but usually terminated with the harvests gathered in at the end of April, from which month to June a period of slackness was afforded the farmer. A great variety of crops was sown, but wheat and barley were the most popular; durra, of which bread was made, lentils, peas, beans, radishes, lettuces, onions, and flax were also cultivated. Fruits were represented by the grape, pomegranate, fig, and date. Timber was scanty and, as has been said, was mostly imported. In early times it was probably more abundant, but the introduction of the camel and the goat proved its ruin, these animals stripping the bark from the trees and devouring the shoots. Wine was chiefly made in the district of Mareotis, near Alexandria, and appears to have possessed a very delicate flavour. The papyrus plant was widely cultivated from the earliest times; the stem was employed for boat-building and rope-making, as well as for writing materials.

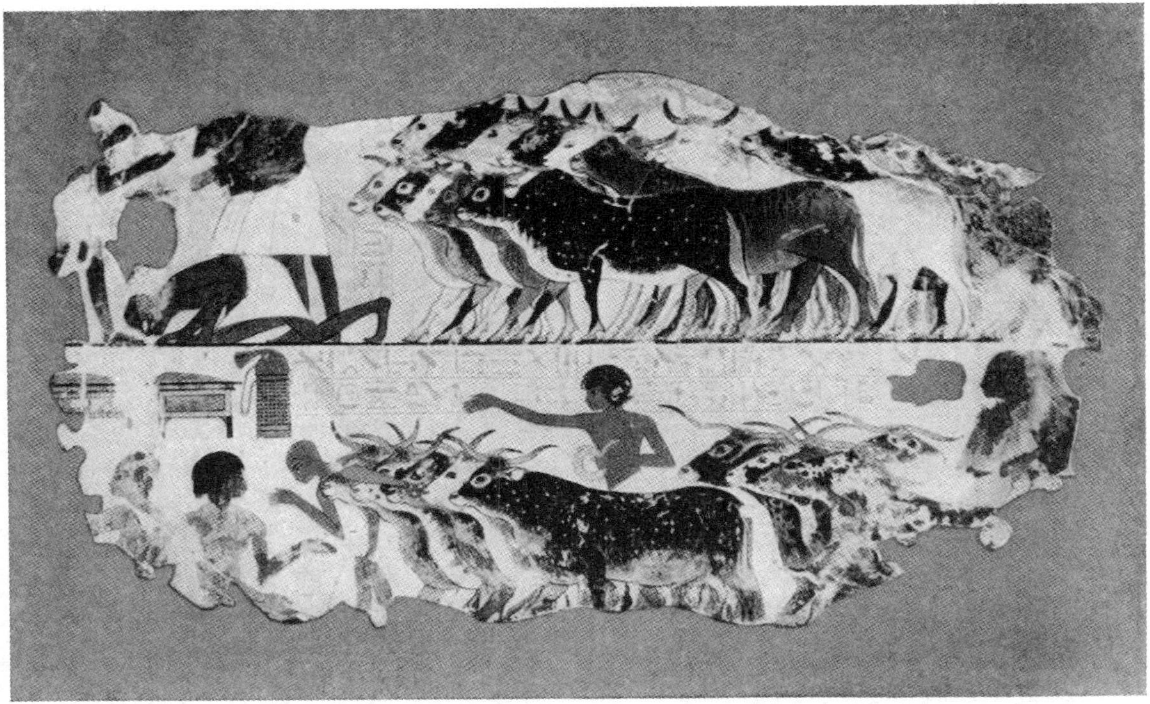

Scene representing the driving of a large herd of cattle on an Egyptian farm

From a Tomb at Thebes, XVIIIth Dynasty

(page 46)

Reproduced by Permission from "Wall Decorations of Egyptian Tombs," published by the Trustees of the British Museum

Rāhetep, a Priest
(IVth or Vth Dynasty)

(page 52)

Legal Code

Egyptian law appears to have been traditional, and no remains of any specific code have come down to us. Royal decrees and regulations were promulgated from time to time, and these were usually engraved on stone and carefully preserved. In the Ptolemaic period travelling courts were instituted, which settled litigation of all descriptions; but the traditional law of the country appears to have been well known to the people and fully recognized by their rulers. A favourite way of having a grievance redressed was to petition the king or one of the great feudal princes. Courts sitting to hear specific cases were nearly always composed of royal or territorial persons in early days, and in later times of officials. The right to appeal to the king existed. Evidence was given upon oath, a favourite oath being "By the king" or "By the life of the king." Only occasionally was torture employed for the purpose of extracting evidence. Penalties were various. In many instances the accused was allowed to take his own life. For minor crimes the bastinado or disfigurement by cutting off the nose, banishment or fine, were the usual punishments. During the Old Kingdom decapitation was the usual means of inflicting death. The drawing up of contracts was universal, and these were, as a rule, duly witnessed. From the time of the Twenty-fifth Dynasty these are discovered in abundance, and usually refer to sales or loans. Although a woman could inherit property, she had not the entire right of dealing with it, but, if divorced, her dowry could not be forfeited. Many of these ancient documents deal with the buying and selling of slaves. It is not clear, however, whether or not the consent of a slave was necessary to his sale.

Science

Knowledge and learning of every description were, of course, subordinated to the religious idea, which was the paramount consideration in Egyptian life. With architecture we have dealt elsewhere. It would seem that scientific operations of all sorts were carried out, not by means of any given formulæ, but merely by rule of thumb. Wonderful results were obtained by the simplest means, and the methods by which the pyramids were raised are still somewhat of a mystery. The dates of festivals were astronomically fixed ; and it has been stated that the pyramids and other large buildings were orientated in the same manner. The beginning of the inundation of the Nile was marked by the rising of the star Sothis or Sirius. A great many Egyptian inventions appear to be of considerable antiquity, but the inventive faculty of the race would seem to have been stunted or altogether lost in later times. Attempts at progress were absolutely unknown even when the Egyptians came into contact with foreigners, and all innovations were looked upon askance.

The Peasantry

It is uncertain to what extent the people followed the nobility in the very rigorous religious programme that these had set themselves. That they were as deeply superstitious as their betters there can be little doubt ; but that they regarded themselves as fit subjects for the same otherworld to which the aristocracy were bound is unlikely in the extreme. Probably at the best they thought they might find some corner in the dark realm of Osiris where they would not be utterly annihilated, or that at least their *kas* would be duly fed and nourished by the offerings made to them by their children. The Egyptian peasant was pre-eminently a son of the soil, hard-working, patient, and content, with little in the way of food, shelter, and raiment—not at all unlike the fellah of the present day. The lot of the Egyptian peasant woman was, like that of her husband, one of arduous toil. She was usually married about the age of fifteen, and by the age of thirty was often a grandmother. The care of her dwelling and children was not, however, permitted to occupy all her time, for at certain seasons she was expected to assist her husband in the field, where she probably received more blows than thanks. Justice was not very even-handed, and redress for any individual of the peasant class was not easily obtained ; it is strange that the conditions under which the peasantry dwelt did not foment rebellion. Probably the only reason that such outbreaks did not take place was that the condition of servitude was too deep and that, like most Orientals, the Egyptians were fatalists.

Costume

The fashion of apparel differed considerably with the dynasties. As we have already noted, the Pharaoh possessed a peculiar attire of his own, upon which that of the upper ranks of society was to some extent modelled. The climate did not permit or encourage the wearing of heavy material, so that fine linen was greatly in use. The upper portions of the body were only partially covered, and amongst the nobility in ancient times a species of linen skirt was worn. The women's dress from the earliest times was a dress reaching from the armpits to the ankles, with straps over the shoulders. The men's dress was usually a form of loin-cloth. The wearing of wigs was practically universal, and originated in prehistoric times. At some early period native ritual had prescribed that the head must be shaved, so that the fashion of the long peruke, or the close-fitting cloth cap with ear-lappets, became practically a necessity. We find, however, that some ladies refused to sacrifice their hair, and in the well-known statue of Nefert we notice the bands of natural hair, neatly smoothed down over the brow, peeping out beneath the heavy wig she is wearing. Practically all classes wore sandals of leather or plaited papyrus.

In general appearance the Egyptian was tall, being considerably above the European average in height. The race were for the most part dolichocephalic, or long-skulled, narrow-waisted and angular. In later life they frequently became corpulent, but during youth and early manhood presented rather a 'wiry' appearance. They had, however, broad shoulders and a well-developed chest-cavity. The examination of thousands of mummies by Dr. Elliot Smith has proved that in later times the Egyptian race greatly improved in physique and muscular qualities. In character the Egyptian was grave, and perhaps a little taciturn, being in this respect not unlike the Scot and the Spaniard; but, like these peoples, he had also a strain of gaiety in his composition, and his popular literature is in places eloquent of the philosophy of *laissez-faire*. It is probable that the stern religious code under which he lived drove him at times to deep disgust of his surroundings. The Egyptian peasant's amusement at times took the form of intoxication, and pictures are extant which show the labourer being borne home on the shoulders of his fellows. Among the upper classes, too, it cannot be denied that a philosophy of pleasure had gained a very strong hold, especially in later times. They probably thought that if they committed the *Book of the Dead* to heart they were sure of a blissful future, and that in this lay their whole moral duty. As regards their ethical standpoint, it may be said that they were rather *unmoral* than *immoral*, and that good and evil, as we understand it, were almost unknown to them. The Egyptians as a race possessed, however, an innate love of justice and right thinking, and they will always take their place in the roll of nations as a people who have done more than perhaps any other to upbuild the fabric of order, decency, and propriety.

CHAPTER III: THE PRIESTHOOD: MYSTERIES AND TEMPLES

The Priesthood

THE power and condition of the Egyptian priesthood varied greatly with the passing of the centuries. It was in all likelihood at all times independent of the royal power, and indeed there were periods in Egyptian history when the sway of the Pharaohs was seriously endangered, or altogether eclipsed, by the ecclesiastical party. Vast grants of land had enriched the hundreds of temples which crowded the Egyptian land, and these gave employment to a veritable army of dependents and officials. Under the New Kingdom, for example, the wealth and power of the god Amen rivalled, if it did not eclipse, that of the Pharaoh himself. In the time of Rameses III this influential cult numbered no fewer than 80,000 dependents, exclusive of worshippers, and its wealth can be assessed by the circumstance that it could count its cattle by the hundred thousand head. The kings, however, periodically attempted to diminish the power of the priesthood by nominating their own relatives or adherents to its principal offices.

In early days the great lords of the soil took upon themselves the title and duties of chief priest in their territory, thus combining the feudal and ecclesiastical offices. Beneath them were a number of priests, both lay and professional. But in later times this system was exchanged for one in which a rigorous discipline necessitated the appointment of a professional class whose duties were sharply outlined and specialized. Despite this, however, and contrary to popular belief, at no time did the priestly power combine itself into a caste that was distinctly separate from the laity, the members of which continued to act along with it. Individuals of the priesthood were generally alluded to as *hen neter* ('servant of the god') or *uab* ('the pure'). In some localities the chief priests possessed distinctive titles, such as *Khorp hemtiu* ('chief of the artificers') in the temple of Ptah, or *Ur ma* ('the Great Seer'—literally, 'Great One of Seeing') at Heliopolis. At Mendes he was known by the title, odd enough for an ecclesiastical dignitary, of 'Director of the Soldiers,' and at Thebes as 'First Prophet of Amen.' Those priests who conducted the ceremonial were known as *kheri-heb*.

The duties of the priesthood were arduous. A most stringent and exacting code had to be followed so far as cleanliness and discipline were concerned. Constant purifications and lustrations succeeded each other, and the garb of the religious must be fresh and unspotted. It consisted entirely of the purest and whitest linen, the wearing of woollen and other fabrics being strictly forbidden, and even abhorred. The head was closely shaven, and no head-dress was worn. The priest's day was thoroughly mapped out for him. If he was on duty, he duly washed himself and proceeded to the Holy of Holies, where he repeated certain formulæ, accompanying them by prescribed gestures, preparatory to breaking the seal which closed the sanctuary. Standing face to face with the god, he prostrated himself, and after performing other ritualistic offices he presented the deity with a small image of Maāt, the goddess of Truth. The god, powerless before this moment to participate in the ceremonial, was then supposedly regaled with a collation the principal items in which seem to have been beef, geese, bread, and beer, having consumed which he re-entered his shrine, and did not appear until the morning following. In the entire ritual of these morning offerings it would appear that the officiating priest represents Horus, son of Osiris, who, like all dutiful Egyptian sons, sees to the welfare of his father after death. Thus the ritual is coloured by the Osirian myth. The remainder of the day was passed in meditation, the study of various arts and sciences, theoretical and manual, and officiation at public religious ceremonies. Even the night had its duties ; for lustration and purification were undertaken in the small hours, the priest being awakened for that purpose about or after midnight.

The College of Thebes

Early Greek travellers in Egypt, and especially Herodotus and Strabo, speak with enthusiasm of the abilities of the Egyptian priests and the high standard of philosophic thought to which they had attained. The great college of priests at Thebes is alluded to with admiration by Strabo. Its members were probably the most learned and acute theologians and philosophers in ancient Egypt. Colleges of almost equal importance existed elsewhere, as at Anu, the On or Heliopolis of the Greeks. Each nome or province had its own great temple, which developed the provincial religion regardless of faiths which existed but a few miles away. The god of the nome was its divinity *par excellence*, Ruler of the Gods, Creator of the Universe, and giver of all good things to his folk.

But it must not be imagined that, if the priesthood as a body was wealthy, some of its members did not suffer the pinch of hardship. Thus, although the best conditions attached to office in the great temples, these were by no means overstaffed. At Abydos only five priests composed the staff, while Siut had ten attached to it. Again, the smaller temples possessed revenues by no means in proportion to their size. A study of this subject shows the stipend of the chief priests of the smaller shrines. "On the western border of the Fayum," says Erman, "on the lake of Moeris, was the temple of *Sobk*[1] *of the Island*, *Soknopaios* as it is called by the Greeks. It had a high-priest who received a small stipend of 344 drachmæ, and all the other priests together received daily about one bushel of wheat as remuneration for their trouble. They were not even immune from the statutory labour on the embankments, and if this was lessened for them, it was owing to the good offices of their fellow-citizens. The revenues of the temple, both in regular incomes and what was given in offerings, was used for the requirements of the ceremonies, for at every festival fine linen must be provided for the clothing of the three statues of the gods, and each time that cost 100 drachmæ; 20 drachmæ were paid on each occasion for the unguents and oil of myrrh employed in anointing the statues, 500 drachmæ were for incense, while 40 drachmæ were required to supply sacrifices and incense for the birthdays of the emperor. And yet these priests, who were in the position of the peasantry and of the lower classes of townspeople, maintained that their position in no way diminished their ancient sanctity."

Priestesses also held offices in the temples. In earlier times these officiated at the shrines of both gods and goddesses, and it is only at a later date that we find them less often as celebrants in the temples dedicated to male deities, where they acted chiefly as musicians.

[1] Sebek.

Mysteries

There is a popular fallacy to the effect that 'volumes' have been written concerning the Egyptian 'mysteries,' those picturesque and unearthly ceremonies of initiation which are supposed to have taken place in subterranean dusk, surrounded by all the circumstances of occult rite and custom. The truth is that works which deal with the subject are exceedingly rare, and are certainly not of the kind from which we can hope to glean anything concerning the mysteries of Egyptian priestcraft. We shall do better to turn to the analogous instances of Grecian practice or even to those of savage and semi-civilized peoples concerning whose mysteries a good deal has been unearthed of recent years.

Regarding the Egyptian mysteries but little is known. We have it on the authority of Herodotus that mysteries existed, possibly those in the case cited being the annual commemoration of the sufferings and death of Osiris. Says Herodotus:

"At Saïs in the Temple of Minerva, beneath the Churche and neere unto the walle of Minerva, in a base Chappell, are standinge certayne greate brooches of stone, whereto is adioyninge a lowe place in manner of a Dungeon, couered over wyth a stone curiously wroughte, the vaute it selfe being on euery side carued with most exquisite arte, in biggnesse matching with that in Delos, which is called Trochoïdes. Herein euery one counterfayteth the shadowes of his owne affections and phantasies in the nyghte season, which the Aegyptians call Mysteryes; touchinge whiche, God forbid, I should aduenture to discouer so much as they vouchsafed to tell mee."

In chapter i of the *Book of the Dead*, too, we

encounter the phrase, " I look upon the hidden things in *Re-stau* "—an allusion to the ceremonies which were performed in the sanctuary of Seker, the god of death at Saqqara. These typified the birth and death of the sun-god, and were celebrated betwixt midnight and dawn. Again, in chapter cxxv of the *Book of the Dead* (Papyrus of Ani) we read, " I have entered into *Re-stau* [the other world of Seker, near Memphis] and I have seen the Hidden One [or mystery] who is therein."

Chapter cxlviii (*Saïte Recension*) is to be recited " on the day of the new moon, on the sixth-day festival, on the fifteenth-day festival, on the festival of Uag, on the festival of Thoth, on the birthday of Osiris, on the festival of Menu, on the night of Heker, during the mysteries of Maāt, during the celebration of the mysteries of Akertet," and so forth. Herodotus, who was supposed to have been initiated into these mysteries, is righteously cryptic concerning them, and just as he has aroused our interest to fever heat he invariably sees fit to remark that his lips are sealed on the subject.

But is there anything so very extraordinary in these terrible doings ? Theosophists and others would lead us to suppose that in the gloomy crypts of Egypt weird spiritistic rites of evocation and magical ceremonies of dark import were gone through. What are the probabilities ?

The Greek Mysteries

Let us briefly examine the mysteries of ancient Greece. We find that these are for the most part pre-Hellenic, and that the conquered populations of the country adopted the mystic attitude in order to shroud their religious ceremonies from the eyes of the invaders. Now those early populations inherited a strong cultural influence from Egypt. The most important of the mysteries was perhaps the Eleusinian, and we may take it as typical of the Greek religious mysteries as a whole. The chief figures in this mysterious cult were Demeter and Kore (or Persephone) and Pluto. Now these are all deities of the underworld and, like many other gods of Hades all the world over, they are also deities possessing an agricultural significance. Much remains uncertain regarding the actual ritual in the hall of the Mystæ, but one thing is certain, and that is that the ceremony was in the nature of a religious drama or Passion-play, in which were enacted the adventures of Demeter and Kore, symbolic of the growth of the corn. Hippolytus also stated that a cornstalk was shown to the worshippers at the Eleusinian mysteries. The whole mystery then resolved itself into symbolism of the growth of the crops. Exactly how the ceremonies in connexion with this came to have the appearance of those usually associated with a savage secret society is not quite clear. The blackfellows of Australia and certain North American Indian tribes possess societies and celebrations almost identical with that of Eleusis, but why they should be wrapped in such mystery it is difficult to understand. It has been stated that the mystic setting of these cults arose in many cases from the dread of the under-world and the miasma which emanated therefrom, and which necessitated a ritual purification; but this does not seem at all explanatory. In the *Popul Vuh* of Central America we find what appear to be the doings of a secret society among the deities of the underworld, some of whom are gods of growth.

We seem to see some such society outlined in

the *Book of the Dead*, which perhaps dates from prehistoric times, and is most probably the remains of a Neolithic cult connected with the phenomena of growth. In its pages we find password and countersign and all the magical material necessary to the existence of such a secret cult as we have been speaking of. We may take it, then, that the Egyptian mysteries strongly resembled those of Greece, that their ritual was of a character similar to that of the *Book of the Dead*, and that it perhaps possessed an origin in common with that work. These mystical associations would appear to be all of Neolithic origin, and to possess an agricultural basis for the most part. When, therefore, we see in Herodotus and elsewhere a strong disposition to preserve these mysteries intact we find ourselves once more face to face with the original question—Why are they mysteries ?

In the first place, all growth is mysterious, and primitive man probably regarded it as in some manner magical. Secondly, it is noticeable that nearly all these mysteries, in the old world at least, took place underground, in darkness, and that there was enacted the symbolism of the growth of corn, probably for the purpose of inciting the powers of growth to greater activity by dint of sympathetic magic.

The Egyptian Temple

The earliest form of temple was a mere hut of plaited wickerwork, serving as a shrine for the symbols of the god ; the altar but a mat of reeds. The earliest temples evolve from a wall built round the name-stelæ, which was afterward roofed in. With the advent of the New Empire the temple-building became of a much more complicated character, though the essential plan from the earliest period to the latest remained practically unchanged. The simplest form was a surrounding wall, the pylon or entrance gateway with flanking towers, before which were generally placed two colossal statues of the king and two obelisks, then the innermost sanctuary, the *naos*, which held the divine symbols. This was elaborated by various additions, such as three pylons, divided by three avenues of sphinxes, then columned courts, and a hypostyle or columnar hall. In this way many of the Egyptian kings enlarged the buildings of their predecessors.

These temples stood in the midst of populous cities, the huge surrounding wall shutting out the noise and bustle of the narrow streets. Leading up to the great pylon, the chief gateway, was a broad road carried right through the inhabited quarter and guarded on each side by rows of lions, rams, or other sacred animals. In front of the gateway were two obelisks, likewise statues of the king who founded the temple, as protector of the sanctuary. On either side of the entrance stood a high tower, square in shape, with the sides sloping inward. These were of course originally designed for defensive purposes, and the passage through the pylon could thus be successfully barred against all foes, while from postern-gates in the wall sorties could be made. Tall masts were fixed in sockets at the foot of the pylon. From these gaily coloured streamers waved to keep afar all menace of evil, as did the symbol of the sun, the Winged Disk, over the great doors. These were often made of wood, a valuable material in Egypt, and covered with a sheathing of glittering gold. The outer walls were decorated with brightly coloured reliefs and inscriptions, depicting the deeds of the founder, for the temple was as much a personal monument as a shrine of the tutelary deity. Inside the pylon was a great court, open to the sky,

Pylon, Karnak, from the North

(page 61)

Photo Bonfils

Osiris

(page 63)

Photo W. A. Mansell & Co.

usually only colonnaded on either side, but in larger temples, as that of Karnak, a series of columns ran the length of the centre. Here the great festivals were held, in which a large number of citizens had the right to take part. By a low doorway from this the hypostyle was entered, the windows of which were near the roof, so that the light was dim, while the sanctuary was in complete and profound darkness.

The Holy Place

This, the Holy Place, was the chief room of the temple. Here stood the *naos*, a box rectangular in shape and open in front, often with a latticework door. This served as the receptacle of the divine symbols or in some cases as the cage of the sacred animal. On either side of the sanctuary were dark chambers, used as the store-rooms for the sacred vestments, the processional standards and sacred barque, the temple furniture, and so on. It is to be noted that as the progression was from the blazing light of the first great court to the complete darkness of the Holy of Holies, so the roofs grew less lofty. The inside walls and columns were decorated with reliefs in brilliant colours depicting the rites and worship connected with the presiding deity in ceremonial order.

Surrounding the temple was the *temenos*, enveloped by a wall in which were situated other and smaller temples, with groves of sacred trees and birds, lakes on which the sacred barque floated, the dwellings of the priests, and sometimes palaces amid the gardens. Outside again were sacred ways that led in different directions, some branching from temple to temple, through cities, villages, and fields, while at the side steps sloped down to the Nile, where boats were anchored. Along these ways went the sacred processions, bearing the images of the gods; by them came the monarch in royal state to make offerings to the gods; and here the dead were carried to their tombs across the Nile.

Greece has frequently been alluded to as the 'Land of Temples.' The appellation might with greater justice be applied to Egypt, where fanes of Cyclopean magnitude rose in every nome ere yet Hellas could boast knowledge of the mason's art. Still they stand, those giant shrines, well-nigh as perfect as when fresh from the chisels of the old hierophants who shaped and designed them. And so long as a fostering love of the past dwells in the heart of man so long shall they remain.

CHAPTER IV : THE CULT OF OSIRIS

Osiris

ONE of the principal figures in the Egyptian pantheon, and one whose elements it is most difficult to disentangle, is Osiris, or As-ar. The oldest and most simple form of the name is expressed by two hieroglyphics representing a throne and an eye. These, however, cast but little light on the meaning of the name. Even the later Egyptians themselves were ignorant of its derivation, for we find that they thought it meant 'the Strength of the Eye'—that is, the strength of the sun-god, Ra. The second syllable of the name, *ar*, may, however, be in some manner connected with Ra, as we shall see later. In dynastic times Osiris was regarded as god of the dead and the under-world. Indeed, he occupied the same position in that sphere as Ra did in the land of the living. We must also recollect that the realm of the under-world was the realm of night.

The origins of Osiris are extremely obscure. We cannot glean from the texts when or where he first began to be worshipped, but that his cult is greatly more ancient than any text is certain. The earliest dynastic centres of his worship were Abydos and Mendes. He is perhaps represented on a mace-head of Narmer found at Hieraconpolis, and on a wooden plaque of the reign of Udy-mu (Den) or Hesepti, the fifth king of the First Dynasty, who is figured as dancing before him. This shows that a centre of Osiris-worship existed at Abydos during the First Dynasty. But allusions in the Pyramid Texts give us to understand that prior to this shrines had been raised to Osiris in various parts of the Nile country. As has been outlined in the chapter on the *Book of the Dead*,

Osiris dwells peaceably in the under-world with the justified, judging the souls of the departed as they appear before him. This paradise was known as Aaru, which, it is important to note, although situated in the under-world, was originally thought to be in the sky.

Osiris is usually figured as wrapped in mummy bandages and wearing the white cone-shaped crown of the South, yet Dr. Budge says of him : "Everything which the texts of all periods record concerning him goes to show that he was an indigenous god of North-east Africa, and that his home and origin were possibly Libyan." In any case, we may take it that Osiris was genuinely African in origin, and that he was indigenous to the soil of the Dark Continent. Brugsch and Sir Gaston Maspero both regarded him as a water-god,[1] and thought that he represented the creative and nutritive powers of the Nile stream in general, and of the inundation in particular. This theory is agreed to by Dr. Budge, but if Osiris is a god of the Nile alone, why import him from the Libyan desert, which boasts of no rivers ? River-gods do not as a rule emanate from regions of sand. Before proceeding further it will be well to relate the myth of Osiris.

The Myth of Osiris

Plutarch is our principal authority for the legend of Osiris. A complete version of the tale is not to be found in Egyptian texts, though these confirm the accounts given by the Greek writers. The following is a brief account of the myth as it is related in Plutarch's *De Iside et Osiride* :

Rhea (the Egyptian Nut, the sky-goddess) was the

[1] See *Zeitschrift für Aeg. Sprache*, li. p. 127 ; "The Cult of the Drowned in Egypt."

wife of Helios (Ra). She was, however, beloved by Kronos (Geb), whose affection she returned. When Ra discovered his wife's infidelity he was wrathful indeed, and pronounced a curse upon her, saying that her child should not be born in any month or in any year. Now the curse of Ra the mighty could not be turned aside, for Ra was the chief of all the gods. In her distress Nut called upon the god Thoth (the Greek Hermes), who also loved her. Thoth knew that the curse of Ra must be fulfilled, yet by a very cunning stratagem he found a way out of the difficulty. He went to Silene, the moon-goddess, whose light rivalled that of the sun himself, and challenged her [1] to a game of tables. The stakes on both sides were high, but Silene staked some of her light, the seventieth part of each of her illuminations, and lost. Thus it came about that her light wanes and dwindles at certain periods, so that she is no longer the rival of the sun. From the light which he had won from the moon-goddess Thoth made five days which he added to the year (at that time consisting of three hundred and sixty days) in such wise that they belonged neither to the preceding nor to the following year, nor to any month. On these five days Nut was delivered of her five children. Osiris was born on the first day, Horus on the second, Set on the third, Isis on the fourth, and Nephthys on the fifth.[2] On the birth of Osiris a loud voice was heard throughout all the world saying, "The lord of all the earth is born!" A slightly different tradition relates that a certain man named Pamyles, carrying water from the temple of Ra at Thebes, heard

[1] The moon is always masculine in Egypt. I am here following Plutarch.—AUTHOR.

[2] Another version gives the children of Nut thus: Osiris, Isis, Set, Nephthys, and Anubis.

a voice commanding him to proclaim the birth of "the good and great king Osiris," which he straightway did. For this reason the education of the young Osiris was entrusted to Pamyles. Thus, it is said, was the festival of the Pamilia instituted.

In course of time the prophecies concerning Osiris were fulfilled, and he became a great and wise king. The land of Egypt flourished under his rule as it had never done heretofore. Like many another 'hero-god,' he set himself the task of civilizing his people, who at his coming were in a very barbarous condition, indulging in cannibalistic and other savage practices. He gave them a code of laws, taught them the arts of husbandry, and showed them the proper rites wherewith to worship the gods. And when he had succeeded in establishing law and order in Egypt he betook himself to distant lands to continue there his work of civilization. So gentle and good was he, and so pleasant were his methods of instilling knowledge into the minds of the barbarians, that they worshipped the very ground whereon he trod.

Set, the Enemy

He had one bitter enemy, however, in his brother Set, the Greek Typhon. During the absence of Osiris his wife Isis ruled the country so well that the schemes of the wicked Set to take a share in its government were not allowed to mature. But on the king's return Set fixed on a plan whereby to rid himself altogether of the king, his brother. For the accomplishment of his ends he leagued himself with Aso, the queen of Ethiopia, and seventy-two other conspirators. Then, after secretly measuring the king's body, he caused to be made a marvellous chest, richly fashioned and adorned, which would contain exactly the body of

Osiris. This done, he invited his fellow-plotters and his brother the king to a great feast. Now Osiris had frequently been warned by the queen to beware of Set, but, having no evil in himself, the king feared it not in others, so he betook himself to the banquet.

When the feast was over Set had the beautiful chest brought into the banqueting-hall, and said, as though in jest, that it should belong to him whom it would fit. One after another the guests lay down in the chest, but it fitted none of them till the turn of Osiris came. Quite unsuspicious of treachery, the king laid himself down in the great receptacle. In a moment the conspirators had nailed down the lid, pouring boiling lead over it lest there should be any aperture. Then they set the coffin adrift on the Nile, at its Tanaitic mouth. These things befell, say some, in the twenty-eighth year of Osiris' life; others say in the twenty-eighth year of his reign.

When the news reached the ears of Isis she was sore stricken, and cut off a lock of her hair and put on mourning apparel. Knowing well that the dead cannot rest till their bodies have been buried with funeral rites, she set out to find the corpse of her husband. For a long time her search went unrewarded, though she asked every man and woman she met whether they had seen the richly decorated chest. At length it occurred to her to inquire of some children who played by the Nile, and, as it chanced, they were able to tell her that the chest had been brought to the Tanaitic mouth of the Nile by Set and his accomplices. From that time children were regarded by the Egyptians as having some special faculty of divination.

The Tamarisk-tree

By and by the queen gained information of a more exact kind through the agency of demons, by whom she was informed that the chest had been cast up on the shore of Byblos, and flung by the waves into a tamarisk-bush, which had shot up miraculously into a magnificent tree, enclosing the coffin of Osiris in its trunk. The king of that country, Melcarthus by name, was astonished at the height and beauty of the tree, and had it cut down and a pillar made from its trunk wherewith to support the roof of his palace. Within this pillar, therefore, was hidden the chest containing the body of Osiris. Isis hastened with all speed to Byblos, where she seated herself by the side of a fountain. To none of those who approached her would she vouchsafe a word, saving only to the queen's maidens, and these she addressed very graciously, braiding their hair and perfuming them with her breath, more fragrant than the odour of flowers. When the maidens returned to the palace the queen inquired how it came that their hair and clothes were so delightfully perfumed, whereupon they related their encounter with the beautiful stranger. Queen Astarte, or Athenais, bade that she be conducted to the palace, welcomed her graciously, and appointed her nurse to one of the young princes.

The Grief of Isis

Isis fed the boy by giving him her finger to suck. Every night, when all had retired to rest, she would pile great logs on the fire and thrust the child among them, and, changing herself into a swallow, would twitter mournful lamentations for her dead husband. Rumours of these strange practices were brought by

Osiris beguiled into the Chest (page 67)
Evelyn Paul

Isis and the Baby Prince (page 68)
Evelyn Paul

the queen's maidens to the ears of their mistress, who determined to see for herself whether or not there was any truth in them. So she concealed herself in the great hall, and when night came sure enough Isis barred the doors and piled logs on the fire, thrusting the child among the glowing wood. The queen rushed forward with a loud cry and rescued her boy from the flames. The goddess reproved her sternly, declaring that by her action she had deprived the young prince of immortality. Then Isis revealed her identity to the awe-stricken Athenais and told her story, begging that the pillar which supported the roof might be given to her. When her request had been granted she cut open the tree, took out the coffin containing the body of Osiris, and mourned so loudly over it that one of the young princes died of terror. Then she took the chest by sea to Egypt, being accompanied on the journey by the elder son of King Melcarthus. The child's ultimate fate is variously recounted by several conflicting traditions. The tree which had held the body of the god was long preserved and worshipped at Byblos.

Arrived in Egypt, Isis opened the chest and wept long and sorely over the remains of her royal husband. But now she bethought herself of her son Harpocrates, or Horus the Child, whom she had left in Buto, and leaving the chest in a secret place, she set off to search for him. Meanwhile Set, while hunting by the light of the moon, discovered the richly adorned coffin and in his rage rent the body into fourteen pieces, which he scattered here and there throughout the country.

Upon learning of this fresh outrage on the body of the god, Isis took a boat of papyrus-reeds and journeyed forth once more in search of her husband's remains. After this crocodiles would not touch a papyrus boat, probably because they thought it contained the goddess, still pursuing her weary search. Whenever Isis found a portion of the corpse she buried it and built a shrine to mark the spot. It is for this reason that there are so many tombs of Osiris in Egypt.[1]

The Vengeance of Horus

By this time Horus had reached manhood, and Osiris, returning from the Duat, where he reigned as king of the dead, encouraged him to avenge the wrongs of his parents. Horus thereupon did battle with Set, the victory falling now to one, now to the other. At one time Set was taken captive by his enemy and given into the custody of Isis, but the latter, to her son's amazement and indignation, set him at liberty. So angry was Horus that he tore the crown from his mother's head. Thoth, however, gave her a helmet in the shape of a cow's head. Another version states that Horus cut off his mother's head, which Thoth, the maker of magic, stuck on again in the form of a cow's.

Horus and Set, it is said, still do battle with one another, yet victory has fallen to neither. When Horus shall have vanquished his enemy, Osiris will return to earth and reign once more as king in Egypt.

Sir J. G. Frazer on Osiris

From the particulars of this myth Sir J. G. Frazer has argued[2] that Osiris was "one of those personifications of vegetation whose annual death and resurrection have been celebrated in so many lands"—that he was a god of vegetation analogous to Adonis and Attis.

"The general similarity of the myth and ritual of

[1] Lang states (art. "Mythology" in *Encyclopædia Britannica*) that "the Osirian myth originated in the same sort of fancy as the Pacullic story of the dismembered beaver out of whose body things were made."

[2] *Golden Bough*, vol. ii. p. 137.

The Departure of Isis from Byblos
Evelyn Paul

(page 69)

A Shrine of Osiris (page 70)
(XIIth Dynasty)

Osiris to those of Adonis and Attis," says Sir J. G. Frazer, "is obvious. In all three cases we see a god whose untimely and violent death is mourned by a loving goddess and annually celebrated by his worshippers. The character of Osiris as a deity of vegetation is brought out by the legend that he was the first to teach men the use of corn, and by the custom of beginning his annual festival with the tillage of the ground. He is said also to have introduced the cultivation of the vine. In one of the chambers dedicated to Osiris in the great temple of Isis at Philæ the dead body of Osiris is represented with stalks of corn springing from it, and a priest is depicted watering the stalks from a pitcher which he holds in his hand. The accompanying legend sets forth that 'this is the form of him whom one may not name, Osiris of the mysteries, who springs from the returning waters.' It would seem impossible to devise a more graphic way of depicting Osiris as a personification of the corn; while the inscription attached to the picture proves that this personification was the kernel of the mysteries of the god, the innermost secret that was only revealed to the initiated. In estimating the mythical character of Osiris, very great weight must be given to this monument. The story that his mangled remains were scattered up and down the land may be a mythical way of expressing either the sowing or the winnowing of the grain. The latter interpretation is supported by the tale that Isis placed the severed limbs of Osiris on a corn-sieve. Or the legend may be a reminiscence of the custom of slaying a human victim as a representative of the corn-spirit, and distributing his flesh or scattering his ashes over the fields to fertilize them.

"But Osiris was more than a spirit of the corn; he was also a tree-spirit, and this may well have been his original character, since the worship of trees is naturally older in the history of religion than the worship of the cereals. His character as a tree-spirit was represented very graphically in a ceremony described by Firmicus Maternus. A pine-tree having been cut down, the centre was hollowed out, and with the wood thus excavated an image of Osiris was made, which was then 'buried' in the hollow of the tree. Here, again, it is hard to imagine how the conception of a tree as tenanted by a personal being could be more plainly expressed. The image of Osiris thus made was kept for a year and then burned, exactly as was done with the image of Attis which was attached to the pine-tree. The ceremony of cutting the tree, as described by Firmicus Maternus, appears to be alluded to by Plutarch. It was probably the ritual counterpart of the mythical discovery of the body of Osiris enclosed in the erica-tree. We may conjecture that the erection of the *Tatu* pillar at the close of the annual festival of Osiris was identical with the ceremony described by Firmicus; it is to be noted that in the myth the erica-tree formed a pillar in the king's house. Like the similar custom of cutting a pine-tree and fastening an image to it, in the rites of Attis, the ceremony perhaps belonged to the class of customs of which the bringing in the Maypole is among the most familiar. As to the pine-tree in particular, at Denderah the tree of Osiris is a conifer, and the coffer containing the body of Osiris is here depicted as enclosed within the tree. A pine-cone often appears on the monuments as an offering presented to Osiris, and a manuscript of the Louvre speaks of the cedar as sprung from him. The sycamore and the tamarisk are also his trees. In inscriptions he is spoken of as residing in them, and his mother Nut is frequently portrayed in a sycamore. In a sepulchre at How

(Diospolis Parva) a tamarisk is depicted overshadowing the coffer of Osiris; and in the series of sculptures which illustrate the mystic history of Osiris in the great temple of Isis at Philæ a tamarisk is figured with two men pouring water on it. The inscription on this last monument leaves no doubt, says Brugsch, that the verdure of the earth was believed to be connected with the verdure of the tree, and that the sculpture refers to the grave of Osiris at Philæ, of which Plutarch tells us that it was overshadowed by a *methide* plant, taller than any olive-tree. This sculpture, it may be observed, occurs in the same chamber in which the god is depicted as a corpse with ears of corn sprouting from him. In inscriptions he is referred to as 'the one in the tree,' 'the solitary one in the acacia,' and so forth. On the monuments he sometimes appears as a mummy covered with a tree or with plants. It accords with the character of Osiris as a tree-spirit that his worshippers were forbidden to injure fruit-trees, and with his character as a god of vegetation in general that they were not allowed to stop up wells of water, which are so important for the irrigation of hot southern lands."

Sir J. G. Frazer goes on to combat the theory of Lepsius that Osiris was to be identified with the sun-god Ra. Osiris, says the German scholar, was named Osiris-Ra even in the *Book of the Dead*, and Isis, his spouse, is often called the royal consort of Ra. This identification, Sir J. G. Frazer thinks, may have had a political significance. He admits that the myth of Osiris might express the daily appearance and disappearance of the sun, and points out that most of the writers who favour the solar theory are careful to indicate that it is the daily, and not the annual, course of the sun to which they understand the myth to apply. But, then, why, pertinently asks Sir J. G. Frazer, was it celebrated by an annual ceremony? "This fact alone seems fatal to the interpretation of the myth as descriptive of sunset and sunrise. Again, though the sun may be said to die daily, in what sense can it be said to be torn in pieces?"

Plutarch says that some of the Egyptian philosophers interpreted Osiris as the moon, "because the moon, with her humid and generative light, is favourable to the propagation of animals and the growth of plants." Among primitive peoples the moon is regarded as a great source of moisture. Vegetation is thought to flourish beneath her pale rays, and she is understood as fostering the multiplication of the human species as well as animal and plant life. Sir J. G. Frazer enumerates several reasons to prove that Osiris possessed a lunar significance. Briefly these are that he is said to have lived or reigned twenty-eight years, the mythical expression of a lunar month, and that his body is said to have been rent into fourteen pieces—"This might be interpreted as the waning moon, which appears to lose a portion of itself on each of the fourteen days that make up the second half of the lunar month." Typhon found the body of Osiris at the full moon; thus its dismemberment would begin with the waning of the moon.

Primitive Conceptions of the Moon

Primitive man explains the waning moon as actually dwindling, and it appears to him as if it is being broken in pieces or eaten away. The Klamath Indians of South-west Oregon allude to the moon as 'the One Broken in Pieces,' and the Dacotas believe that when the moon is full a horde of mice begin to nibble at one side of it until they have devoured the whole. To continue Sir J. G. Frazer's argument, he quotes Plutarch to the effect that at the new moon of the month Phanemoth, which was the beginning of spring, the Egyptians celebrated what they called 'the entry of Osiris into the moon'; that at the ceremony called the 'Burial of Osiris' they made a crescent-shaped chest, "because the moon when it approaches the sun assumes the form of a crescent and vanishes"; and that once a year, at the full moon, pigs (possibly symbolical of Set, or Typhon) were sacrificed simultaneously to the moon and to Osiris. Again, in a hymn supposed to be addressed by Isis to Osiris it is said that Thoth

> Placeth thy soul in the barque Maat
> In that name which is thine of god-moon.

And again:

> Thou who comest to us as a child each month,
> We do not cease to contemplate thee.
> Thine emanation heightens the brilliancy
> Of the stars of Orion in the firmament.

In this hymn Osiris is deliberately identified with the moon.[1]

In effect, then, Sir James Frazer's theory regarding Osiris is that he was a vegetation or corn god, who later became identified, or confounded, with the moon. But surely it is as reasonable to suppose that it was because of his status as moon-god that he ranked as a deity of vegetation.

A brief consideration of the circumstances connected with lunar worship might lead us to some such supposition. The sun in his status of deity requires but little explanation. The phenomena of growth are attributed to his agency at an early period of human thought, and it is probable that wind, rain, and other atmospheric manifestations are likewise credited to his

[1] See M. A. Murray, *Osireion at Abydos*, p. 26.

action, or regarded as emanations from him. Especially is this the case in tropical climates, where the rapidity of vegetable growth is such as to afford to man an absolute demonstration of the solar power. By analogy, then, that sun of the night, the moon, comes to be regarded as an agency of growth, and primitive peoples attribute to it powers in this respect almost equal to those of the sun. Again, it must be borne in mind that, for some reason still obscure, the moon is regarded as the great reservoir of magical power. The two great orbs of night and day require but little excuse for godhead. To primitive man the sun is obviously godlike, for upon him the barbarian agriculturist depends for his very existence, and there is behind him no history of an evolution from earlier forms. It is likewise with the moon-god. In the Libyan desert at night the moon is an object which dominates the entire landscape, and it is difficult to believe that its intense brilliance and all-pervading light must not have deeply impressed the wandering tribes of that region with a sense of reverence and worship. Indeed, reverence for such an object might well precede the worship of a mere corn and tree spirit, who in such surroundings could not have much scope for the manifestation of his powers. We can see, then, that this moon-god of the Neolithic Nubians, imported into a more fertile land, would speedily become identified with the powers of growth through moisture, and thus with the Nile itself.

Osiris in his character of god of the dead affords no great difficulties of elucidation, and in this one figure we behold the junction of the ideas of the moon, moisture, the under-world, and death—in fact, all the phenomena of birth and decay.

Osiris and the Persephone Myth

The reader cannot fail to have observed the very close resemblance between the myth of Osiris and that of Demeter and Kore, or Persephone. Indeed, some of the adventures of Isis, notably that concerning the child of the king of Byblos, are practically identical with incidents in the career of Demeter. It is highly probable that the two myths possessed a common origin. But whereas in the Greek example we find the mother searching for her child, in the Egyptian myth the wife searches for the remains of her husband. In the Greek tale we have Pluto as the husband of Persephone and the ruler of the under-world also regarded, like Osiris, as a god of grain and growth, whilst Persephone, like Isis, probably personifies the grain itself. In the Greek myth we have one male and two female principles, and in the Egyptian one male and one female. The analogy could perhaps be pressed further by the inclusion in the Egyptian version of the goddess Nephthys, who was a sister-goddess to Isis or stood to her in some such relationship. It would seem, then, as if the Hellenic myth had been sophisticated by early Egyptian influences, perhaps working through a Cretan intercommunication.

It remains, then, to regard Osiris in the light of ruler of the underworld. To some extent this has been done in the chapter which deals with the *Book of the Dead.* The god of the underworld, as has been pointed out, is in nearly every instance a god of vegetable growth, and it was not because Osiris was god of the dead that he presided over fertility, but the converse. To speak more plainly, Osiris was first god of fertility, and the circumstance that he presided over the underworld was a later innovation. But it was not adventitious; it was the logical outcome of his status as god of growth.

A New Osirian Theory

We must also take into brief consideration his personification of Ra, whom he meets, blends with, and under whose name he nightly sails through his own dominions. This would seem like the fusion of a sun and moon myth; the myth of the sun travelling nightly beneath the earth fused with that of the moon's nocturnal journey across the vault of heaven. A moment's consideration will show how this fusion took place. Osiris was a moon-god. That circumstance accounts for one half of the myth; the other half is to be accounted for as follows: Ra, the sun-god, must perambulate the underworld at night if he is to appear on the fringes of the east in the morning. But Osiris as a lunar deity, and perhaps as the older god, as well as in his character as god of the underworld, is already occupying the orbit he must trace. The orbits of both deities are fused in one, and there would appear to be some proof of this in the fact that, in the realm of Seker, Afra (or Ra-Osiris) changes the direction of his journey from north to south to a line due east toward the mountains of sunrise. The fusion of the two myths is quite a logical one, as the moon during the night travels in the same direction as the sun has taken during the day—that is, from east to west.

It will readily be seen how Osiris came to be regarded not only as god and judge of the dead, but also as symbolical of the resurrection of the body of man. Sir James Frazer lays great stress upon a picture of Osiris in which his body is shown covered with sprouting shoots of corn, and he seems to be of opinion that this is positive evidence that Osiris was a corn-god. In our view the picture is simply symbolical of resurrection. The circumstance that Osiris is represented in the picture as in the recumbent position of the dead lends added weight to this supposition. The corn-shoot is a world-wide symbol of resurrection. In the Eleusinian mysteries a shoot of corn was shown to the neophytes as typical of physical rebirth, and a North American Indian is quoted by Loskiel, one of the Moravian Brethren, as having spoken : "We Indians shall not for ever die. Even the grains of corn we put under the earth grow up and become living things." Among the Maya of Central America, as well as among the Mexicans, the maize-goddess has a son, the young, green, tender shoot of the maize plant, who is strongly reminiscent of Horus, the son of Osiris, and who may be taken as typical of bodily resurrection. Later the vegetation myth clustering round Osiris was metamorphosed into a theological tenet regarding human resurrection, and Osiris was believed to have been once a human being who had died and had been dismembered. His body, however, was made whole again by Isis, Anubis and Horus acting upon the instructions of Thoth. A good deal of magical ceremony appears to have been mingled with the process, and this in turn was utilized in the case of every dead Egyptian by the priests in connexion with the embalmment and burial of the dead in the hope of resurrection. Osiris, however, was regarded as the principal cause of human resurrection, and he was capable of giving life after death because he had attained to it. He was entitled 'Eternity and Everlastingness,' and he it was who made men and women to be born again. This conception of resurrection appears to have been in vogue in Egypt from very early times. The great authority upon Osiris is the *Book of the Dead*, which might well be called the 'Book of Osiris,' and in which are recounted his daily doings and his nightly journeyings in his kingdom of the underworld.

Isis

Isis, or Ast, must be regarded as one of the earliest and most important conceptions of female godhead in ancient Egypt. In the dynastic period she was regarded as the feminine counterpart of Osiris, and we may take it that before the dawn of Egyptian history she occupied a similar position. The philology of the name appears to be unfathomable. No other deity has probably been worshipped for such an extent of time, for her cult did not perish with that of most other Egyptian gods, but flourished later in Greece and Rome, and is seriously carried on in Paris to-day.

Isis was perhaps of Libyan origin, and is usually depicted in the form of a woman crowned with her name-symbol and holding in her hand a sceptre of papyrus. Her crown is surmounted by a pair of horns holding a disk, which in turn is sometimes crested by her hieroglyph, which represents a seat or throne. Sometimes also she is represented as possessing radiant and many-coloured wings, with which she stirs to life the inanimate body of Osiris.

No other goddess was on the whole so popular with the Egyptians, and the reason for this is probably to be found in the circumstances of travail and pity which run through her myth. These drew the sympathies of the people to her, but they were not the only reasons why she was beloved by the Egyptian masses, for she was the great and beneficent mother-goddess and represented the maternal spirit in its most intimate and affectionate guise. In her myth, perhaps one of the most touching and beautiful which ever sprang

Isis (page 80)

Photo W. A. Mansell & Co.

Winged Isis (page 81)

(The wings are in the attitude of protecting Horus)

Photo W. A. Mansell & Co.

from the consciousness of a people, we find evolved from what may have been a mere corn-spirit a type of wifely and maternal affection mourning the death of her cherished husband, and seeking by every means in her power to restore him to life.

Isis as the Wind

Although Isis had undoubtedly many forms, and although she may be regarded as the great corn-mother of Egypt, the probabilities are that in one of her phases she represents the wind of heaven. This does not appear to have been recognized by students of Egyptology, but the record seems a fairly clear one. Osiris in his guise of the corn dies and comes to life again and is sown broadcast over the land. Isis is disconsolate and moans terribly over his loss ; in fact, so loud and heartrending is her grief that the child of the King of Byblos, whom she is nursing, dies of terror. From her, grateful odours emanate, as the women of the Queen of Byblos experience. She transforms herself into a swallow. She restores the dead Osiris to life by fanning him with her wings and filling his mouth and nostrils with sweet air. It is noteworthy that she is one of the few Egyptian deities who possess wings. She is a great traveller, and unceasingly moans and sobs. If these qualities and circumstances are not allegorical of the wind, a much more ingenious hypothesis than the above will be necessary to account for their mythological connexion. Isis wails like the wind, she shrieks in tempest, she carries the fragrance of spices and flowers throughout the country, she takes the shape of a swallow, one of the swiftest of birds and typical of the rapidity of the wind, she employs the element of which she is mistress to revivify the dead Osiris, she possesses wings, as do all deities connected with the wind, and like the rest of her kind she is constantly travelling up and down the land. We do not advance the hypothesis that she is a wind-goddess *par excellence*, but in one of her phases she certainly typifies the revivifying power of the spring wind, which wails and sobs over the grave of the sleeping grain, bringing reanimating breath to the inert seeds.

Isis is one of those deities who from fortuitous and other circumstances are fated to achieve greatness. From a Libyan spirit connected in some manner with the growth of the crops, she rose to such supreme importance during her reign of nearly four thousand years in Egypt that every description of attribute was heaped upon her in abundance. This is invariably the case with successful deities. Not only do they absorb the attributes of their contemporaries in the pantheon, but qualities which are actually at variance with their original character are grafted upon them because of their very popularity. This was the case, for instance, with Tezcatlipoca, a Mexican deity, originally god of the air, who later became god of fate and fortune, and practically head of the Aztec pantheon ; and many other instances might be adduced. Thus Isis is a giver of life and food to the dead in the Duat—that is, she brings with her the fresh air of heaven into the underworld—and as the air-god Tezcatlipoca was identified with justice, so Isis is identified with Maāt, the goddess of justice.

Isis may also typify the wind of morning, from which the sun is born. In most countries at the moment of sunrise a wind springs up which may be said to usher the sun into existence. In her myth, too, we find that on leaving the house where she had been imprisoned by Set (the summer dwelling of the wind, which during that season leaves Egypt altogether) she is preceded by seven scorpions, the fierce-stinging blasts of winter. They show her the way through swamps and marshes. Women shut the doors in her face ; a child is stung by one of the scorpions, but Isis restores it to life—that is, the child recovers with the approach of better weather. Her own son Horus is stung by a scorpion—that is, the heat of the sun is rendered weak by the cold of winter until it is restored by Isis, the genial spring wind.

Manifold Attributes of Isis

The myth of Isis became so real to the people of Egypt that they came to regard her very intimately indeed, and fully believed that she had once been a veritable woman. In a more allegorical manner she was of course the great feminine fructifier of the soil. She was also a powerful enchantress, as is shown by the number of deities and human beings whom she rescued from death. Words of great and compelling power were hers. Her astronomical symbol was the star Sept, which marked the spring and the approach of the inundation of the Nile, an added evidence that in one of her phases she was goddess of the winds of spring. As the light-giver at this season of the year she was called Khut, and as goddess of the fruitful earth Usert. As the force which impelled the powers of spring and sent forth the Nile flood she was Sati, and as the goddess of fertile waters she was Anqet. She was further the deity of cultivated lands and fields, goddess of harvest and goddess of food. So that from first to last she personified the forces which make for growth and nourishment. She personifies the power of the spring season, the power of the earth to grow and yield grain, motherhood and all the attributes and affinities which spring therefrom. It is not necessary in this place to trace her worship into Greece, Rome, and Western Europe, where it became greatly degraded from its pristine purity. The dignified worship of the great mother took on under European auspices an orgiastic character which appealed to the false mystic of Greece, Rome, Gaul, and Britain just as it does to-day to his Transatlantic or Parisian prototype. But the strength of the cult in the country of its origin is evinced by the circumstance that it was not finally deserted until the middle of the fifth century A.D.

Horus

As we have seen, the god Ra was depicted as a falcon, but there was another god of similar form who had been worshipped before him in the land of Egypt. This was the god Heru, or Horus, 'He who is above.' This god had many shapes. As Horus the Elder he is delineated as a man with the head of a falcon, and was believed to be the son of Geb and Nut. Horus proper was perhaps regarded as the face of heaven, the countenance of the sky, and as Horus the Elder he represented the face by day in contradistinction to Set, who was the face by night. Horus the Younger, or Harpocrates as he was called by the Greeks to distinguish him from Horus the Elder, is represented as a youth, and was the son of a Horus-god and the goddess Rat-Tauit, who appears to have been worshipped at Hermonthis in the form of a hippopotamus. Horus the Younger represented the earliest rays of the rising sun, and had no fewer than seven aspects or forms. To detail all the variants of Horus would be foreign to the purpose of this work, so it must suffice to enumerate the more important of them. The Horus of the Two Horizons, the Harmachis of the Greeks, was one

Cippus of Horus (page 84)

Photo W A. Mansell & Co.

Horus in Battle
Evelyn Paul

(page 92)

of the chief forms of the sun-god Ra, and represented the sun in his diurnal course from sunrise to sunset. He thus included the personalities of Ra, Tem, and Khepera, and this affords a good example of the widespread system of overlapping which obtained in Egyptian mythology, and which does not appear to such an extent in any other mythology. Probably a number of these Horus-gods were local. Thus we find Harmachis worshipped principally at Heliopolis and Apollinopolis. His best-known monument is the famous Sphinx, near the pyramids of Gizeh. We find the first mention of the Sphinx in inscriptions in the days of Thothmes IV, when we read in the text inscribed on the stele between the paws of the Sphinx the following legend of Thothmes and the Sphinx.

The Dream of Thothmes

There was a king in Egypt called Thothmes, a mighty monarch, skilled in the arts of war and of the chase. He was good to look upon, too, with a beauty like unto that of Horus, whom Isis bare in the Northern Marshes, and greatly was he loved by gods and men.

He was wont to hunt in the burning desert, alone, or with only a few companions, and this is told of one of his hunting expeditions.

One day, before he had ascended the throne of Egypt, he was hunting unattended in the desert. It was noontide, and the sun beat fiercely down upon him, so that he was fain to seek the shadow of the mighty Harmachis, the Sphinx. Great and powerful was the god, and very majestic was his image, with the face of a man and the body of a lion, a snake upon his brow. In many temples were sacrifices made to him, in many towns did men worship with their faces turned toward him.

In the great cool shadow Thothmes laid himself

down to rest, and sleep enchained his senses. And as he slept he dreamed, and behold! the Sphinx opened its lips and spoke to him; it was no longer a thing of motionless rock, but the god himself, the great Harmachis. And he addressed the dreamer thus:

"Behold me, O Thothmes, for I am the Sun-god, the ruler of all peoples. Harmachis is my name, and Ra, and Khepera, and Tem. I am thy father, and thou art my son, and through me shall all good come upon thee if thou wilt hearken to my words. The land of Egypt shall be thine, and the North Land, and the South Land. In prosperity and happiness shalt thou rule for many years."

He paused, and it seemed to Thothmes as if the god were struggling to free himself from the overwhelming sands, for only his head was visible.

"It is as thou seest," Harmachis resumed; "the sands of the desert are over me. Do that quickly which I command thee, O my son Thothmes."

Ere Thothmes could reply the vision faded and he awoke. The living god was gone, and in his place was the mighty image, hewn from the solid rock.

And here the story must perforce end. It is inscribed on a stele in the little temple which lies between the paws of the Sphinx, and the remainder of the inscription is so defaced as to be indecipherable.

Heru-Behudeti

One of the greatest and most important of all the forms of Horus is Heru-Behudeti, who typifies midday, and therefore the greatest heat of the sun. It was in this form that Horus waged war against Set. His principal shrines were at Edfû, Philæ, Mesen, Aat-ab, and Tanis, where he was worshipped under the form of a lion trampling upon its enemies. In general, however, he is depicted as hawk-headed and bearing in his hand a weapon, usually a club or mace to symbolize his character as a destroyer. In the old Arthurian romances, and, indeed, in many mediæval tales which have a mythological ancestry, we read of how certain knights in combat with their enemies grew stronger as the sun waxed in the heavens, and when his beams declined their strength failed them. So was it with Sir Belin, with King Arthur, who in his frenzy slew thousands, and with St George, the patron saint of England, originally an Egyptian hero. These figures were all probably sun-gods at some early period of their development. They are obscure in birth and origin, as is the luminary they symbolize—that is, they spring from the darkness. Arthur's origin, for example, was unknown to him until the age of manhood, and the same holds good of Beowulf. As they grew in power, like the sun which they typify, the solar heroes frequently became insane, and laid about them with such pitiless fury that they slaughtered thousands in a manner of which no ordinary paladin would be capable. This is typical of the strength and fury of the sun at midday in Eastern climates. Heru-Behudeti, then, because he was god of the midday sun, was the pitiless warrior wielding the club, perhaps typifying sunstroke, and the bow and arrows, symbolizing his fierce beams which were to destroy the dragon of night and his fiendish crew. He was well represented as a lion, for what is so fierce as the tropical sun? At midday he was all-conquering and had trampled the night-dragon out of sight. In this manner, too, he represented the force of good against that of evil. The following is the myth of his battles with Set and the battalions of his evil companions.

The Myth of the Winged Disk

In the year 363 of the reign of Ra-Horakhti upon the earth it befell that the god was in Nubia with a mighty army. Set, the Evil One, had rebelled against him, for Ra was advanced in years, and Set was of all beings the most cunning and treacherous. He it was also who had slain his twin-brother Osiris, the great and good king; and for this reason Horus, the brother of Osiris, desired greatly to have his life.

With his chariots and horsemen and foot-soldiers Ra embarked on the Great River and came to Edfû, where Horus of Edfû joined him.

"O Ra," said Horus, "great are thine enemies, and cunningly do they conspire against thee!"

"My son," answered Ra, "arm thee and go forth against mine enemies, and slay them speedily."

Thereupon Horus sought the aid of the god Thoth, the master of all magic, by whose aid he changed himself into a great sun-disk, with resplendent wings outstretched on either side. Straight to the sun he flew, and from the heavens he looked so fiercely upon his enemies and Ra's, that they neither heard nor saw aright. Each man judged his neighbour to be a stranger, and a cry went up that the foe were upon them. Each turned his weapon against the other, the majority were slain, and the handful of survivors scattered. And Horus hovered for a while over the battle-plain, hoping to find Set, but the arch-enemy was not there; he was hiding in the North Country.

Then Horus returned to Ra, who embraced him kindly. And Horus took Ra and the goddess Astarte, and showed them the battlefield strewn with corpses.

Ra, king of the gods, said to those in his train: "Come, let us voyage to the Nile, for our enemies are slain." But Set still had a large following, and some of his associates he commanded to turn themselves into crocodiles and hippopotami, so that they might swallow the occupants of the divine barque and yet remain invulnerable by reason of their thick hides. Horus, however, had gathered his band of smiths, each of whom made for himself an iron lance and a chain, on which Thoth bestowed some of his ever-powerful magic. Horus also repeated the formulæ in the *Book of Slaying the Hippopotamus*. So that when the fierce animals charged up the river the god was ready for them ; many of them were pierced by the magic weapons and died, while the remainder fled. Those who fled to the south were pursued by Horus, and were at length overtaken. Another great conflict ensued, wherein the followers of Set were again vanquished. According to the desire of Ra, a shrine was raised to commemorate the victory, and his image placed therein. Yet another encounter, however, was to take place in the South Land ere the followers of Set were utterly destroyed.

The Slaughter of the Monsters

Then Horus and Ra sailed northward toward the sea in search of Set and his allies, hoping to slay all the crocodiles and hippopotami, which were the bodily forms of their foes. But the beasts kept under water, and four days had elapsed ere Horus caught sight of them. He at once attacked them, and wrought great havoc with his glittering weapons, to the delight of Ra and Thoth, who watched the conflict from the boat. A hundred and forty-two prisoners were taken on this occasion. Yet did Horus continue to pursue his enemies, always in the form of a burning disk with wings like unto the sunset, and attended by the goddesses Nekhbet and Uazet in the shape of two snakes.

Once more he overtook the allies of Set, this time at the Western Waters of Mert. On this occasion, as on the others, Horus was victorious, and nearly four hundred prisoners were brought to the boat of Ra and slain.

Then was Set very greatly incensed, and decided to come forth in person to do battle with Horus. Horrible indeed were his cries and curses when he heard the losses his army had sustained. And Horus and his followers went out to meet the army of Set, and long and furious was the battle. At length Horus took a prisoner whom he believed to be Set. The wretched being was dragged before Ra, who gave him into the hands of his captor, bidding the latter do with him what he would. Then Horus killed his prisoner, cut off his head, dragged him through the dust, and cut his body in pieces, even as Set had done to Osiris. But, after all, it was only one of Set's associates who had perished thus miserably. The Evil One himself was still at large, vowing vengeance on his enemies. In the form of a large snake he hid himself under the earth, while his followers took courage from the knowledge that he had eluded his enemy. Yet again, however, were they defeated by Horus, who slew great numbers of them. The gods remained for six days on the canal, waiting for the reappearance of the foe, but none were to be seen. Then Horus scattered abroad his followers to destroy the remnant of Set's army.

The last two battles were fought at Thalû (Zaru), and at Shaïs, in Nubia. At Thalû Horus took the form of a fierce lion, and slew a hundred and forty-two enemies. At Shaïs he appeared once more in the shape of a great shining disk with wings of splendid plumage, and with the goddesses Nekhbet and Uazet on either side of it in the shape of crowned snakes. On these occasions also Horus was victorious.

There are various endings to this myth. It is said that the prisoner whom Horus caused to be decapitated was none other than Set, whose fate, however, did not hinder him from living again and taking the form of a serpent. According to this version Horus of Edfû was accompanied by Horus the Child, son of Isis and Osiris. In the same inscription which gives an account of the battles Horus the Elder and Horus the Child are utterly confused at the end. So while Horus the Elder fights the battles, Horus the Child kills Set. They are looked upon as one and the same. On capturing Set, therefore, Horus, according to one account, delivered him into the hands of Isis, who cut off his head.

Another version, again, has it that the decisive battle has not yet been fought, and that Horus will finally destroy his enemy, when Osiris and the gods once more return to earth.

Other Horus Legends

Yet another account states that when Horus the Child had become a man Set came forth and challenged him to mortal combat. So Horus set out in a boat splendidly decorated by Isis, who also laid magic spells upon it, so that its occupant might not be overcome. Meanwhile the arch-foe of the gods had taken upon himself the shape of a huge red hippopotamus. And he caused a raging storm to break over the boats of Horus and his train, so that the waters were lashed into fury; and had it not been that the boats were protected by magic, all would assuredly have perished. Horus, however, held on his course undismayed. He had taken the form of a youth of giant stature, and towered at the gilded prow of his boat, which shone like sunlight amid the storm and the darkness. A great harpoon was poised in his hand, such a weapon as an ordinary mortal could not lift. In the water the red hippopotamus waited for the wrecking of the boat, so that he might swallow his enemies. But this he was destined never to do, for directly he showed himself above water the mighty harpoon was launched at his head and sank into his brain. And this was the end of Set, the Evil One, the murderer of Osiris and the enemy of Ra. In honour of Horus the Conqueror hymns and triumphal choruses were sung throughout the land.

In the myth of the battles of Horus it is easy to discern what is perhaps the most universal of all mythological conceptions—the solar myth. Horus (called in the Edfû text Horbehûdti, *i.e.* Horus of Edfû) was originally a sun-god, and as such was equivalent to Ra, but in time the two gods came to be regarded as separate and distinct personages, Ra being the highest, and Horus serving him as a sort of war-captain. The winged disk, therefore, and all his train represented the powers of light, while the wicked Set and his companions symbolized darkness. Thus it is that while Horus was always victorious over his enemies, he never succeeded (according to the most widespread form of the tradition) in destroying them utterly.

When Horus had routed the enemy in the form of a winged disk, that symbol came to be regarded as an excellent protective against violence and destruction. It was therefore repeated many times—especially in the New Kingdom—in temples, on monuments, stelæ, and so on, and it was believed that the more numerous the representations of it, the more efficacious did the charm become. In its simplest form the image is merely that of a winged disk, but at times there is a serpent on either side of the disk, representing the goddesses Nekhbet and Uazet.

The principal version of the myth, dealing with Hor-Behûdti, or Horus of Edfû, was really a local form belonging to Edfû, though in time it gained a wider acceptance. In other forms of the legend other gods took the chief *rôle* as destroyer of the enemies of Ra.

With this legend of light and darkness came to be fused another, that which relates how Horus avenged the death of Osiris. It is noticeable that in this second myth there exists some confusion between Horus the Elder and Horus the Child, respectively brother and son of Osiris. No mention is made of Osiris in the Edfû text, but that this myth is a sequel to the legend of Osiris is implied by the circumstance that Set is handed over for punishment to Isis and Horus the Child. In the later form of the story the conflict is not properly between light and darkness, but rather between the forces of good and evil.

In this legend one of the most noteworthy circumstances is that the followers of Horus were armed with weapons of metal. His followers are called in the Egyptian text Mesniu, or Mesnitu, which in all probability signifies 'workers in metal,' or 'blacksmiths.' The worshippers of Horus of Behudet continually alluded to him as 'Lord of the Forge-city,' or Edfû, where tradition asserted he carried on the work of a blacksmith. At Edfû, indeed, the great golden disk of the sun itself had been forged, as we see from a certain inscription, and in the temple of that city was a chamber behind the sanctuary called Mesnet, or 'the foundry,' where the blacksmith caste of priests attended upon the god. From sculptures upon the walls of the temple we see that these are arrayed in short robes and a species of collar which is almost a cape, that they carry their spears head downward, and a weapon of metal resembling a dagger. Horus of Behudet, who accompanies them, is dressed in a similar fashion, and is represented as spearing a hippopotamus, round which he has wound a double chain of metal. This illustrates the story of the defeat of Set by Horus of Behudet, and we may be justified in believing that the legend possessed a more or less historic basis. Here we have a tribe or caste of metal-workers at war with what is obviously a more primitive race, whom they defeat with their weapons of metal and bind with their chains, afterward slaughtering them at leisure. It is significant that they do not slay them out of hand. For what, then, do they reserve them ? Obviously for human sacrifice. They are a caste of sun-worshippers, and human blood was as necessary to the sustenance of the sun in early Egypt as it was in ancient Mexico, where the military caste, living under the patronage of the sun, always refrained from slaying an enemy in battle if they could make him prisoner, to be sacrificed at leisure. The circumstances of the legend would appear to indicate that we are here following the adventures of some West Asiatic invader who, with followers armed with metal, landed on the soil of Egypt, made himself master of Edfû, and, marching northward, established himself in the land by force of arms. This story, or portion of history, probably became amalgamated, perhaps by priestly influence, with the legend of Horus, the god of heaven in the earliest times.

Another important form of Horus was that known as Horus, son of Isis, and of Osiris. He represented the rising sun, as did several other forms of Horus, and possessed many aspects or variants. His shrines were so numerous that at one epoch or another he was identified with all the other Horus-gods, but he chiefly represented the new sun, born daily, and he was son and successor of Osiris. He was extremely popular, as being a well-marked type of resurrection after death. As Osiris represented 'yesterday,' so Horus, his son, stood for 'to-day' in the Egyptian mind. Although some texts state that Osiris was his father, others claim this position for Ra, but the two in this instance are really one and the same and interchangeable.

Osiris became the father of Horus after he was dead; such is the origin of several sun-heroes. As has been said, the birth of such is usually peculiar and obscure. Isis, while tending the infant Horus and in fear of the persecutions of Set, took shelter in the swamps of the Delta, and hid herself and her child amidst a dense mass of papyrus plants. To the Egyptian of the Delta it would of course seem as if the sun took its rise from amidst the papyrus-covered swamps which stretched on every side to the horizon, so we may regard this part of the myth as allegory pure and simple. The circumstances of the escape of Isis from Set have already been detailed in the myth of Osiris.

The filial respect which Horus displayed for the memory of his father Osiris won him much honour from the Egyptians. He it was who fixed the details of the god's mummification, and who set the standard for the pious Egyptian son. In this respect he was regarded as a helper of the dead, and was thought to mediate between them and the judges of the Taut. In his work of caring for the deceased he had a number of helpers, known as the followers of Horus, who were regarded as gods of the cardinal points. They are given positions of great importance in the *Book of the Dead*, and shared the protection of the body of the deceased, as has been mentioned in the paragraph concerning the mummy. They were four in number and were named Hapï, Tuamutef, Amset, and Qebhsennuf.

Horus, son of Isis and Osiris, was regarded as of such importance that he absorbed the attributes of all the other Horus-gods, but in certain texts he is represented as a child, with forefinger to lip, and wearing the lock of hair at the side of the head which indicates youth. In later times he was figured in a great many different fanciful forms.

The Black Hog

Ra, Set, and Horus are concerned in an Egyptian myth which attempts an explanation of eclipses of the sun and moon. Set and Horus were bitter enemies, yet Set did not dare to enter the fray openly, for he feared Horus as evil must ever fear good. So he devised subtle and underhand schemes whereby he might compass the fall of Horus, and this is how the matter fell out.

One day Horus sought Ra with a request to be allowed to read the future in his eyes. This request Ra granted willingly because of his love for Horus, the beloved of gods and men. Whilst they conversed there passed them a black hog, a huge, sinister animal, ferocious of aspect, and with eyes that glinted with cunning and cruelty. Now, though neither Ra nor Horus was aware of the fact, the black hog was Set himself, who had the power to take upon him the shape of any animal he chose.

"What an evil monster!" cried Ra, as he looked upon the animal.

Horus also turned his gaze in the direction of the black hog, in whom he still failed to recognize his enemy. This was Set's opportunity. He shot a bolt of fire straight into the eye of the god. Horus was half crazed with the violence of the pain. "Set hath done me this evil," he cried; "he shall not go unpunished." But Set had vanished, and was not to be found anywhere. Yet for the evil that had come upon Horus Ra cursed the pig.

When the young god recovered his sight Ra gave to him the city of Pé, whereat he was much delighted; and at his smile the cloud of darkness passed away, and all the land rejoiced.

A Greek version of the myth has it that the black hog tore out the eye of Horus and swallowed it, but was forced by Ra (Helios) to restore it. The eyes of Horus are of course the sun and moon, one of which is swallowed or destroyed by the 'black hog' during an eclipse. The restoration of light to the earth is occasioned by the joy of Horus on being presented with the city of Pé.

Nephthys

The female counterpart of Set was Nephthys. She was the daughter of Geb[1] and Nut, the sister and wife of Set, and the mother of Anubis, but whether by Osiris or Set is not clear. The words Nebt-het mean 'the lady of the house,' or sky. Although Nephthys is associated with Set, she appears to remain more faithful to her sister Isis, whom she assists to regain the scattered limbs of Osiris. She is represented in the form of a woman wearing upon her head the symbol of her name, *i.e.* a basket and a house (reading Nebt-het). She appears in some ways in the *Book of the Dead* as an assistant of her sister Isis, standing behind Osiris when the hearts of the dead are weighed,

[1] Or Seb.

and kneeling at the head of Osiris' bier. She was supposed to possess great magical powers like her sister, and resembles her in possessing many forms. She is also supposed to protect Osiris in his form of moon-god. Plutarch throws some light upon Egyptian belief concerning this goddess. He says that Anubis was the son of Osiris and Nephthys, and that Typhon or Set was first apprised of their amour by finding a garland of flowers which had been left behind him by Osiris. As Isis represents fruitfulness, so, he says, Nephthys signifies corruption. Dr. Budge, commenting upon this passage, says that it is clear that Nephthys is the personification of darkness and of all that belongs to it, and that her attributes were of a passive rather than of an active character. " She was the opposite of Isis in every respect. Isis symbolized birth, growth, development, and vigour ; but Nephthys was the type of death, decay, diminution, and immobility." The two goddesses were, however, associated inseparably with each other. " Isis, according to Plutarch, represents the part of the world which is visible, whilst Nephthys represents that which is invisible. . . . Isis and Nephthys represent respectively the things which are and the things which are yet to come into being, the beginning and the end, birth and death, and life and death. We have unfortunately no means of knowing what the primitive conception of the attributes of Nephthys was, but it is most improbable that it included any of the views on the subject which were current in Plutarch's time. Nephthys is not a goddess with well-defined characteristics, but she may, generally speaking, be described as the goddess of the death which is not eternal." Dr. Budge proceeds to say that Nephthys, although a goddess of death, was associated with the coming into existence of the life

Nephthys (page 97)

Photo W. A. Mansell & Co.

Set

(page 99)

which springs from death. With Isis she prepared the funeral bed of Osiris and made his mummy-wrappings. Along with Isis she guarded the corpse of Osiris. In later times the goddesses were represented by two priestesses whose hair was shaved off and who wore ram's-wool garlands upon their heads. On the arm of one was a fillet inscribed to Isis, and the other wore a like band inscribed to Nephthys.

Set

The cult of Set was of the greatest antiquity, and although in later times he was regarded as evil personified, this was not his original *rôle*. According to the priests of Heliopolis he was the son of Geb and Nut, and therefore brother of Osiris, Isis, and Nephthys, husband of the latter goddess and father of Anubis. These relationships, however, were all manufactured for him at a comparatively late period. In the Pyramid Texts we find Set acting as a friend to the dead, and he even assisted Osiris to reach heaven by means of a ladder. He is also associated with Horus and is regarded as his equal. But in time they came to be regarded as mortal enemies, who were only prevented from entirely destroying one another by the wise Thoth. Horus the Elder was the god of the sky by day, and Set the god of the sky by night. The one was in fact the direct opposite of the other.

The derivation of the name Set presents many difficulties of elucidation. The determinative of his hieroglyph is either the figure of an animal or a stone, which latter seems to symbolize the stony or desert country on either side of the Nile. As to the animal which pictorially represents him, it has by no means been identified, but various authorities have likened it to a camel and an okapi. In any case it must have been a denizen of the desert inimical to man.

As Horus was the god of the North, so was Set god of the South. Dr. Brugsch considered Set symbolized the downward motion of the sun in the lower hemisphere, thus making him the source of the destructive heat of summer. As the days began to shorten and the nights to lengthen it was thought that he stole the light from the sun-god. He was likewise instrumental in the monthly destruction of the moon. Storms, earthquakes, and eclipses and all natural phenomena which caused darkness were attributed to him, and from an ethical point of view he was the god of sin and evil.

We find the myths of the combat between Set and Horus evolving from a simple opposition of day and night into a combat between the two gods. Ra and Osiris, instead of Horus, are sometimes ranged against Set. The combat symbolized the moral idea of the victory of good over evil, and those of the dead who were justified were regarded as having overcome Set as Osiris had done. In his combat with the sun-god Set took the form of the monster serpent Apep and was accompanied by an army of lesser serpents and reptiles of every description. In later times we find him identified with Typhon. All desert animals and those which inhabited the waters were regarded as the children of Set, as were animals with red hair or skins, or even red-haired men. Such animals were often sacrificed ritually in propitiation of Set. In the month Pachons an antelope and a black pig were sacrificed to him in order to deter him from attacking the full moon, and on the great festival of Heru-Behudeti such birds and fish as were thought to be of his following were trodden underfoot to the cry that Ra had triumphed over his enemies.

Set had also a kingdom in the northern sky, and his peculiar abode was the Great Bear. As in some other countries, the north was considered by the Egyptians as the place of darkness, cold, and death. Thus we find that by the Mexicans and Maya the abode of the god of death was considered to be the north, and that among the latter people the hieroglyph for the north is a human bone placed before the head of the death-god. The goddess Reret, who has the head and body of a hippopotamus, was supposed to have the evil influence of Set in restraint. She is pictured as holding darkness fettered by a chain, and is considered to be a form of Isis.

It was probably about the Twenty-second Dynasty that the worship of Set began to decline, and that he took on the shape of an evil deity. The theory has been put forward that the Hyksos invaders identified him with certain of their gods, and that this sufficed to bring him into disrepute with the Egyptians.

Set and the Ass

Plutarch, in his *De Iside et Osiride*, has an interesting passage concerning the alleged resemblance between the ass and Set. He says (the translation is the old one of Squire):

"Hence their ignominious treatment of those persons, whom from the redness of their complexions they imagine to bear a resemblance to him; and hence likewise is derived the custom of the Coptites of throwing an Ass down a precipice; because it is usually of this colour. Nay, the inhabitants of Busiris and Lycopolis carry their detestation of this animal so far, as never to make any use of trumpets, because of the similitude between their sound and the braying of an ass. In a word, this animal is in general regarded by them as unclean and impure, merely on account of the resemblance which they conceive it bears to Typho; and in consequence of this notion, those cakes which they offer with their sacrifices during the last two months Païni and Phaophi, have the impression of an ass, bound, stamped upon them. For the same reason likewise, when they sacrifice to the Sun, they strictly enjoyn all those who approach to worship the God, neither to wear any gold about them, nor to give provender to any ass. It is moreover evident, say they, that even the Pythagoreans looked upon Typho to have been of the rank or order of Demons, as, according to them, 'he was produced in the even number fifty-six.' For as the power of the Triangle is expressive of the nature of Pluto, Bacchus, and Mars, the properties of the Square of Rhea, Venus, Ceres, Vesta, and Juno; of the Dodecagon of Juppiter; so, as we are informed by Eudoxus, is the figure of 56 angles expressive of the nature of Typho: as therefore all the others above-mentioned in the Pythagorean system are looked upon as so many Genii or Demons, so in like manner must this latter be regarded by them. 'Tis from this persuasion likewise of the red complexion of Typho, that the Egyptians make use of no other bullocks in their sacrifice but what are of this colour. Nay, so extremely curious are they in this respect, that if there be so much as one black or white hair in the beast, 'tis sufficient to render it improper for this service. For 'tis their opinion, that sacrifices ought not to be made of such things as are in themselves agreeable and well-pleasing to the Gods, but, on the contrary, rather of such creatures wherein the souls of wicked and unjust men have been confined during the course of their transmigration. Hence sprang that custom, which was formerly observed by them, of pronouncing a solemn curse upon the head of the beast which was to be offered in sacrifice, and afterwards of cutting it off and throwing it into the Nile, though now they dispose of it to foreigners. No bullock therefore is permitted to be offered to the Gods, which has not the seal of the Sphragistæ first stamped upon it, an order of priests peculiarly set apart for this purpose, from whence likewise they derive their name. Their impress, according to Castor, is 'a man upon his knees with his hands tied behind him and a sword pointed at his throat.' Nor is it from his colour only that they maintain a resemblance between the ass and Typho, but from the stupidity likewise and sensuality of his disposition; and agreeably to this notion, having a more particular hatred to Ochus than to any other of the Persian monarchs who reigned over them, looking upon him as an execrable and abominable wretch, they gave him the nickname of the Ass, which drew the following reply from that prince, 'But this ass shall dine upon your ox,' and accordingly he slew the Apis: this story is thus related by Dino."

In certain phases of his myth Set is symbolized as a black pig. Especially is this the case when he is shown by Ra to Horus, and tears the latter's eye out of his head.

Anubis

Anubis, or, as the Egyptians called him, An-pu, was, according to some, the son of Osiris and Nephthys, and to others the son of Set. He had the head of a jackal and the body of a man, and was evidently symbolical of the animal which prowled about the tombs of the dead. His worship was of great antiquity, and it may be that in early times he had been a totem. He was the guide of the dead in the underworld on their way to the abode of Osiris. In many mythologies a dog is the companion of the dead man to the otherworld. Its remains are found in prehistoric graves ; in both Mexico and Peru dogs were sacrificed at burial, and, indeed, the custom is a very widespread one. Now it is not improbable that Anubis may have typified the prehistoric half-domesticated jackal, or early type of dog that was supposed to guide the wanderer through the underworld. Plutarch says of Anubis that the Egyptians imagine a resemblance between him and the dog.

Anubis was particularly worshipped at Lycopolis, Abt, and elsewhere. He plays a prominent part in the *Book of the Dead*, especially in those passages which are connected with the justification and the embalming of the deceased. He it was who embalmed the body of Osiris. Indeed, he rendered great assistance to the mourning sisters, and in this he may typify the faithful and helpful qualities of the dog. This is all the more striking if he is to be accepted as the son of Set, and the whole evolution of the deity would seem to imply that whereas the semi-savage, half-domesticated dog was originally nocturnal and of doubtful value, under domestication its virtues became apparent. It is probable that, could research be pushed back to a sufficiently remote epoch, and did paintings of such an early period exist, we should find Anubis pictured as the faithful dog preceding the deceased on the journey to the Duat. Later, when every deity in the picture had received a special function through the aid of priestly ingenuity, and perhaps in an area where the jackal or dog was totemic, we find the companion of the dead still accompanying him indeed, still his guide through the darkness, but in the guise and with the attributes of a full-grown deity. How he came to be the mummifier of Osiris it would, indeed, be hard to say ; probably

Anubis (page 103)

Thoth (page 106)

Maāt (page 108)

Photo W. A. Mansell & Co.

the association of the jackal with the burial-ground would account for this. He was symbolical of the grave. Professor Petrie has put it on record that the best guides to Egyptian tombs are the jackal-trails. A speech of Anubis in the *Book of the Dead*, chapter cli, is suggestive of his protective character. "I have come," he says, "to protect Osiris." In many countries the dog is dispatched with the deceased for the purpose of protecting him against various grisly enemies he may meet on the way to Hades, and it is not unlikely that Anubis played a similar part in very early times.

It is the duty of Anubis to see that the beam of the great balance wherein the heart of the deceased is weighed is in its proper position. As Thoth acts for the gods, so Anubis appears for the dead man, whom he also protects against the 'Eater of the Dead.' He also guided the souls of the dead through the underworld, being assisted in this duty by Up-uaut, another jackal-headed deity, whose name signifies 'Opener of the Ways.' These gods have sometimes been confounded with one another, but in certain texts they are separately alluded to. The name of the latter deity is significant of his probable early function. Anubis, thinks Dr. Budge, was the opener of the roads of the north, and Up-uaut of those of the south. "In fact," he says, "Anubis was the personification of the summer solstice, and Ap-uat [Up-uaut] of the winter solstice." He goes on to say that when they appear with the two Utchats, or eyes of Ra, they symbolize the four quarters of heaven and of earth, and the four seasons of the year. Plutarch has also a passage upon the astronomical significance of Anubis which seems far from clear.

At Heliopolis, Anubis was to some extent fused with Horus as regards his attributes, and in some manner he took on the character of the old fusion between Horus and Set, in this latter connexion personifying death and decay. In the *Golden Ass* of Apuleius we find that Anubis had votaries in Rome, and it is noticeable that in this account he is spoken of as having a dog's head.

Thoth

Thoth, or Tehuti, was a highly composite deity. His birth was coeval with that of Ra. Let us enumerate his attributes before we seek to disentangle his significance. He is alluded to as the counter of the stars, the measurer and enumerator of the earth, as being twice great and thrice great lord of books, scribe of the gods, and as possessing knowledge of divine speech, in which he was 'mighty.' In general he was figured in human form with the head of an ibis, but sometimes he appears in the shape of that bird. He wears upon his head the crescent moon and disk, the Atef crown, and the crowns of the North and South. In the *Book of the Dead* he is drawn as holding the writing reed and palette of the scribe, and as placing on his tablets the records of the deceased whose heart is being weighed before him. There is no reason to suppose that Thoth was totemic in character, as he belongs to the cosmogonic or nature deities, few or none of whom were of this type. Another form of Thoth is that of the dog-headed ape, which, it has been stated, symbolizes his powers of equilibrium. His principal seat of worship was Hermopolis, where Ra was supposed to have risen for the first time. To Thoth was ascribed the mental powers of Ra, and, indeed, the dicta of Ra seem to have come from his lips. He was the Divine Speech personified. But we are looking ahead. Let us discover his primitive significance before we enumerate the more or less complex attributes which are heaped upon him in later times.

It is pretty clear that Thoth is originally a moon-god. He is called the 'great god' and 'lord of heaven.' Among primitive peoples the moon is the great regulator of the seasons. A lunar calendar is invariably in use prior to the introduction of the computation of time by solar revolution. The moon is thus the 'great measurer' of primitive life. Thus primitive peoples speak about the 'seed moon,' the 'deer moon,' the 'grain' or 'harvest moon,' and so on. Thoth, then, was a measurer because he was a moon-god, and conversely because of his lunar significance he was *the* measurer. As Aah-Tehuti he symbolizes the new moon, as it is from the first appearance that time is measured by primitive peoples. His eye signifies the full moon in the same manner that the eye of Ra signifies the sun at mid-day. But it also symbolizes the left eye of Ra, or the cold half of the year, when the sun's rays were not so strong. It is sometimes also called the 'black eye of Horus,' the 'white eye' being the sun. This serves to illustrate how greatly the attributes of the Egyptian deities had become confused. As he was a moon-god, so he was to some extent connected with moisture, and we find him alluded to in chapter xcv of the *Book of the Dead* as a rain and thunder god.

Thoth as Soul-Recorder

It is, however, as the recorder of souls before Osiris that Thoth was important in the eyes of the Egyptian priesthood. He held this office because of his knowledge of letters and his gift of knowing what was right or in equilibrium. Again, he had the power of imparting the manner in which words should be correctly spoken. As has already been said, the mode of speech, the tone in which words were pronounced, spelt success or failure in both prayer and magical incantations. The secret of this Thoth taught to men, and this it was that the Egyptians especially desired to learn. Through the formula of Thoth the gates of the Duat were opened to the deceased, and he was safeguarded against its terrors. The *Book of the Dead* was indeed believed to be the work of Thoth, as was the *Book of Breathings*, a much later work.

The Greek writers upon things Egyptian imagined Thoth, whom they called Trismegistos, or Hermes the Thrice Great, as the prime source of all learning and wisdom. They ascribed to him the invention of the sciences of astronomy and astrology, mathematics, geometry, and medicine. The letters of the alphabet were also his invention, from which sprang the arts of reading and writing. According to them the 'Books of Thoth' were forty-two in number, and were divided into six classes, dealing with law and theology, the service of the gods, history, geography and writing, astronomy and astrology, religious writings and medicine. It is almost certain that most of this mass of material was the work of Alexandrian Greeks sophisticated by ancient Egyptian lore.

Maāt

The goddess Maāt closely resembles Thoth, and has indeed been regarded as the female counterpart of that god. She was one of the original goddesses, for when the boat of Ra rose above the waters of the primeval abyss of Nu for the first time she had her place in it beside Thoth. She is symbolized by the ostrich feather, which she either holds or which decorates her head-dress. Dr. Budge states that the reason for the association of the ostrich feather with Maāt is unknown, as is the primitive conception which underlies her name. But it is likely that the equal-sidedness of the feather, its division into halves, rendered it a fitting symbol of balance or equilibrium. Among the Maya of Central America the feather denoted the plural number. The word, we are told, indicates "that which is straight." The name Maāt with the ancient Egyptians came to imply anything which was true, genuine, or real. Thus the goddess was the personification of law, order, and truth. She indicated the regularity with which Ra rose and set in the sky, and, assisted by Thoth, wrote down his daily course for him every day. In this capacity she is called the 'daughter of Ra' and the 'eye of Ra.' As the personification of justice her moral power was immense and inexorable. In fact, she came to be regarded as that fate from whom every man receives his deserts. She sat in a hall in the underworld to hear the confessions of the dead, the door of which was guarded by Anubis. The deceased had to satisfy forty-two assessors or judges in this hall, after which he proceeded to the presence of Osiris, whom he assured that he had 'done Maāt,' and had been purified by her.

The Book of the Dead

The *Book of the Dead*, the Egyptian title of which, *Pert em hru*, has been variously translated 'coming forth by day' and the 'manifestation day,' is a great body of religious compositions compiled for the use of the dead in the otherworld. It is probable that the name had a significance for the Egyptians which is incapable of being rendered in any modern language, and this is borne out by another of its titles—'The chapter of making perfect the Khu' (or spirit).

Texts dealing with the welfare of the dead and their life in the world beyond the grave are known to have been in use among the Egyptians as early as 4000 B.C. The oldest form of the *Book of the Dead* known to us is represented in the Pyramid Texts. With the invention of mummification a more complete funerary ritual arose, based on the hope that such ceremonies as it imposed would ensure the corpse against corruption, preserve it for ever, and introduce it to a beatified existence among the gods. Almost immediately prior to the dynastic era a great stimulus appears to have been given to the cult of Osiris throughout Egypt. He had now become the god of the dead *par excellence*, and his dogma taught that from the preserved corpse would spring a beautified astral body, the future home of the spirit of the deceased. It therefore became necessary to adopt measures of the greatest precaution for the preservation of human remains.

The generality of the texts comprised in the *Book of the Dead* are in one form or another of much greater antiquity than the period of Mena, the first historical king of Egypt. Indeed, from internal evidence it is possible to show that many of these were revised or edited long before the copies known to us were made. Even at as early a date as 3300 B.C. the professional writers who transcribed the ancient texts appear to have been so puzzled by their contents that they hardly understood their purport.[1] Dr. Budge states: "We are in any case justified in estimating the earliest form of the work to be contemporaneous with the foundation of the civilization which we call 'Egyptian' in the valley of the Nile."[2]

[1] Maspero, *Recueil de Travaux*, vol. iv, p. 62.
[2] *Book of the Dead*, Papyrus of Ani, vol. i, p. 7.

A 'Discovery' 3400 Years Old

A hieratic inscription upon the sarcophagus of Queen Khnem-nefert, wife of Mentu-hetep, a king of the Eleventh Dynasty (*c.* 2500 B.C.), states that a certain chapter of the *Book of the Dead* was discovered in the reign of Hesep-ti, the fifth king of the First Dynasty, who flourished about 4266 B.C. This sarcophagus affords us two copies of the said chapter, one immediately following the other. That as early as 2500 B.C. a chapter of the *Book of the Dead* should be referred to a date almost 2000 years before that time is astounding, and the mind reels before the idea of a tradition which, during comparatively unlettered centuries, could have conserved a religious formula almost unimpaired. Thus thirty-four centuries ago a portion of the *Book of the Dead* was regarded as extremely ancient, mysterious, and difficult of comprehension. It will be noted also that the inscription on the tomb of Queen Khnem-nefert bears out that the chapter in question was 'discovered' about 4266 B.C. If it was merely discovered at that early era, what periods of remoteness lie between that epoch and the time when it was first reduced to writing? The description of the chapter on the sarcophagus of the royal lady states that "this chapter was found in the foundations beneath the Dweller in the Hennu Boat by the foreman of the builders in the time of the king of the South and North, Hesep-ti, whose word is truth"; and the Nebseni Papyrus says that the chapter was found in the city of Khemennu or Hermopolis, on a block of alabaster, written in letters of lapis-lazuli, under the feet of the god. It also appears from the Turin Papyrus, which dates from the period of the Twenty-sixth Dynasty, that the name of the finder was Heru-ta-ta-f, the son of Cheops, who was at the time engaged in a tour of inspection of the temples. Sir Gaston Maspero is doubtful concerning the importance which should be attached to the statement regarding the chapter on the tomb of Queen Khnem-nefert, but M. Naville considers the chapter in question one of the oldest in the *Book of the Dead.*

A bas-relief of the Second Dynasty bears an inscription dedicating to the shade of a certain priest the formula of the "thousands of loaves of bread, thousands of jugs of ale," and so forth, so common in later times. We thus see that 4000 years B.C. it was regarded as a religious duty to provide offerings of meat and drink for the dead, and there seems to be good evidence, from the nature of the formula in question, that it had become fixed and ritualistic by this period. This passage would appear to justify the text on the sarcophagus of the wife of Mentu-hetep. A few centuries later, about the time of Seneferu (*c.* 3766 B.C.), the cult of the dead had expanded greatly from the architectural point of view, and larger and more imposing cenotaphs were provided for them. Victorious wars had brought much wealth to Egypt, and its inhabitants were better able to meet the very considerable expenditure entailed upon them by one of the most expensive cults known to the history of religion. In the reign of Men-kau-Ra a revision of certain parts of the text of the *Book of the Dead* appears to have been undertaken. The authority for this is the rubrics attached to certain chapters which state that they were found inscribed upon a block of alabaster in letters of lapis-lazuli in the time of that monarch.

We do not find a text comprising the *Book of the Dead* as a whole until the reign of Unas (3333 B.C.), whose pyramid was opened in 1881 by Sir G. Maspero. The stone walls were covered with texts extremely difficult of decipherment, because of their archaic character and spelling, among them many from the *Book of the Dead*. Continuing his excavations at Saqqarah, Maspero made his way into the pyramid of Teta (3300 B.C.), in which he discovered inscriptions, some of which were identical with those in the pyramid of Unas, so that the existence of a fully formed *Book of the Dead* by the time of the first king of the Sixth Dynasty was proven. Additional texts were found in the tomb of Pepi I (3233 B.C.). From this it will be seen that before the close of the Sixth Dynasty five copies of a series of texts, forming the *Book of the Dead* of that period, are in evidence, and, as has been observed, there is substantial proof that its ceremonial was in vogue in the Second, and probably in the First, Dynasty. Its text continued to be copied and employed until the second century of the Christian era.

It would appear that each chapter of the *Book of the Dead* had an independent origin, and it is probable that their inclusion and adoption into the body of the work were spread over many centuries. It is possible that some of the texts reflect changes in theological opinion, but each chapter stands by itself. It would seem, however, that there was a traditional order in the sequence of the chapters.

The Three Recensions

There were three recensions or versions of the *Book of the Dead*—the Heliopolitan, the Theban, and the Saïte. The Heliopolitan Recension was edited by the priests of the College of Anu, or On, known to the Greeks as Heliopolis, and was based upon texts not now recoverable. The Pyramids of Unas, Teta, and Pepi contain the original texts of this recension, which represent the theological system introduced by the priests of Ra. The essentials of the primitive Egyptian religion are, however, retained, the only modification in them being the introduction of the solar doctrine of Ra. In later times the priesthood of Ra were forced to acknowledge the supremacy of Osiris, and this theological defeat is visible in the more modern texts. Between the Sixth and Eleventh Dynasties the priests of On edited a number of fresh chapters from time to time.

The Theban Recension was much in vogue from the Eighteenth to the Twenty-second Dynasties, and was usually written upon papyri and painted upon coffins in hieroglyphs. Each chapter was preserved distinct from the others, but appears to have had no distinct place in the entire collection.

The Saïte Recension was definitely arranged at some date prior to the Twenty-sixth Dynasty, and is written upon coffins and papyri, and also in hieratic and demotic script. It continued to be employed to the end of the Ptolemaic period.

As we have previously noticed, the *Book of the Dead* was for their use from the moment when they found themselves inhabitants of the otherworld. Magic was the very mainspring of existence in that sphere, and unless a spirit was acquainted with the formulæ which compelled the respect of the various gods and demons, and even of inanimate objects, it was helpless. The region to which the dead departed the primitive Egyptians called Duat. They believed it to be formed of the body of Osiris. It was regarded as dark and gloomy, containing pits of fire and dreadful monsters which circled the earth, and was in its turn bounded by a river and a lofty chain of mountains. The part of it that was nearest to Egypt was regarded as a description of mingled desert and forest, through which the soul of the deceased might not hope to struggle unless guided by some benevolent spirit who knew the paths through this country of despair. Thick darkness covered everything, and under veil of this the hideous inhabitants of the place practised all sorts of hostility to the new-comer, unless by the use of words of power he could prove his superiority over them. But there was one delectable part in this horrid region—the Sekhet Hetepet, the Elysian fields which contained the Sekhet Aaru, or the Field of Reeds, where dwelt the god Osiris and his company. At first he had domain over this part of the Duat alone, but gradually he succeeded in extending it over the entire country of the dead, of which he was monarch. We find also a god of the Duat named Duati, but who appears to have been more a personification of the region than anything else. Now the wish of all good men was to win to the kingdom of Osiris, and to that end they made an exhaustive study of the prayers and ritual of the *Book of the Dead*, in order that they might the more easily penetrate to the region of bliss. This they might reach by two ways—by land and by water. The path by water was no whit less dreadful than that by land, the passage of the soul being barred by streams of fire and boiling water, and the banks of the rivers navigated were populous with evil spirits.

The Place of Reeds

We learn from the Theban Recension that there were seven halls or mansions in the Field of Reeds, all of which had to be passed through by the soul before it was received by the god in person. Three gods guarded the door of each hall—the doorkeeper, watchman, and questioner. It was necessary for the new-comer to address each god by his name. There were also names for the doors which must be borne in mind. The name of each god was in reality a spell consisting of a number of words. The Place of Reeds was divided into fifteen regions, each of which was presided over by a god. The first of these was called Amentet, where dwelt those souls who lived upon earth-offerings; it was ruled over by Menuqet. The second was Sekhet Aaru, the Field of Reeds proper, the walls surrounding which were formed of the stuff of which the sky is made. Here dwelt the souls, who were nine cubits high, under the rule of Ra Heru-Khuti, and this place was the centre of the kingdom of Osiris. The third was the place of the spirit-souls, a region of fire. In the fourth dwelt the terrible serpent Sati-temui, which preyed on the dead who dwelt in the Duat. The fifth region was inhabited by spirits who fed upon the shadows of the weak and helpless souls. They appear to have been a description of vampire. The remaining regions were very similar to these.

The Journey of Osiris

We find other descriptions of the Duat in the *Book of Gates* and the *Book of Him that is in the Duat*, in which is outlined the journey that the sun-god makes through the otherworld after he has set upon the earth-world. Immediately after sinking he takes the form of Osiris, which in this instance is that of a ram with a man's head. Coming to the antechamber of the Duat in the west, his entrance is heralded by songs of praise, raised by the Ape-gods, while serpents blow fire from their mouths by the light of which his Pilot-gods steer his craft. All the doors are thrown open, and the dead, revived by the earthly air which Osiris carries with him, come to life again for a brief hour. All the creatures of this portion of the Duat are provided with meat and drink by command of the god. Such of the dead as dwell here are those who have failed to pass the various tests for entrance to his court, and all that they exist for is the material comfort provided for them by the brief diurnal passage of the deity. When the sun, who in this form is known as Af Ra, reaches the entrance to the second part of the Duat, which is called Urnes, the gods of the first section depart from him, and do not again behold his face until the following night. At this point the boat of Af Ra is met by the boats of Osiris and his attendant gods, and in this place also Osiris desires that the dead should receive food, light, and air. Here he grapples with the serpents Hau and Neha-her, as do most sun-gods during the time of darkness, and, having overcome them, is led into the Field of the Grain-gods, where he reposes for a while. When there he hearkens to the prayers of the living on behalf of the dead, and takes account of the offerings made by them. Continuing his journey, he traverses the twelve sections of the Duat. In some of these we see what were probably quite separate realms of the dead, such as the Realm of Seker, a god who is perhaps of greater antiquity than Osiris. In this place his boat is useless, as there is no river in the gloomy kingdom of Seker, which appears completely alien to Osiris. He therefore repeats words of awful power, which compel the gods of the place to lead him by subterranean passages from which he emerges into Amhet, where is situated a stream of boiling water. But he is not out of the kingdom of Seker until he reaches the sixth section, where dwell the dead kings of Egypt and the 'Khu' or Spirit-souls. It is at this point of his journey that Af Ra turns his face toward the east and directs his course to the Mountain of the Sunrise; previous to this he has been journeying from the south to the north. In the seventh section he is joined by Isis and other deities, and here his path is obstructed by the wicked serpent Apep, through whose body the attendant deities drive their daggers. A company of gods tow him through the eighth section, but his vessel sails itself through the ninth, and in the tenth and eleventh he seems to pass over a series of lakes, which may represent the lagoons of the eastern delta. In the latter section his progress is lighted by a disk of light, encircled by a serpent, which rests upon the prow of the boat. The twelfth section contains the great mass of celestial waters called Nu, and here dwells Nut, the personification of the morning. Before the boat looms the great serpent Ankh-neteru, and twelve of the gods, taking hold of the tow-line, enter this serpent at the tail and draw the god in his boat through the monstrous body, bringing Af Ra out at its mouth; but not as Af Ra, for during this passage he has been transformed into Khepera, in which shape he is towed into the sky by twelve goddesses, who lead him before Shu, the god of the atmosphere of the terrestrial world. Shu places him in the opening in the semicircular wall which forms the end of the twelfth section, and he now appears to mortal eyes as a disk of light, having discarded his mummified form, in which he traversed the Duat. His progress is followed by the acclamations of his company of gods, who fall upon and destroy his enemies and sing hymns of praise to him. The Duat, as described in the *Book of Gates*, differs considerably from that of the *Book of Him that is in the Duat*, but it also possesses twelve sections, and a similar journey is outlined in it.

The principal gods alluded to in the *Book of the Dead* are: Tem or Atmu, Nu, Ra, Khepra, Ptah, Ptah-Seker, Khnemu, Shu, Set, Horus, Thoth, Nephthys, Anubis, Amen, and Anu—in fact, the majority of the principal divinities of Egypt. Besides these there were many lesser gods and a great company of spirits, demons, and other supernatural beings. Many of these demons were very ancient forms of half-forgotten deities. It will be noticed that at practically every stage of his journey Osiris left behind him one or more of his divine companions, who henceforth were supposed to become the rulers or satraps of the regions in which he had quitted them. So might an earthly Pharaoh reward his courtiers for services rendered.

It was only during the Middle Kingdom that the conception of Osiris as judge of the dead took definite form and received general recognition. In one of the chapters of the *Book of the Dead* we find him seated in a large hall the roof of which is covered with fire and symbols of truth. Before him are the symbol of Anubis, the four sons of Horus, and the Devourer of the West, a monster who serves as his protector. In the rear sit the forty-two judges of the dead. The deceased makes his appearance before the god and his heart is placed in a great balance to be weighed by Anubis, Thoth, the scribe of the gods, standing by to note the result upon his tablets. Having communicated this to Osiris, the dead man, if found worthy, is presented to the deity, to whom he repeats a long prayer, in which he states that he has not committed any evil. Those who could not pass the test were hurried away, and so far as is known were in danger of being devoured by a frightful monster called Beby, which awaited them outside. The justified deceased took part in the life of Osiris and the other gods, which appears to have been very much the same as that of the Egyptian aristocracy. As has been said, the deceased might also transform himself into any animal form he cared. The life of the justified dead is well outlined in an inscription on the tomb of Paheri, prince of El Kab, which is as follows: "Thou goest in and out with a glad heart, and with the rewards of the gods. . . . Thou becomest a living soul; thou hast power over bread, water, and air. Thou changest thyself into a phœnix or a swallow, a sparrow-hawk or a heron, as thou desirest. Thou dost cross in the boat and art not hindered. Thou sailest upon the water when a flood ariseth. Thou livest anew and thy soul is not parted from thy body. Thy soul is a god together with the illuminated, and the excellent souls speak with thee. Thou art among them and (verily) receivest what is given upon earth; thou possessest water, possessest air, hast superabundance of that which thou desirest. Thine eyes are given to thee to see, and thine ears to hear speech, thy mouth speaketh, thy legs move, thy hands and arms bestir themselves for thee, thy flesh grows, thy veins are in health, and thou feelest thyself well in all thy limbs. Thou hast thine upright heart in thy possession, and thy earlier heart belongs to thee. Thou dost mount up to heaven, and art summoned each day to the libation table of Wennofre, thou receivest the good which has been offered to him and the gifts of the Lords of the necropolis."

The *Book of the Dead* is obviously an allegory of the passage of the sun through the underworld. The sinking of the sun at nightfall would naturally arouse in primitive man thoughts as to where the luminary dwelt during the hours of gloom, for the sun was to early man a living thing. He could watch its motion

The Weighing of the Heart (page 119)

From the Papyrus of Ani

Reproduced from the Facsimile by Permission of the Director of the British Museum

Ra

(page 130)

across the sky, and the light and other benefits which he received from it came to make him regard it as the source of all good. It appeared plain to him that its diurnal career was cut short by the attacks of some enemy, and the logical sequel of the belief in the solar deity as a beneficent power was of course that the force hostile to him must be of evil disposition. It came to be figured as a serpent or dragon which nightly battled with the luminary and for a season prevailed. The gods of many religions have to descend into the otherworld to do battle with the forces of death and hell. We may see an analogy to the *Book of the Dead* in the Central American *Popol Vuh*, in which two hero-gods, the sons and nephews of the sun and the moon, descend into the dark abyss of the Maya Hades, rout its forces, and return triumphant. It has been suggested that the *Book of the Dead* was nothing more or less than the ritual of a secret brotherhood, and that the various halls mentioned in it symbolized the several stages of initiation through which the members had to pass.

It is curious that in his recent interesting book on *Mexican Archæology* Mr. T. Athol Joyce, of the British Museum, has mentioned that the court of the Maya underworld, as alluded to in the *Popol Vuh*, "seems to have been conducted on the principle of a secret society with a definite form of initiation." It is practically certain that the mysteries of Eleusis, and similar Greek initiatory ceremonies, were concerned with the life of the underworld, especially with the story of Demeter and Kore, or Ceres, and that a theatric representation of the wanderings of the mother in search of her daughter in the underworld was given in the course of the ceremonial. These Greek deities, besides being gods of the dead, were gods of agriculture—corn-gods;

but gods of the underworld often presided over the growth of the crops, as it was believed that the grain germinated underneath the earth by their influence. For example, we find in the *Popol Vuh* that Xquiq, daughter of one of the lords of the underworld, was able to reap a field of maize in a few minutes in a spot where before there had been none. All this would seem to point to the probability that if the *Book of the Dead* did not contain an early type of initiatory ceremonial, it may have powerfully influenced the ceremonial of mysteries when they arose. The mysteries of the Cabiri, for example, are supposed to be of Egyptian origin. On the other hand, it may be possible that the *Book of the Dead* represents the ceremonial of an older prehistoric mystery, which had been forgotten by the dynastic Egyptians. Savage races all over the world possess such mysteries. The Indians of North America and the Blackfellows of Australia possess most elaborate initiatory ceremonies; and it is quite possible that the *Book of the Dead* may preserve the ritual of Neolithic savages who practised it thousands of years prior to its connexion with the worship of Osiris.

The Place of Punishment

Although there does not appear to have been a portion of the Duat specially reserved for the wicked, they were sufficiently tormented in many ways to render their existence a punishment for any misdeeds committed during life. At one end of this region were pits of fire where grisly deities presided, superintending the destruction of the bodies of the deceased and hacking them to pieces before they were burned. Their punishment was, however, mitigated by the appearance of Ra-Osiris on his nightly journey, for as he advanced their torments ceased for the time being.

The deities who inflicted punishment upon the damned were the enemies of Ra-Osiris—personifications of darkness, night, fog, mist, vapour, tempest, wind, and so forth, and these were destroyed daily by the fiery beams of the luminary. These were pictured in human form, and the scenes of their destruction by fire have often been mistakenly supposed to represent the burning of the souls of the doomed. This evil host was renewed with every revolution of the sun, so that a fresh phalanx of enemies appeared to attack Ra each night and morning. It was during the interval between dawn and sunrise that they were discomfited and punished. The souls of the doomed were in no wise enabled to hinder the progress of Ra, but in later times these were in some measure identified with the enemies of Ra, with whom they dwelt and whom they assisted to attack the sun-god. In the strife which ensued they were pierced by the fiery sun-rays, symbolized as darts or spears, and the knives which hacked their bodies in pieces were typical of the flames of fire emanating from the body of Ra. The lakes and pits of fire in which they were submerged typified the appearance of the eastern heavens at sunrise.

There was nothing in the Egyptian creed to justify the belief in everlasting punishment, and such a view is unsupported by the material of the texts. There is, in fact, no parallel in the Egyptian religion to the Gehenna of the Hebrews, or the Purgatory and Hell of medieval Europe. The Egyptian idea of death did not include the conception of the resurrection of a second physical body in the underworld, but, should the physical body be destroyed, they considered that the *ka* or double, the shadow and spirit of man, might also perish. It is strange, all the same, to observe that the Egyptian idea of temporary punishment after death appears to have coloured the medieval Christian conception of that state through Coptic sources. Indeed, the Coptic Christians of Egypt appear to have borrowed the idea of punishment in the Duat almost entire from their pagan ancestors or contemporaries. Amélineau cites a Coptic work in which a dead Egyptian tells how at the hour of dissolution avenging angels collected around him with knives and other weapons, which they thrust through and through him. Other spirits tore his soul from his body and, securing it to the back of a black horse, galloped off with it to Amentet. On arrival there he was first tortured in a place filled with noisome reptiles, and was then thrust into outer darkness. He fell into another pit at least two hundred feet deep, in which were assembled reptiles of every description, each having seven heads, and here he was given over to a serpent which had teeth like iron stakes. From Monday to Friday of each week this monster gnawed and tore at the doomed wretch, who rested only from this torment on Saturday and Sunday. In the circumstance that it does not posit eternal punishment, the region of torment, if so it can be named, differs from similar ideas in other mythologies; but in the essence concerning the nature of the punishment meted out, the cutting with knives, stabbing with spears, burning with fire, and so forth, it is practically at one with the underworlds of other faiths. The scenery of the Egyptian infernal regions also closely resembles that of its equivalents in other mythologies. It was not to be supposed that the Egyptians, with their elaborate precautions against bodily attack after death, should believe in eternal punishment. They may have believed in punishment for each other, but it is highly improbable that any Egyptian who had devoted any time to the study of the *Book of the Dead* believed that he himself was doomed. His whole future, according to that book, hung upon his knowledge of the words of power written therein, and surely no one with such a comparatively easy means of escape could have been so foolish as to neglect it.

The Egyptian Heaven

As has been said, the exact position of heaven does not appear to have been located, but it may be said in a general sense that the Egyptians believed it to be placed somewhere above the sky. They called it Pet, which expression they used in contradistinction to the word Nu, meaning sky. The heavens and the sky they regarded as a slab, each end of which rested on a support formed of the two mountains Bakhau and Manu, the mountains of sunrise and sunset. In primitive times heaven was conceived as consisting of two portions, the east and the west; but later it was divided into four parts, each of which was placed under the sovereignty of a god. This region was supported by four pillars, each of which again was under the direction of a deity, and at a comparatively late period an extra pillar was added to support the middle. In one myth we find the heavens spoken of as representing a human head, the sun and moon forming the eyes, and the supports of heaven being formed by the hair. The gods of the four quarters who guarded the original pillars were those deities known as Canopic (see p. 28), or otherwise called the Children of Horus.

In heaven dwelt the great god Ra, who sat upon a metal throne, the sides of which were embossed with the faces of lions and the hoofs of bulls. His train or company surrounded him, and was in its turn encircled by the lesser companies of deities. Each of the gods who presided over the world and the Duat had also his own place in heaven. Beneath the lesser gods again came beings who might well be described as angelical. First among these were the Shemsu-heru, or followers of Horus, who waited upon the sun-god, and, if necessary, came to his protection. They were regarded as being essential to his welfare. Next came the Ashemu, the attributes of which are unknown, and after those the Henmemet, perhaps souls who were to become human beings, but their status is by no means clear. They were supposed to live upon grain and herbs. There were also beings called Utennu and Afa, regarding the characteristics of which absolutely nothing is known. Following these came an innumerable host of spirits, souls and so forth, chiefly of those who had once dwelt upon the earth, and who were known collectively as 'the living ones.' The Egyptians thought these might wander about the earth and return to heaven at certain fixed times, the idea arising probably because they wished to provide a future for the body as well as for the soul and spirit. As explained previously, the gods of heaven had their complements or doubles on earth, and man in some degree was supposed to partake of this dual nature. The Egyptian conception of heaven altered slowly throughout the centuries. An examination of the earliest records available shows that the idea of existence after death was a sort of shadowy extension of the life of this world. Such an idea is common to all primitive races. As they progressed, however, this conception became entirely changed and a more spiritual one took its place. The soul, *ba*, and the spirit, *khu*, which were usually represented as a hawk and a heron in the hieroglyphic texts, partook of heavenly food and became one with the gods, and in time became united with the glorified body or heavenly frame, so that the soul-spirit, power, shade, double, and name of the deceased were all collected in the one heavenly body known as *sahu*, which may be described as the spiritual body. It was considered to grow out of the dead body, and its existence became possible through the magic ceremonies performed and the words of power spoken by the priests during the burial service.

How the Blessed Lived

In the *Book of the Dead* it is stated that the spirits of heaven are in number 4,601,200. It has been suggested that this number was probably the Egyptian enumeration of all those human spirits who had died and had attained to heaven; but this is hardly probable, for obvious reasons. The manner in which these spirits employed their time is a little obscure. Some directed the revolutions of the heavenly bodies; others accompanied the great gods in their journey through the heavens; while still others superintended mundane affairs. They chanted eternal praises of Ra as supreme monarch of the gods, and their hymns described the wonders of his power and glory. They lived upon the rays of light which fell from the eye of Horus—that is, they were nourished upon sunlight, so that in time their bodies became wholly composed of light. According to one myth the gods themselves lived upon a species of plant called the 'plant of life,' which appears to have grown beside a great lake. But such a conception is in consonance with an almost separate theological idea to the effect that the deceased dwelt in a Paradise where luxuriant grain-fields were watered by numerous canals, and where material delights of every kind abounded. It was perhaps this place in which the 'bread of eternity' and the 'beer of eternity,' the celestial fig-tree, and other such conceptions were supposed to form the food of the dead. The blessed were supposed to be arrayed in garments similar to those which clothed the gods, but certain of them seem to have worn white linen apparel, with white sandals on their feet.

All this goes to show that the heaven of the primitive Egyptians was nothing more than an extension of terrestrial conditions, or perhaps it might be said an improvement upon them. So long as the Egyptian had the wherewithal to make bread and to brew beer, and had cleanly garments, and shelter under a homestead the ground round which was intersected with numerous canals, he considered that to be the best of all possible heavens. The crops, of course, would grow of themselves. The whole idea was quite a material one, if the life was simple but comfortable. There is nothing sophisticated about the Egyptian heaven like the Mohammedan or Christian realms of bliss ; even the manner of reaching it was primitive, the early dwellers by the Nile imagining that they could reach it by climbing on to its metal floor by way of the mountains which supported it, and their later descendants believing that a ladder was necessary for the ascent. In many tombs models of these ladders were placed so that the dead people might make use of their astral counterparts to gain the celestial regions. Even Osiris required such a ladder, and was helped to ascend it by Ra and Horus, or by Horus and Set. Many pictures of such ladders are also found in various papyri of the *Book of the Dead* which were placed in tombs. Its length was regulated by the deceased himself according to the power of the magical words he pronounced over it. The deceased by words of power was further enabled to turn himself into many bird and animal shapes. It is difficult to understand the reason for these animal transformations in Paradise, but the conception has a parallel in the idea of the Aztec warriors that when they entered the domain of the sun-god they would accompany him in his course and would descend to earth during part of his daily journey in the shape of humming-birds.

CHAPTER V : THE GREAT GODS

Ra, the Sun-God

RA, the great god of the sun, appears to have occupied a prominent position in the Egyptian pantheon at a very early period. The Egyptians of later days appear to have thought that the name was in some way associated with creation. Sun-worship in Egypt was very ancient, and it is probable that a number of sun-cults became fused in that of Ra. It is certain, indeed, that this was the case with the cult of the hawk-god Heru or Horus. Both of these deities are usually figured with the body of a man and the head of a hawk, but they sometimes have the veritable form of that bird. The hawk in Egypt appears to have been identified with the sun from the earliest times. Its power of flight and the heights to which it can rise were probably the reasons assigned for its association with the great luminary of day. But in many lands birds of heaven-aspiring flight have symbolized the sun. Among several of the North American Indian tribes the eagle typifies the sun. The condor typified the orb of day in ancient Peru, and perhaps the eagle did the same in some aspects of the Mexican religion. But it is not always birds of lofty flight which typify the sun. Thus the quetzal bird seems to have stood for it in Mexico and Central America, and in the same countries the humming-bird or colibri was sometimes associated with it. It is strange that just as we find the bird and the serpent combined in the Mexican god Quetzalcoatl, so we discover them to some extent associated in Ra, who wears as his symbol the disk of the sun encircled by the serpent Khut.

The Egyptians had several varying conceptions as to the manner in which the sun crossed the heavens. One of these was that it sailed over the watery mass of the sky in relays of boats or barques. Thus the rising sun occupied the barque Manzet, which means 'growing strong,' and the evening sun was ferried to the place of setting by the barque Mesektet, which means 'growing weak,' in both of which names will be readily discovered allegorical titles for the rising and setting sun. The definite path of Ra across the sky had been planned at the time of creation by the goddess Maāt, who personified justice and order.

The daily voyage of Ra was assisted by a company of friendly deities, who navigated his barque to the place of the setting sun, the course being set out by Thoth and Maāt, while Horus acted as steersman and commander. On each side of the boat swam one of two pilot fishes called Abtu and Ant, but, notwithstanding the assistance of his fellow deities, the barque of Ra was constantly beset by the most grisly monsters and demons, who strove to put every obstacle in the way of its successful passage.

By far the most potent of these was the serpent Apep, who personified the darkness of night, and concerning whom we gain much information from the *Book of Overthrowing Apep*, which gives spells and other instructions for the checkmating of the monster, which were recited daily in the temple of Amen-Ra at Thebes. In these Apep is referred to as a crocodile and a serpent, and it is described how by the aid of sympathetic magic he is to be speared, cut with knives, decapitated, roasted, and finally consumed by fire, and his evil followers also. These magical acts were duly carried out at Thebes day by day, and it was supposed that they greatly assisted the journey of the sun-god. In Apep we have a figure such as is known in nearly every mythology. He is the monster who daily combats with, and finally succeeds in devouring, the sun. He is the same as the dragons which fought with Beowulf the sun-hero, as the night-dragon of Chinese mythology, as the Fenris-wolf of Scandinavian story, and the multitudinous monsters of fable, legend, and romance. We find his counterpart also in the Babylonian dragon Tiamat, who was slain by Marduk.

Rat

In the late period there was invented for Ra a female counterpart, Rat, who is depicted as a woman having on her head a disk with horns and a uræus. She does not seem to have been of any great importance, and perhaps only sprang from the idea that every great deity must have his female double. The worship of Ra in Egypt during the dynastic period was centred in the city of Anu, On, or Heliopolis, about five miles from the modern Cairo. The priests of the god had settled there during the Fifth Dynasty, the first king of which, User-ka-f, was high-priest of the god, a circumstance which denotes that the cult must even at this early period (3350 B.C.) have gained great ascendancy in that part of Egypt.

An ancient legend describes how the progeny of Ra first gained the Egyptian throne, and will be found on page 200.

This tradition proves that in early times the kings of Egypt believed themselves to have been descended from Ra, who, it was affirmed, had once ruled over the country, and whose blood flowed in the veins of the entire Egyptian royal family. Indeed, Ra was said to have been the actual father of several Egyptian kings, who were therefore regarded as gods incarnate. Such priestly fictions gave the theocratic class added power, until at last the worship of Ra practically superseded that of almost every other deity in the Nile valley, these being absorbed into the theological system of the priests of Heliopolis, and granted subordinate positions in the group which surrounded the great sun-god.

Fusion of Myths

It is not in Egypt alone that we find such astute subterfuges made to subserve the purposes of the priesthood. In most mythologies we discover that legends of creation and of the origin of deities have in many cases been manufactured from two or more myths which have been so skilfully amalgamated that it is only by the most careful and patient study that they can be resolved into their original components. Thus we find in the Book of Genesis that beside the existence of Jahveh, the creative power, we have evidences of a polytheistic pantheon called Elohim. This shows that two accounts of the Hebrew creation, the one monotheistic and the other polytheistic, have become fused together. Perhaps one of the best examples of this dovetailing of myths is to be found in one of the creation legends of Peru, in which philosophic skill has fused all the forms of worship through which Peruvian thought passed into one definite whole. Thus the various stages of belief from simple animism to anthropomorphism are visible to the student of mythology in perusing this one legend. That the same feat had been accomplished by the Kiches of Central America in their wonderful book, the *Popol Vuh*, was shown by the writer in an article printed in the *Times* some years ago.

The original local god of Heliopolis was Tem or Atum, who was united with Ra as Ra-Tem. The power of the priests of Ra declined somewhat about the close of the Sixth Dynasty, but in the reign of Senusert I[1]

[1] Or Usertsen.

(*c.* 2433 B.C.) the temple at Heliopolis was rebuilt, being dedicated to Ra and to two of his forms, Horus and Temu. In this temple were kept models of the sacred boats of Ra, the Manzet, containing a hawk-headed figure of Ra, and the Mesektet, a man-headed statue of him.

Primitive as is the nature of sun-worship, it possesses elements which enable it to survive where many more advanced and complicated cults succumb. Even in such a country, side by side with an aristocracy of real intelligence but limited opportunities, there must naturally have existed millions of peasants and helots who were only to be distinguished from savages because of their contact with their superiors and their settlement as an agricultural race. To them the sun would, it might be thought, appear as the god *par excellence*, the great quickener and fructifier; but we find the cult of Ra more or less of an aristocratic theological system, in early times at least; and for the cult of the people we have to turn to the worship of Osiris. Undoubtedly the best parallel to the worship of Ra in Egypt is to be found in that of the sun in ancient Peru. Just as the monarch of Peru personified the sun on earth, and acted as his regent in the terrestrial sphere, so the Egyptian monarchs styled themselves 'sons of the sun.' In both instances the solar cult was eminently aristocratic in character. This is proved by the circumstance that the paradise of Ra was a sphere more spiritual by far than that of Osiris, with its purely material delights. Those happy enough to gain the heaven of the sun-god were clothed with light, and their food was described as 'light.' The Osirian paradise, again, it will be recalled, consisted of converse with Osiris and feasting with him. Indeed, the aristocratic caste in all countries shrinks from the conception that it must in the afterlife rub shoulders with the common herd. This was definitely the case in ancient Mexico and Scandinavia, where only warriors killed in battle might enter paradise. These beliefs, however, were never sufficiently powerful to obliterate the cult of Osiris, and as the Egyptian mind was of a strongly material cast, it greatly favoured the conception of a 'field of reeds' and a 'field of peace,' where man could enjoy the good things and creature-comforts that he so much desired upon earth, rather than the unsubstantial fare and raiment of the more superlative sphere of Ra.

Ra and Osiris

A great but silent struggle was waged for many centuries between the priesthoods of Ra and Osiris, but in the end the beliefs clustering around the latter deity gained pre-eminence, and he took over the titles, powers, and attributes of the great god of the sun. Then it was probable, as has elsewhere been stated, that the conception of a moon- and a sun-god became fused in his person. The worship of Osiris was fundamentally African and Egyptian in character, but there is strong reason to believe that the cult of Ra possessed many foreign elements, possibly West Asiatic in origin, which accounts for the coldness with which the masses of Egypt regarded his worship. Heliopolis, his city, contained many inhabitants of Asiatic birth, and this may account to some extent for the introduction of some of the tenets in his creed which the native Egyptians found unpalatable.

There is no doubt, however, that, to the aristocracy of Egypt at least, Ra stood in the position of creator and father of the gods. Osiris stood in relation to him as a son. In fact, the relations of these two deities may be regarded as that between god the father and god the son, and just as in certain theologies the figure of god the son has overshadowed that of god the father, so did Osiris overshadow Ra.

The god Tem, or Atum, who, as has been said, was originally the local deity of Heliopolis, was in the dynastic period held to be one of the forms of Ra, and a personification of the setting sun. Tem was one of the first gods of the Egyptians. He is depicted as sailing in the boat of Ra, with whom he was clearly united in early times as Ra-Tem. He appears to have been a god who possessed many attributes in common with Ra, and later on he seems to have been identified with Osiris as well. In the myth of Ra and Isis Ra says, "I am Khepera in the morning, and Ra at noonday, and Tem in the evening," which shows that to the Egyptians the day was divided into three parts, each of which was presided over by a special form of the sun-god. Tem was worshipped in one of his forms as a serpent, a fairly common shape for a sun-god, for in many countries the snake or serpent, tail in mouth, symbolizes the disk of the sun.

The Sacred Beetle

Khepera, the remaining form of Ra, is generally represented in human form with a beetle upon his head. The worship of the beetle was very ancient in Egypt, and we must regard its fusion with the cult of Ra as due to priestly influence. The scarabæus, having laid its eggs in the sand of Egypt, rolls them into a little ball of manure, which it then propels across the sand with its hind legs to a hole which it has previously dug, where the eggs are hatched by the rays of the sun. This action of the beetle seemed to the ancient Egyptians to resemble the rolling of the sun across the heavens, so that Khepera, the rising luminary, was symbolized by it.

Isis and Ra (page 136)
Evelyn Paul

Amen-Ra (page 139)

Photo W. A. Mansell & Co.

Khepera is a deity of some importance, for he is called creator of the gods and father of the gods. He was also looked upon as a type of the resurrection, because of his symbolizing the ball enclosing living germs, and probably in a secondary sense, because the rising sun steps as it were from the grave of night morning after morning with the greatest certainty. The scarabs which were found on Egyptian mummies typified this hope of resurrection, and have been found in Egyptian tombs as old as the time of the Fourth Dynasty.

Amen

Although the god Amen appears to have been numbered among the deities of Egypt as early as the Fifth Dynasty, when he was alluded to as one of the primeval gods,[1] it was not until a later period that his votaries began to exercise the enormous power which they wielded throughout Egypt. With the exception of Ra and Osiris, the worship of Amen was more widespread than that of any other god in the Nile valley; but the circumstances behind the growth of his cult certainly point to its having been disseminated by political rather than religious propaganda. What his attributes were in the time of the Ancient Empire we do not know. The name means 'what is hidden,' or what cannot be seen, and we are constantly informed in votive hymns and other compositions that he is "hidden to his children" and "hidden to gods and men." It has been advanced that these expressions refer to the setting of the sun, but there is far better reason for supposing that they

[1] There is a mention in the pyramid of Unas (Sixth Dynasty) of a deity which may mean Amen, but may also mean 'The Hidden One,' and the epithet which follows appears to apply to Osiris.

imply that Amen is a god who cannot be viewed by mortal eyes, invisible and inscrutable. It is not difficult to see that the conception of such a deity would speedily win favour with a priestly and theological class, who would quickly tire of the more material cults by which they were surrounded, and who would strain after a form of godhead less crude than the purely symbolical systems which held sway in the country. In fact, the whole theological history of Amen is that of a priesthood who were determined to impose upon a rather materialistic population a more spiritual type of worship and a higher conception of God.

Amen was represented in numerous forms:[1] in the shape of a man seated on a throne, with the head of a frog and the body of a man, with a serpent's head, as an ape and as a lion. But the most general form in which he was drawn was that of a bearded man wearing on his head two long and very straight plumes, which are coloured alternately red and green or red and blue. He is clothed in a linen tunic, wears bracelets, and necklet, and from the back of his dress there hangs an animal's tail, which denotes that he was a god originating in early times. In a later form he has the head of a hawk when fused with Ra. The great centre of his worship and of his rise to power was the city of Thebes, where in the Twelfth Dynasty a temple was built in his honour. At that period he was a mere local god, but when the princes of Thebes came into power and grasped the sovereignty of Egypt the reputation of Amen rose with theirs, and he became a prominent god in Upper Egypt. His priesthood, seizing upon the new political conditions, cleverly succeeded in identifying him with Ra and his subsidiary forms, all of whose attributes they

[1] Budge, *The Gods of Egypt*, ii. p. 2.

ascribed to Amen ; but they further stated that although their deity included in himself all their characteristics, he was much greater and loftier than they. As we have already observed, the god of the capital of Egypt for the time being was the national deity, and when this lot fell to the fortune of Amen his priesthood took full advantage of it. Never was a god so exploited and, if the term may be employed, advertised as was Amen. When evil days fell upon Egypt and the Hyksos overran the country, Amen, thanks to his priestly protagonists, weathered the storm and, because of internecine strife, had become the god *par excellence* of the Egyptians. When the country recovered from its troubles and matters began to right themselves once more, the military successes of the kings of the Eighteenth Dynasty redounded greatly to the power and glory of Amen, and the spoil of conquered Palestine and Syria loaded his temples. There was of course great dissatisfaction on the part of the worshippers of Ra at such a condition of affairs. Osiris, as the popular god, could not well be displaced, as he had too large a hold on the imagination of the people, and his cult and character were of too peculiar a nature to admit of usurpation by another deity. His cult had been slowly evolved, probably through many centuries, and the circumstances of his worship were unique. But the cult of Ra was challenged by that of a deity who not only presented like attributes, but whose worship was on the whole more spiritual and of a higher trend than that of the great sun-god. We do not know what theological battles were waged over the question of the supremacy of the two gods, but we do know that priestly skill was, as in other cases, more than equal to the occasion. A fusion of the gods took place. It would be rash to assert that this amalgamation was a planned affair between the two warring cults, and it is more probable that their devotees quietly acquiesced in a gradual process of fusion. The Theban priests would come to recognize that it was impossible to destroy altogether the worship of Ra, so they would as politic men bow to the inevitable and accept his amalgamation with their own deity.

Amen's Rise to Power

Many hymns of Amen-Ra, especially that occurring in the papyrus of Hu-nefer, show the completeness of this fusion and the rapidity with which Amen had risen to power. In about a century from being a mere local god he had gained the title of 'king of the gods' of Egypt. His priesthood had become by far the most powerful and wealthy in the land, and even rivalled royalty itself. Their political power can only be described as enormous. They made war and peace, and when the Ramessid Dynasty came to an end the high-priest of Amen-Ra was raised to the royal power, instituting the Twenty-first Dynasty, known as the 'dynasty of priest-kings.' But if they were strong in theology, they were certainly not so in military genius. They could not enforce the payment of tribute which their predecessors had wrung from the surrounding countries, and their poverty increased rapidly. The shrines of the god languished for want of attendants, and even the higher ranks of the priesthood itself suffered a good deal of hardship. Robber bands infested the vicinity of the temples, and the royal tombs were looted. But if their power waned, their pretensions certainly did not, and even in the face of Libyan aggression in the Delta they continued to vaunt the glory of the god whom they served. Examining the texts and hymns which tell us what we know of Amen-Ra, we find that in them he is considered as the general source of life, animate and inanimate, and is identified with the creator of the universe, the 'unknown god.' All the attributes of the entire Egyptian pantheon were lavished upon him, with the exception of those of Osiris, of whom the priests of Amen-Ra appear to have taken no notice. But they could not displace the great god of the dead, although they might ignore him. In one of his forms certainly, that of Khensu the Moon-god, Amen bears a slight likeness to Osiris, but we cannot say that in this form he usurps the *rôle* of the god of the underworld in any respect. Amen-Ra even occupied the shrines of many other gods throughout the Nile valley, absorbing their attributes and entirely taking their place. One of his most popular forms was that of a goose, and the animal was sacred to him in many parts of Egypt, as was the ram. Small figures of him made in the Ptolemaic form have the bearded face of a man, the body of a beetle, the wings of a hawk, human legs with the toes and claws of a lion. All this, of course, only symbolizes the many-sided character of him who was regarded as the greatest of all gods, and typified the manner in which attributes of every description resided in him. The entire *pesedt* or company of the gods was supposed to be unified in Amen, and indeed we may describe his cult as one of the most serious attempts of antiquity to formulate a system of monotheism, the worship of a single god. That they did not achieve this was by no means their fault. We must look upon them as a band of enlightened men animated by a spiritual fire, which burned very brightly among the sadly material surroundings of Egypt. But, like all priestly hierarchies, they possessed the inherent weakness of ambition and the love of overweening power. Had they relegated politics to its proper sphere, they might have been much more successful than they were; but the true cause of their ultimate failure to conquer entirely the other cults of Egypt lay in the circumstance of the very ancient and deep-seated nature of these cults, and of the primeval and besotted ignorance of those who supported them.

The Oracle of Jupiter-Ammon

No part of Egypt was free from the dominion of Amen-Ra, which spread north and south, east and west, and had ramifications in Syria, Nubia, and other Egyptian dependencies. Its most powerful centres were Thebes, Hermonthis, Coptos, Panopolis, Hermopolis Magna, and in Lower Egypt Memphis, Saïs, Heliopolis, and Mendes. In one of the oases in later times he had a great oracle, known as that of Jupiter-Ammon, a mysterious spot frequented by superstitious Greeks and Romans, who went there to consult the deity on matters of state or private importance. Here every roguery of priestcraft was practised. An idol of the god was on occasion carried through the temple by his priests, responding, if he were in a good humour, to his votaries, not by speech, but by nodding and pointing with outstretched arm. We know from classical authors that the Egyptians possessed the most wonderful skill in the manufacture of automata, and there is no room for doubt that the god responded to the questions of the eager devotees who had made the journey to his shrine by means of cleverly concealed strings. But the oracle of Jupiter-Ammon in Libya is surrounded in obscurity. Even Alexander the Great paid a visit to this famous shrine to satisfy himself whether or not he was the son of Jupiter. Lysander and Hannibal also journeyed thither, and the former received a two-edged answer from the deity, not unlike that which Macbeth received from the witches.

Mut the Mother

The great female counterpart of Amen-Ra was Mut, the 'world-mother.' She is usually represented as a woman wearing the united crowns of north and south, and holding the papyrus sceptre. In some pictures she is delineated with wings, and in others the heads of vultures project from her shoulders. Like her husband, she is occasionally adorned with every description of attribute, human and animal, probably to typify her universal nature. Mut, like Amen, swallowed up a great many of the attributes of the female deities of Egypt. She was thus identified with Bast, Nekhebet, and others, chiefly for the reason that because Amen had usurped the attributes of other gods, she, as his wife, must do the same. She is a striking example in mythology of what marriage can do for a goddess. Even Hathor was identified with her, as was Ta-urt and every other goddess who could be regarded as having the attributes of a mother. Her worship centred at Thebes, where her temple was situated a little to the south of the shrine of Amen-Ra. She was styled the 'lady of heaven' and 'queen of the gods,' and her hieroglyphic symbol, a vulture, was worn on the crowns of Egypt's queens as typical of their motherhood. The temple of Mut at Thebes was built by Amen-hetep III about 1450 B.C. Its approach was lined by a wonderful avenue of sphinxes, and it overlooked an artificial lake. Mut was probably the original female counterpart of Nu, who in some manner became associated with Amen. She is mentioned only once in the *Book of the Dead* in the Theban Recension, which is not a little strange considering the reputation she must have enjoyed with the priesthood of Amen.

Ptah

Ptah was the greatest of the gods of Memphis. He personified the rising sun, or, rather, a phase of it—that is, he represented the orb at the time when it begins to rise above the horizon, or immediately after it has risen. The name is said to mean 'opener,' from the circumstance that Ptah was thought to open the day; but this derivation has been combated. Dr Brugsch suggests 'sculptor' or 'engraver' as the true translation, and as Ptah was the god of all handicrafts it seems most probable that this is correct. Ptah seems to have retained the same characteristics from the period of the Second Dynasty down to the latest times. In early days he seems to have been regarded as a creator, or perhaps he was confounded with one of the first Egyptian creative deities. We find him alluded to in the Pyramid Text of Teta as the owner of a 'workshop,' and the passage seems to imply that it was Ptah who fashioned new boats in which the souls of the dead were to live in the Duat. From the *Book of the Dead* we learn that he was a great worker in metals, a master architect, and framer of everything in the universe; and the fact that the Romans identified him with Vulcan greatly assists our understanding of his attributes.

It was Ptah who, in company with Khnemu, carried out the commands of Thoth concerning the creation of the universe. To Khnemu was given the fashioning of animals, while Ptah was employed in making the heavens and the earth. The great metal plate which was supposed to form the floor of heaven and the roof of the sky was made by Ptah, who also framed the

Mut (page 143)

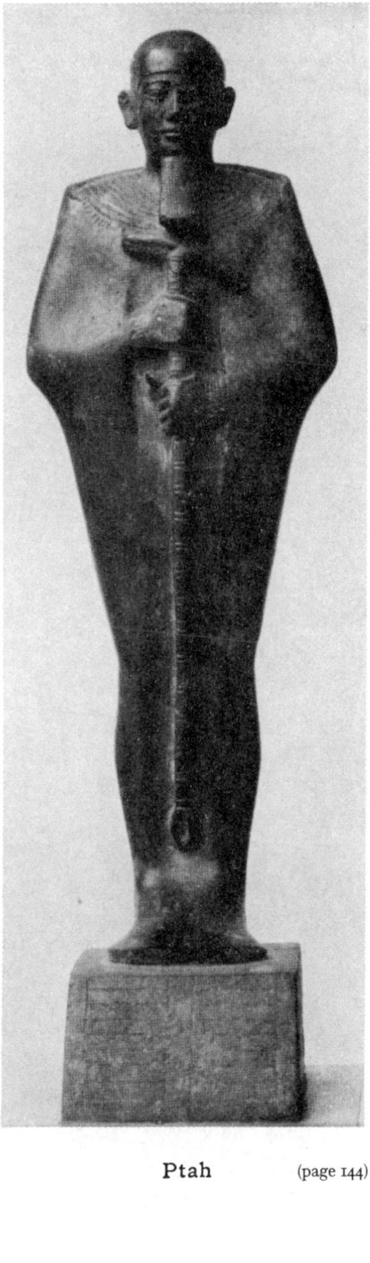

Ptah (page 144)

Sekhmet (page 147)

Photo W. A. Mansell & Co.

Bast (page 147)

Photo W. A. Mansell & Co.

supports which upheld it. We find him constantly associated with other gods—that is, he takes on the attributes or characteristics of other deities for certain fixed purposes. For example, as architect of the universe he partakes of the nature of Thoth, and as the god who beat out the metal floor of heaven he resembles Shu.

Ptah is usually represented as a bearded man having a bald head, and dressed in habiliments which fit as closely as a shroud. From the back of his neck hangs a Menat, the symbol of happiness, and along with the usual insignia of royalty and godhead he holds the symbol of stability. As Ptah-Seker he represents the union of the creative power with that of chaos or darkness:[1] Ptah-Seker is, indeed, a form of Osiris in his guise of the Night-sun, or dead Sun-god. Seker is figured as a hawk-headed man in the form of a mummy, his body resembling that of Ptah. Originally Seker represented darkness alone, but in later times came to be identified with the Night-sun. Seker is, indeed, confounded in places with Sept, and even with Geb. He appears to have ruled that portion of the underworld where dwelt the souls of the inhabitants of Memphis and its neighbourhood.

The Seker-boat

In the great ceremonies connected with this god, and especially on the day of his festival, a boat called the Seker-boat was placed upon a sledge at sunrise, at the time when the rays of the sun were slowly beginning to diffuse themselves over the earth. It was then drawn round the sanctuary, which act typified the revolution of the sun. This boat was known as Henu, and is mentioned several times in the *Book of the Dead.*

[1] Budge, *op. cit.* i. p. 503.

It did not resemble an ordinary boat, but one end of it was much higher than the other, and was fashioned in the shape of the head of an animal resembling a gazelle. In the centre of the vessel was a coffer surmounted by a hawk with outspread wings, which was supposed to contain the body of Osiris, or of the dead Sun-god. The Seker- or Henu-boat was probably a form of the Mesektet-boat, in which the sun sailed over the sky during the second half of his daily journey, and in which he entered the underworld in the evening. Although Seker was fairly popular as a deity in ancient Egypt, his attributes seem to have been entirely usurped by Ptah. We also find the triple-named deity Ptah-Seker-Asar or Ptah-Seker-Osiris, who is often represented as a hawk on coffers and sarcophagi. About the Twenty-second Dynasty this triad had practically become one with Osiris, and he had even variants which took the attributes of Min, Amsu, and Khepera. He has been described as the 'triune god of the resurrection.' There is very little doubt that the amalgamation of these gods was brought about by priestly influence.

Ptah was also connected with the god known as Tenen, who is usually represented in human form and wearing on his head the crown with ostrich feathers. He is also drawn working at a potter's wheel, upon which he shapes the egg of the world. In other drawings he is depicted as holding a scimitar. Dr Budge suggests that this weapon shows that he is the destructive power of nature or the warrior-god, but this is most unlikely. The scimitar of Ptah in his guise as Tenen is precisely the same as those axes which are the attributes of creative deities all over the world. With this scimitar he carves out the earth, as the god of the Ainu of Japan shapes it with his hatchet, or as other deities which have already been mentioned use their axes or hammers. Tenen was probably a primeval creative god, but for that reason was co-ordinated with Ptah.

Sekhmet

The principal centre of the worship of Ptah was Memphis, in which were also situated the temples of Sekhmet,[1] Bast, Osiris, Seker, Hathor, and I-em-hetep, as well as that of Ra. The female counterpart of Ptah was Sekhmet, and they were the parents of Nefer-tem. Sekhmet was later identified with forms of Hathor. She had the head of a lioness, and may be looked upon as bearing the same relation to Bast as Nephthys bears to Isis. She was the personification of the fierce destroying heat of the sun's rays. One of her names is Nesert, flame, in which she personifies the destroying element.

The Seven Wise Ones

We occasionally find Ptah in company with certain beings called the Seven Wise Ones of the goddess Meh-urt, who was their mother. We are told that they came forth from the water, from the pupil of the eye of Ra, and that they took the form of seven hawks, flew upward, and, together with Thoth, presided over learning and letters. Ptah as master-architect and demiurge, carrying out the designs of Thoth and his assistants, partook of the attributes of all of them, as did his female counterpart Sekhmet.

Bast

Bast, the Bubastis of the Greeks, possessed the attributes of the cat or lioness, the latter being a more modern development of her character. The

[1] Or Sekmet.

name implies 'the tearer' or 'render,' and she is also entitled 'the lady of Sept'—that is, of the star Sothis. She was further sometimes identified with Isis and Hathor. In contradistinction to the fierce Sekhmet, she typified the mild fertilizing heat of the sun. The cat loves to bask in the sun's rays, and it is probably for this reason that the animal was taken as symbolizing this goddess. She is amalgamated with Sekhmet and Ra in a deity known as Sekhmet-Bast-Ra, and as such is represented as a woman with a man's head, and wings sprouting from her arms, and the heads of two vultures springing from her neck. She has also the claws of a lion. She was the goddess of the eastern part of the Delta, and was worshipped at Bubastis, in Lower Egypt. Her worship seems to have been of very considerable antiquity in that region, and although she is mentioned in the Pyramid Texts, it is only occasionally that she figures in the *Book of the Dead.* In all probability she was originally a cat totem, and in any case was first worshipped in the shape of a cat pure and simple. It has been stated that she possesses the characteristics of a foreign goddess, but there do not appear to be any very strong grounds for this assumption. Although she is connected with fire and with the sun, it would appear that she also has some association with the lunar disk, for her son Khensu is a moon-god. Cat-gods are often associated with the moon, chiefly because of the fertility of the animal which typified the ideals of fruitfulness and growth connected with the lunar orb.

The Festival of Bast

Herodotus gives a very picturesque description of a festival of this goddess, which took place in the months of April and May. He says that the inhabitants of the city of Bubastis sailed toward it in ships, playing upon drums and tabors and making a great noise, those who did not play clapping their hands and singing loudly. Having arrived at the city, they danced and held festival with drinking and song.

Of the city of Bubastis he gives a vivid picture, which has been translated by an old English author as follows : "The noble city of Bubastis seemeth to be very haughty and highly planted, in which city is a temple of excellent memory dedicate to the goddesse Bubastis, called in our speech Diana, than the which, albeit there be other churches both bigger and more richly furnished, yet for the sightly grace and seemelynesse of building, there is none comparable unto it. Besides, the very entrance and way that leadeth unto the city, the rest is in forme of an Ilande, inclosed round about with two sundry streames of the river Nilus, which runne to either side of the path way, and leauing as it were a lane or causey betweene them, without meeting, take their course another way. These armes of the floud are each of them an hundred foote broade, beset on both sides the banckes with fayre braunched trees, ouershadowing ye waters with a coole and pleasant shade. The gate or entry of the city is in heighth 10. paces, hauing in the front a beautifull image, 6. cubites in measure. The temple it selfe situate in the middest of ye city, is euermore in sight to those yt passe to and fro. For although ye city by addition of earth was arrered and made higher, yet ye temple standing as it did in ye beginning, and neuer mooued, is in maner of a lofty and stately tower, in open and cleare viewe to euery parte of ye city. Round about the which goeth a wall, ingrauen with figures and portraitures of sundry beasts. The inner temple is enuironed with an high grove of trees, set and planted by the hande and industrie of men : in the whiche temple is standing an image. The length of the temple is in euery way a furlong. From the entrance of the temple Eastward, there is a fayre large causey leading to the house of Mercury, in length three furlongs and four acres broade, all of faire stone, and hemmed in on each side with a course of goodly tall trees planted by the hands of men, and thus as touching the description of ye temple."

Nefer-Tem

Nefer-tem was the son of Ptah and Sekhmet, or of Ptah and Bast. He is drawn as a man surmounted by plumes and sometimes standing upon a lion. Indeed, occasionally he is painted as having the head of a lion and with a body in mummy-shape. In early times he was symbolized by the lotus-flower. He was the third member of the triad of Memphis, which was made up of himself with Ptah and Sekhmet. His attributes are anything but well defined, but he is probably the young Tem, god of the rising sun. He is perhaps typified by the lotus because the sun would often seem to the Egyptians to rise from beds of this plant in the Delta of the country. In later texts he is identified with numerous gods all of whom appear to be forms of Horus or Thoth.

I-em-hetep

I-em-hetep, another son of Ptah, was also regarded as the third member of the great triad of Memphis. The name means ‘ Come in peace,’ and was given him because he was supposed to bring the art of healing to mankind. Like his father Ptah, he is depicted as wearing a skull-cap. Before him is stretched a roll of papyrus to typify his character as a god of study and learning ; but it is as a god of medicine that he was

Khnemu (page 152)

Photo W. A. Mansell & Co.

I-em-hetep (page 150)

Nefer-Tem (page 150)

Photo W. A. Mansell & Co.

Aten

(page 156)

most popular in Egypt. In later times he took the place of Thoth as scribe of the gods, and provided the words of magic power which protected the dead from their enemies in the Duat. He had also a funerary character, which perhaps implies that physicians may have been in some manner connected with the art of embalmment. He is addressed in a text of the Ptolemies in his temple on the island of Philæ as "he who giveth life to all men." He was also supposed to send the boon of sleep to the suffering, and indeed the sorrowful and afflicted were under his especial patronage. Dr Budge ventures the opinion that "if we could trace his history to its beginning, we should find probably that he was originally a very highly skilled medicine-man, who had introduced some elementary knowledge of medicine amongst the Egyptians, and who was connected with the practice of the art of preserving the bodies of the dead by means of drugs and spices and linen bandages." The supposition is a very likely one indeed, only the medicine-man must have become fairly sophisticated in later times, as is evidenced by his perusing a roll of papyrus. I-em-hetep was the god of physicians and those who dealt in medical magic, and his worship was certainly of very ancient date in Memphis. Dr Budge goes so far as to suggest that I-em-hetep was the deified form of a distinguished physician who was attached to the priesthood of Ra, and who flourished before the end of the rule of the kings of the Third Dynasty. In the songs which were sung in the temple of Antuf occurs the passage : "I have heard the words of I-em-hetep and of Heru-tata-f, which are repeated over and over again, but where are their places this day ? Their walls are overthrown, their seats have no longer any being, and they are as if they had never existed. No man cometh to declare unto us what manner of beings they were, and none telleth us of their possessions." Heru-tata-f was a man of great learning, who, as we find in the Tale of the Magician given elsewhere in this book, brought that mysterious person to the court of his father Khufu. He also discovered certain chapters of the *Book of the Dead*. It is likely, thinks Dr Budge, that the said I-em-hetep who is mentioned in connexion with him was a man of the same type, a skilled physician, whose acts and deeds were worthy of being classed with the words of Heru-tata-f. The pictures and figures of I-em-hetep suggest that he was of human and local origin, and he had a great hold upon the imagination of later Egyptians of the Saïte and Ptolemaic periods. He was indeed a species of Egyptian Hippocrates, who had probably, as Dr Budge infers, become deified because of his great medical skill.

Khnemu

At the city of Elephantine or Abu a great triad of gods was held in reverence. This consisted of Khnemu, Satet, Anqet. The worship of the first-mentioned deity was of great antiquity, and even in the inscription of King Unas we find him alluded to in a manner which proves that his cult was very old. His position, too, had always been an exalted one, and even to the last he appears to have been of importance in the eyes of the Gnostics. Khnemu was probably a god of the predynastic Egyptians. He was symbolized by the flat-horned ram, which appears to have been introduced into the country from the East. We do not find him referred to in any inscription subsequent to the Twelfth Dynasty. He is usually represented in the form of a ram-headed man wearing the white crown, and sometimes the disk. In some instances he is pictured as pouring water over the earth, and in others with a jug above his horns—a sure indication that he is connected in some way with moisture. His name signifies the builder or framer, and he it was who fashioned the first man upon a potter's wheel, who made the first egg from which sprang the sun, who made the bodies of the gods, and who continued to build them up and maintain them.

Khnemu had been worshipped at Elephantine from time immemorial and was therefore the god of the First Cataract. His female counterparts, Satet and Anqet, have been identified as a form of the star Sept and as a local Nubian goddess. From the texts it is pretty clear that Khnemu was originally a river-god who, like Hapi, was regarded as the god of the Nile and of the annual Nile flood, and it may be that he and Hapi were Nile gods introduced by two separate races, or by the people of two different portions of the country. In the texts he is alluded to as "father of the fathers of the gods and goddesses, lord of created things from himself, maker of heaven and earth and the Duat and water and mountains," so we see that, like Hapi, he had been identified with the creative deities. He is sometimes represented as having four rams' heads upon a human body, and as he united within himself the attributes of Ra, Shu, Geb, and Osiris, these heads may have typified the deities in question. Dr Brugsch considered, however, that they symbolized the four elements–fire, air, earth, and water. But it is a little difficult to see how this could be so. In any case, when represented with four heads Khnemu typified the great primeval creative force.

The Legend of the Nile's Source

The powers that were ascribed to Khnemu-Ra as god of the earthly Nile are exemplified in a story found inscribed on a rock on the island of Sahal in 1890. The king mentioned in the inscription has been identified as Tcheser, the third monarch of the Third Dynasty.

The story relates that in the eighteenth year of this king's reign a famine spread over Egypt because for seven years the Nile had not risen in flood. Thus grain of all kinds was scarce, the fields and gardens yielded naught, so that the people had no food. Strong men tottered like the aged, the old fell to the ground and rose no more, the children cried aloud with the pangs of hunger. And for the little food there was men became thieves and robbed their neighbours. Reports of these terrible conditions reached the king upon his throne, and he was stricken with grief. He remembered the god I-em-hetep, the son of Ptah, who had once delivered Egypt from a like disaster, but when his help was invoked no answer was vouchsafed. Then Tcheser the king sent to his governor Māter, who ruled over the South, the island of Elephantine, and Nubia, and asked him where was the source of the Nile and what was the name of the god or goddess of the river. And to answer this dispatch Māter the governor went in person before the king. He told him of the wonderful island of Elephantine, whereon was built the first city ever known; that out of it rose the sun when he wanted to bestow life upon mankind. Here also was a double cavern, Querti, in shape like two breasts, and from this cavern rose the Nile flood to bless the land with fruitfulness when the god drew back the bolts of the door at the proper season. And this god was Khnemu. Māter described to his royal master the temple of the Nile god at Elephantine, and stated that other gods were in it, including the great deities Osiris, Horus, Isis, and Nephthys. He told of the products of the country around, and said that from these, offerings should be made to Khnemu. Then the king rose and offered sacrifices unto the god and made supplication before him in his temple. And the god heard and appeared before the grief-stricken king. He said, "I am Khnemu the Creator. My hands rest upon thee to protect thy person and to make sound thy body. I gave thee thine heart . . . I am he who created himself. I am the primeval watery abyss, and I am the Nile who riseth at his will to give health to those who toil. I am the guide and director of all men, the Almighty, the father of the gods, Shu, the mighty possessor of the earth." And then the god promised unto the king that henceforward the Nile should rise every year as in the olden time, that the famine should be ended and great good come upon the land. But also he told the king how his shrine was desolate and that no one troubled to restore it even although stone lay all around. And this the king remembered and made a royal decree that lands on each side of the Nile near the island where Khnemu dwelt were to be set apart as the endowment of his temple, that priests were to minister at his shrine, and for their maintenance a tax must be levied on the products of the land near by. And this decree the king caused to be cut upon a stone stele and set up in a prominent place as a lasting token of gratitude unto the god Khnemu, the god of the Nile.

Satet

Satet,[1] the principal female counterpart of Khnemu, was also a goddess of the inundation. The name

[1] Or Setet = shooter (with arrows).

probably means 'to pour out' or 'to scatter abroad,' so that it might signify a goddess who wielded the powers of rain. She carries in her hands a bow and arrows, as did Neith, typical of the rain or thunderbolt. She was regarded as a form of Isis from the circumstance that both were connected with the star Sept, and in this guise she appears in the *Book of the Dead* as a counterpart of Osiris.

Anqet

Anqet, the third member of the triad of Elephantine, was a sister-goddess of Satet. She wears a crown of feathers, which would go to show that her origin is a purely African one, and she may have been a goddess of some of the islands in the First Cataract. She had been associated with the other members of the triad from very early dynastic times, however, and her cult was fairly widely disseminated through Northern Nubia. In later times her worship was centred at Sahal, where she was regarded as a goddess of that island, and where she had a temple built perhaps in the Eighteenth Dynasty. She had also a shrine at Philæ, where she was identified with Nephthys, as was almost necessary, seeing that Osiris had been identified with Khnemu and Satet with Isis. Dr Brugsch considered her a personification of the waters of the Nile, and thought that her name signified 'to surround,' 'to embrace,' and that it had reference to the embracing and nourishing of the fields by the river.

Aten

Aten, the disk of the sun, stands in a class by himself in Egyptian mythology. Although he possesses certain broad characteristics in common with other sun-gods of Egypt, yet an examination of this deity shows that he differs widely from these in many respects, and that his cult is indeed entirely foreign to the religious genius of the Egyptian people. The cult of Aten, of which there is little record before the time of Amen-hetep IV, sprang into sudden prominence during that monarch's reign and became for a time the State religion of Egypt. Of its origin nothing is known, and it would appear that under the Middle Kingdom Aten was an obscure local deity, worshipped somewhere in the neighbourhood of Heliopolis. His important position in the Egyptian pantheon is due to the fact that his cult was directly responsible for a great religious, social, and artistic revolution which occurred during the reign of Amen-hetep IV.

With the overthrow of the Hyksos kings and the consequent establishment of the Theban monarchy (at the beginning of the Eighteenth Dynasty), Amen, the local god of Thebes, took the place of honour in the Egyptian pantheon, and was worshipped as Amen-Ra. However, it is known that Thothmes IV did much to restore the worship of Ra-Harmachis. His son, Amen-hetep III, built temples to this deity and to Aten at Memphis and Thebes. In this he would appear to have been supported by his wife Tyi,[1] daughter of Iuaa and Thuau, who, though not connected with the Egyptian royal line, became chief of the royal wives. Possibly she herself was originally a votary of Aten, which would account for the reverence with which her son, Amen-hetep IV, regarded that deity. On the accession of the last-named monarch he adopted the title of 'high-priest of Ra-Heru-Akhti,[2] the exalted one in the horizon, in his name of Shu who is in Aten,' this implying that, according to the view generally current at that period, he regarded Aten as the abode of the

[1] Or Thi.

[2] Or Ra-Heru-Khuti.

sun-god rather than as the divinity himself. In the early part of his reign Amen-hetep worshipped both Amen and Aten, the former in his *rôle* of monarch, the latter in his private capacity, while he also built a great obelisk at Thebes in honour of Ra-Harmachis. Then it became apparent that the king desired to exalt Aten above all the other gods. This was by no means pleasing to the worshippers of Amen, whose priesthood was recruited from the noblest families in the land. A struggle ensued between the votaries of Amen-Ra and those of Aten, and finally the king built a new capital, dedicated to the faith of Aten, on the site of what is now Tell-el-Amarna, in Middle Egypt. Thence he withdrew with his followers when the struggle reached its height. To the new city he gave the name of Akhet-Aten ('Horizon of Aten'). His own name, Amen-hetep, he changed to Akh-en-Aten ('Glory of Aten').

A Religion of One God

One of the features of the new religion was that it was essentially monotheistic, and could not tolerate the inclusion of other deities. Thus whereas certain sun-gods in like circumstances might have become fused with Ra, such fusion was impossible in the case of Aten. Not only was he king of the gods, he was *the* god, the divinity *par excellence.* Yet did this monotheistic religion retain many of the forms and rites of other cults, paradoxical as this must have appeared. The king retained his title of 'son of the sun' (Aten), while he exchanged his Horus and other titles for Aten titles. The burial customs and the use of scarabs were still continued. Yet the name of Amen-Ra, with which they had previously been associated, was everywhere obliterated by order of the king, even where it formed part of proper names. The temple which the king built to his god in Akhet-Aten he called Het-Benben, the 'House of the Pyramidion.' It was never completed.

The religion thus thrust upon the people of Egypt met with a by no means ready acceptance. The deities which had hitherto been evolved in each nome or province had each his special attributes and ritual, any or all of which might be absorbed by the central deity. But, as has been said, Aten was incapable of this fusion with the local gods. He was indeed a much more colourless deity than Amen or Horus.

It is interesting to speculate upon the probable motives of Akh-en-Aten in introducing this new cult into Egypt. It has been suggested that his inauguration of Aten-worship was an enlightened, if somewhat misplaced, attempt to unite Egypt under the sway of one religion, a religion in which all could participate, which did not bear the *cachet* of any one race or caste, and which in consequence would prove equally acceptable to Syrian, Ethiopian, or Egyptian. If such were his aim, it is evident that the people of Egypt were not prepared for the upheaval. The drastic and fanatical measures, too, of Akh-en-Aten defeated his own ends and roused distrust and hatred of the 'Aten heresy.'

A Social Revolt

Accompanying this religious revolution came a social and artistic revolt of no less striking proportions. Aten as a deity was freed, in theory at least, from the trammels of myth and ritual which had grown up round his predecessors in Egypt. His was essentially a naturalistic cult. Social life in Akhet-Aten, therefore, tended to become much freer and more natural. The king and queen moved among the people with less formality than had hitherto obtained; family life was subject to fewer restraints ; in short, a decided tendency to all that was natural and spontaneous was observable. The movement spread in time even to the art of the nation, which shows a certain departure from established traditions in the matter of colouring, while during this reign Egyptian artists show for the first time that they appreciated the effects of light and shade as well as of mere outline.

We have unfortunately no means of knowing the exact period of Akh-en-Aten's reign. Probably it covered about a score of years. After him came various other rulers, but none of these upheld the Aten cult, which speedily declined, while the supremacy of Amen-Ra was triumphantly restored. All monuments and temples in honour of Aten were effaced, and only recovered within recent times by Lepsius, Petrie, and Davies. The last refuge of the god was at Heliopolis, where a sanctuary remained to him.

Aten's Attributes

Now as to the attributes of Aten. As already stated he was a somewhat colourless deity, and is perhaps better to be distinguished by the attributes which are not ascribed to him than by those which are, though in time some of the attributes of Ra, Horus, and other forms of the sun-god were given to him. From his original subordinate position as the abode of Ra—the material disk wherein the sun-god had his dwelling (' Ra in his Aten ')—Aten came in time to signify both the god and the actual solar disk. Attempts made to identify him with the Semitic Adonai, the Greek Adonis, have met with no success. Evidence of Aten's early position in the pantheon is to be found in the *Book of the Dead*, where Ra is addressed thus : "O thou beautiful being, thou dost renew thyself and make thyself young again under the form of Aten." "Thou turnest thy face toward the underworld, and thou makest the earth to shine like fine copper. The dead rise up to see thee, they breathe the air and they look upon thy face when Aten shineth in the horizon."

A Hymn to Aten

During the period when his cult was supreme in Egypt Aten was regarded by his worshippers as the creator, self-existent and everlasting, fructifier and nourisher of the earth and all it contains, measurer of the lives of men. Aten was invested with a cartouche, wherein he is styled 'Lord of heaven,' 'Lord of earth,' 'He who liveth for ever,' 'He who illumineth the earth,' 'He who reigneth in truth.' A singularly beautiful and poetic version of a hymn to Aten, in which he is exalted as the giver of life and fruitfulness to all things, has been found in the tomb of Aï, a high official under Amen-hetep, or Akh-en-Aten. It begins thus:

> Beauteous is thy resplendent appearing on the horizon of heaven,
> O Aten, who livest and art the beginning of life!

He it was who made the Nile in the Duat and conducted it to men, causing its waters to rise; he, also, who sent the rain to those lands which were beyond the reach of the Nile's beneficent flood.

> Thou makest the Nile in the underworld, thou conductest it hither at thy pleasure,
> That it may give life to men whom thou hast made for thyself, Lord of All!
> Thou givest the Nile in heaven that it descendeth to them.
> It causeth its waters to rise upon the rocks like the sea; it watereth their fields in their districts.

So are thy methods accomplished, O Lord of Eternity!
 thou who art thyself the celestial Nile:
Thou art the king of the inhabitants of the lands,
And of the cattle going upon their feet in every land,
 which go upon feet.
The Nile cometh out of the underworld to Egypt.

The Aten hymns, then, ascribe to the deity such attributes as any people might see in their sun-god. All the paraphernalia of the cult of Ra, Osiris, and like divinities are absent. There is no mention of the barques in which they sailed across the heavens; of Apep, the great serpent, and the other enemies of Ra; of the companies of gods and goddesses which formed his train. We find in the cult of Aten no myths such as that of the battles of Horus, nor do the ceremonies and ritual of the domain of Osiris enter into it. All these are without parallel in the Aten-worship. It is easily understood why it failed in its appeal to the Egyptian people.

Aten was not even figured as anthropomorphic, as were Ra and Osiris, but was invariably represented as the sun-disk, with rays emanating from it in a downward direction. Each ray terminated in a human hand, to which were sometimes attached the sign of life, the sign of power, and so on. Reliefs of this period frequently depict the king and queen seated with their children, over their heads the symbol of Aten, one of whose numerous hands presents the sign of life to each member of the royal family.

In short, the cult of Aten was the worship of the sun-god pure and simple, shorn of the picturesque story and ritual so dear to the heart of the Egyptian.

Hathor

It is no easy matter to gauge the true mythological significance of the Egyptian goddess Hathor, patron of

Hathor (page 162)

Photo W. A. Mansell & Co.

Hapi

(page 169)

women, of love, and of pleasure, Lady of Heaven, and Mistress of the Underworld. She occupied a very important position in the pantheon of ancient Egypt, dating as she did from archaic or even pre-dynastic times. We find a multitude of mythological ideas fused in the Hathor conception : she is a moon-goddess, a sky-goddess, a goddess of the east, a goddess of the west, a cosmic deity, an agricultural goddess, a goddess of moisture, even on occasion a solar deity. Though her original status is thus in a measure obscured, it is supposed that she is primarily a moon-goddess, for reasons which follow hereafter.

The original form under which Hathor was worshipped was that of a cow. Later she is represented as a woman with the head of a cow, and finally with a human head, the face broad, kindly, placid, and decidedly bovine, sometimes retaining the ears or horns of the animal she represents. She is also shown with a head-dress resembling a pair of horns with the moon-disk between them. Sometimes she is met with in the form of a cow standing in a boat, surrounded by tall papyrus-reeds. Now in mythology the cow is often identified with the moon—why it is hard to say. Perhaps it may not be too far-fetched to suppose that the horned appearance of the moon at certain seasons has suggested its association with the cow. Mythology is largely based on such superficial resemblances and analogies ; it is by means of these that the primitive mind first learns to reason. Or it may be that the cow, naturally of great importance to agricultural peoples, was, by reason of this importance, associated with the moon, mistress of the weather and principle of growth and fruitfulness. The fact that Hathor the cow is sometimes shown in a boat suggests that she was also a water-goddess, and heightens the probability that she was identified with the moon, for the latter was regarded by the Egyptians as the source of all moisture.

The name Hathor signifies 'House of Horus'—that is, the sky, wherein dwelt the sun-god Horus, and there is no doubt that at one time Hathor was regarded as a sky-goddess, or a goddess of the eastern sky, where Horus was born; she has also been identified with the night sky and with the sunset sky. If, however, we regard her as a moon-goddess, a good deal of the mythology concerning her will become clear. She is, for example, frequently spoken of as the 'Eye of Ra,' Ra, the sun-god, probably possessing in this instance the wider significance of sky-god. She is also designated 'The Golden One,' who stands high in the south as the Lady of Teka, and illumines the west as the Lady of Saïs. That she is mistress of the underworld is likewise not surprising when we consider her as identical with the moon, for does not the moon make a daily pilgrimage through Amentet? Neither is it astonishing that a goddess of moisture and vegetation should be found in the underworld dispensing water to the souls of the dead from the branches of a palm or a sycamore.

Hathor as Love-Goddess

On the same hypothesis we may explain the somewhat paradoxical statement that Hathor is 'mother of her father, daughter of her son'—that she is mother, wife, and daughter to Ra. The moon, when she appears in the heavens before the sun, may be regarded as his mother; when she reigns together with him she is his wife; when she rises after he has set she is his daughter. It is possible that the moon, with her generative and sustaining powers, may have been considered the creative and upholding force of the universe, the great cosmic mother, who brought forth not only the gods and goddesses over whom she rules, but likewise herself as well. It was as the ideal of womanhood, therefore whether as mother, wife, or daughter, that she received the homage of Egyptian women, and became the patron deity of love, joy, and merry-making, "lady of music and mistress of song, lady of leaping, and mistress of wreathing garlands." Temples were raised in her honour, notably one of exceptional beauty at Denderah, in Upper Egypt, and she had shrines without number. She became in time associated or even identified with many local goddesses, and, indeed, it has been said that all Egyptian goddesses were forms of Hathor.

As guardian of the dead Hathor is figured as a cow, issuing from the Mountain of the West, and she is also represented as standing on its summit receiving the setting sun and the souls of the dead (the latter travelling in the footsteps of the sun-god). In this case Hathor might be regarded as the western sky, but the myth might be equally significant of the moon, which sometimes "stands on the mountains of the west" after the time of sunset, with horns resembling hands outstretched to welcome the unseen souls. Yet another point is worthy of note in connexion with the mythological aspect of Hathor. When she was born as the daughter of Ra (her mother was Nut, the sky-goddess) she was quite black. This fact admits of several interpretations. It may be that Hathor's swarthy complexion is indicative of an Ethiopian origin, or it may be that she represents the night sky, which lightens with the growth of day. It is still possible, however, to regard her as typifying the moon, which is 'born black,' with only a narrow crescent of light, but which grows brighter as it becomes older. It is unlikely that the keen eyes of these primitive peoples would fail to observe the dark disk of the new moon, faintly outlined with light reflected from the earth.

The Slaying of Men

In the following myth of Ra and Hathor the latter is plainly identified with the lunar deity:

Long ago there dwelt on earth Ra, the sun-god, the creator of men and things, and ruler over the gods. For a time men gave to him the reverence due to his exalted position, but at length he began to grow old, and they mocked him, saying, "Behold! his bones are like silver, his limbs are like gold, his hair is like unto real lapis-lazuli." Now Ra was very wroth when he heard their blasphemy, so he called together his followers, the gods and goddesses of his train, Shu and Tefnut, Geb and Nut, and Hathor, the eye of Ra.

The gods assembled secretly, so that the race of mankind might know nothing of their meeting. And when they were all gathered about the throne of Ra, he said to Nun, the oldest of the gods:

"O Nun, thou first-born of the gods, whose son I am, I pray thee give me thy counsel. The men whom I have created have conceived evil against me, even those men who have issued forth from mine eye. They have murmured in their hearts, saying, 'Behold! the king has become old, his bones are like silver, his limbs like gold, his hair like unto real lapis-lazuli.' Tell me what shall be done unto them? For this have I sought thy counsel. I will not destroy them till thou hast spoken."

Then answered Nun:

"O thou great god, who art greater than he who made thee, thou son who art mightier than his father, do thou but turn thine eye upon them who blaspheme thee, and they shall perish from off the earth."

Ra turned his eye upon the blasphemers, according to the counsel of Nun. But the men fled from the eye of Ra, and hid them in deserts and rocky places. Then did all the gods and goddesses give counsel to Ra that he should send his eye down among men to smite them sorely. And the eye of Ra descended in the form of the goddess Hathor, and smote the men in the desert and slew them. Then Hathor returned to the court of Ra, and when the king had given her welcome she said, "I have been mighty among mankind. It is well pleasing to my heart."

All night Sekhmet[1] waded in the blood of those who had been slain, and on the morrow Ra feared that Hathor would slay the remnant of the human race, wherefore he said unto his attendants, "Fetch to me swift messengers who can outstrip the wind." When the messengers appeared the majesty of Ra bade them bring a great number of mandrakes from Elephantine. These Ra gave to Sekhmet, bidding her to pound them, and when this was done he mixed the mandrakes with some of the blood of those whom Hathor had slain. Meanwhile servant-maids were busy preparing beer from barley, and into this Ra poured the mixture. Thus were seven thousand jars of beer made.

In the morning Ra bade his attendants carry the beer to the place where Hathor would seek to slay the remnant of mankind, and there pour it out. For the sun-god said within himself, "I will deliver mankind out of her hands."

And it came to pass that at dawn Hathor reached the place where the beer lay, flooding the fields four spans

[1] Or Sekhet. Sekhmet is the same personage as Hathor in the original text. The beer was made by the people of On, who mixed the 'mandrake' with it, and Sekhmet-Hathor drank it.

deep. She was pleased with her beautiful reflection, which smiled at her from the floods ; and so deeply did she drink of the beer that she became drunken, and was no more able to destroy men.

Henceforward festivals were celebrated with high revelry in commemoration of this event.

There is no doubt that in this myth the beer represents the annual rise of the Nile, and if further evidence be required than that contained in the story, it lies in the fact that the Intoxication festivals of Hathor fall in the month of Thoth, the first month of the inundation.

The vengeance of Ra is doubtless the plagues and starvation which accompany the dry season immediately preceding the rise of the river. The eye of Ra—that is, Hathor—must be either the sun or the moon ; but Ra himself is the sun-god, therefore Hathor is most probably the moon. It must be borne in mind, of course, that the Egyptians believed the moon wilfully to prevent the inundation, and thus were likely to regard her as the source of disasters arising from the drought. It is evident, too, that the eye of Ra wrought havoc among men *during the night*—"Day dawned, after this goddess had been slaughtering men as she went upstream."

The Forms of Hathor

Hathor is sometimes identified with the star Sept, or Sothis (Sirius), which rose heliacally on the first day of the month of Thoth. When Ra entered his boat Sothis, or the goddess Hathor, took her place on his head like a crown.

Reference has already been made to the numerous forms of this goddess. She was identified with Aphrodite by the Greeks, and by the Egyptians with a multitude of local deities. The *Seven Hathors*, sometimes stated to be independent deities, were in reality but a selection of forms of the goddess, which selection varied in the various localities. Thus the Seven Hathors worshipped at Denderah were Hathor of Thebes, Hathor of Heliopolis, Hathor of Aphroditopolis, Hathor of the Sinaitic Peninsula, Hathor of Momemphis, Hathor of Herakleopolis, and Hathor of Keset. These were represented as young women carrying tambourines and wearing the Hathor head-dress of a disk and a pair of horns. In the Litanies of Seker other groups of Seven Hathors are mentioned, while Mariette includes yet a different company under that title.

Briefly, Hathor is a personification of the female principle—primitive, fruitful, attractive—such as is known to most barbaric peoples, and becoming more sophisticated as the centuries pass.

Hapi, the God of the Nile

This deity was especially connected with the great river whence Egypt drew her sustenance, and as such was a god of very considerable importance in the Egyptian pantheon. In time he became identified with Osiris. The name Hapi still baffles translation, and is probably of pre-dynastic origin. Perhaps the first mention of this deity is in the Text of Unas, where the Nile god is exhorted to fructify grain for the requirements of the dead monarch. In the same texts Hapi is alluded to as a destructive force, symbolizing, of course, the inundations so frequently caused by the River Nile.

In appearance Hapi possesses both male and female characteristics, the latter indicating his powers of nourishment. As god of the North Nile he is crowned with papyrus plants, and as god of the southern part of the river with lotus plants. These two forms of Hapi resulted from the geographical division of the country into Upper and Lower Egypt, and they are sometimes combined in a single figure, when the god is shown holding in his hands both plants. On the thrones of certain of the Pharaohs we often find the lotus and papyrus conjoined with the emblem of union, to signify the sovereignty of the monarch over both regions.

The very position of Hapi made it certain that he would become successful as a deity. The entire country looked to the Nile as the source of all wealth and provender, so that the deity which presided over it rapidly rose in public estimation. Thus Hapi quickly became identified with the greater and more outstanding figures in early Egyptian mythology. He thus became a partner with the great original gods who had created the world, and finally came to be regarded as the maker and moulder of everything within the universe. We find him credited with the attributes of Nu, the primeval water-mass, and this in effect made him a father of Ra, who had emerged from that element. Hapi, indeed, stood in more immediate relationship to the Egyptians than almost any other god in their pantheon. Without the sun Egypt would have been plunged into darkness, but without the Nile every living creature within its borders would assuredly have perished.

The circumstance, too, that the source of the River Nile was unknown to the Egyptians tended to add a mystery to the character of its presiding deity. The people of the country could not understand the rise and fall of the river, which appeared to them to take place under supernatural auspices.

On the occasion of the annual rise of the Nile a great festival was held in honour of Hapi, and statues of the god were carried about through the towns and villages. It is noticeable in many mythologies that gods of fructification are those honoured by the circulation of their images throughout the region where they are worshipped, and it is a little difficult to see why this should be so. It cannot be said that none but deities with an agricultural significance were thus carried about, but it is noteworthy that these are by far the most numerous to receive such honours.

Counterparts of Hapi

Isis was in a manner regarded as the female counterpart of Hapi, but we also find that in the north of Egypt the goddess Natch-ura was regarded as the female companion of Hapi, and that Nekhebet reigned in the south in a like capacity. The following hymn to Hapi, found in a papyrus of the Eighteenth or Nineteenth Dynasty, clearly shows the great importance of his worship in Egypt: "Homage to thee, O Hapi, thou appearest in this land, and thou comest in peace to make Egypt to live. Thou art the Hidden One, and the guide of the darkness on the day when it is thy pleasure to lead the same. Thou art the waterer of the fields which Ra hath created, thou givest life unto all animals, thou makest all the land to drink unceasingly as thou descendest on thy way from heaven. Thou art the friend of bread and of Tchabu, thou makest to increase and be strong Nepra, thou makest prosperous every workshop, O Ptah, thou lord of fish; when the Inundation riseth, the waterfowl do not alight upon the fields that are sown with wheat. Thou art the creator of barley, and thou makest the temples to endure, for millions of years repose of thy fingers hath been an abomination to thee. Thou art the lord of the poor and needy. If thou wert overthrown in the heavens the gods would fall upon their faces and men would perish. He causeth the whole earth to be opened by the cattle, and princes and peasants lie down and rest. . . . Thy form is that of Khnemu. When thou shinest upon the earth shouts of joy ascend, for all people are joyful, and every mighty man receiveth food, and every tooth is provided with food. Thou art the bringer of food, thou art the mighty one of meat and drink, thou art the creator of all good things, the lord of divine meat, pleasant and choice. . . . Thou makest the herb to grow for the cattle, and thou takest heed unto what is sacrificed unto every god. The choicest incense is that which followeth thee, thou art the lord of the two lands. Thou fillest the storehouses, thou heapest high with corn the granaries, and thou takest heed unto what is sacrificed unto every god. The choicest incense is that which followeth thee, thou art the lord of the two lands. Thou fillest the storehouses, thou heapest high with corn the granaries, and thou takest heed to the affairs of the poor and needy. Thou makest the herb and green things to grow that the desires of all may be satisfied, and thou art not reduced thereby. Thou makest thy strength to be a shield for man."

Nut

The goddess Nut was the daughter of Shu and Tefnut, the wife of Geb, and the mother of Osiris and Isis, Set and Nephthys. She personified the sky and the vault of heaven. A good many other goddesses probably became absorbed in her from time to time. She is, however, the personification of the day sky, a certain Naut representing the sky of night, but this distinction was an early one. She was indeed the counterpart of Nu, and represented the great watery abyss, out of which all things originally came, so that Nut, the spouse of Nu, and Nut, the spouse of Geb, are one and the same being. She is usually represented as a woman carrying upon her head a vase of water, which plainly indicates her character. Sometimes she wears the horns and disk of Hathor, but she has many other guises as the great mother of the gods.

Her most general appearance, however, is that of a woman resting on hands and feet, her body forming an arch, thus representing the sky. Her limbs typified the four pillars on which the sky was supposed to rest. She was supposed originally to be reclining on Geb, the earth, when Shu raised her from this position. This myth is a very common one among the aborigines of America, but in an inverted sense, as it is usually the sky which takes the place of the original father, and the earth that of the great mother. These are usually separated by the creative deity, just as were Geb and Nut, and the allegory represents the separation of the earth from the waters which were above it, and the creation of the world.

According to another myth Nut gave birth daily to the sun-god, who passed across her body, which represented the sky. In a variant account he is represented as travelling across her back. The limbs and body of the goddess are bespangled with stars. In another pictorical description of Nut we see a second female figure drawn inside the first, and within that again the body of a man, the last two conforming to the semicircular shape of the sky-goddess. This is explained as meaning that the two women personify the day and night skies, but it does not account for the male body, which may represent the Duat. Again we read that Nut was transformed into a great cow, and she is frequently represented in this form. The deceased are described in the *Book of the Dead* as relying on her for fresh air in the underworld, over the waters of which she was supposed to have dominion. She possessed a sacred tree, the sycamore, which was situated at Heliopolis, at the foot of which the serpent Apep was slain by the great cat Ra. The branches of this tree were regarded as a place of refuge for the weary dead in noonday during the summer, and in its shade they were refreshed by the food on which the goddess herself lived.

It was asserted by the priests of Denderah that Nut had her origin in their city, and that there she became the mother of Isis. Her five children, Osiris, Horus, Set, Isis, and Nephthys, were born on the five epagomenal days of the year—that is, the five days over the three hundred and sixty. As in Mexico, certain of these were regarded as unlucky. Nut plays a prominent part in the underworld, and the dead are careful to retain her good offices, probably in order that they may have plenty of air. Indeed, her favour renewed their bodies and they were enabled to rise and journey with the sun-god each day, even as did Ra, the son of Nut. A portrait of the goddess was often painted on the cover of the coffin as a mark of her protection, and this was rarely omitted in the Egyptian burial ceremonies.

Taurt

Taurt is usually pictured as a hippopotamus standing upon her hind legs, holding in her hand an amulet which has not yet been satisfactorily explained. She wears on her head the solar disk and two tall feathers. Occasionally she is pictured in human form with the cow-horns worn by all Egyptian goddesses. She was regarded as the mother and nurse of the gods, and had a counterpart in Apet, the hippopotamus-goddess of

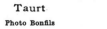

Taurt (page 174)

Photo Bonfils

Khonsu (page 176)

The Maiden of Bekhten (page 177)

Evelyn Paul

Thebes, who was supposed by some Egyptians to have been the mother of Osiris. In later times Taurt was known as Rert or Reret, the female hippopotamus, but she was also identified with Isis, Hathor, Bast, and other goddesses. Her image in faience formed a favourite amulet, which, indeed, was almost as popular as that of Bes. Indeed, figures which appear to have been copied from that of Taurt are to be seen on Mykenæan wall-scenes, so widespread was her fame. She was supposed to be the guardian of the mountain of the west, through which lay the road to Hades. It would appear that she was certainly of totemic origin. Her popularity seems to have been greatest during the New Empire, and increased greatly during the latter period.

Hekt

Hekt, the frog-headed goddess, was regarded as the wife of Khnemu, although in some degree she may be looked upon as a form of Hathor. Her character has not been made very clear by writers on Egyptian mythology, but the circumstance that she possesses the head of a frog obviously shows her connexion with water, and therefore with the powers of fructification. She appears also to have been associated with the deities of growth. Many corn-gods are deities of resurrection and re-birth. At the festival of a certain Mexican goddess of the maize a frog was placed upon the top of a sheaf of grain as being symbolical of the goddess. It might be hazardous to identify Hekt with the Greek Hecate, who was perhaps a moon-goddess, and as such associated with water. It is noticeable that Hecate is regarded by Farnell as a foreign importation from Thrace. She is, of course, the goddess of the lower world as well, just as Osiris, the moon-god, was god of the Egyptian dead. She was also worshipped at the Samothracian mysteries, which probably had an Egyptian origin. We find that Hecate was also a goddess of fertility.

Khonsu

Khonsu was a lunar deity, and as such was often identified with Thoth. Indeed, at Hermopolis and Edfû the two were occasionally joined under the name of Khonsu-Thoth. The name is derived from the root *khens*, to traverse, showing that he was the traveller who nightly crossed the heavens. He was depicted as a hawk-headed god crowned with the lunar crescent and the solar disk. Rameses III built him a great temple at Thebes between those of Amen and Mut. He had two distinct forms: Khonsu in Thebes Nefer-hetep, and Khonsu the carrier out of plans. The Greeks compared Khonsu to Heracles, for what reason it would be difficult to say. Occasionally the Egyptians fused him with Horus, Shu, and Ra, which shows that he could assume a solar character, as is indicated by his hawk-head. It would appear as if Khonsu, originally a moon-god, became also a sun-god when the lunar calendar was merged into or abandoned for the solar method of computation.

The following tale illustrates the healing power of Khonsu:

The Princess and the Demon

In the reign of King Rameses there were many fair women in Egypt, but lovelier than them all was the daughter of the prince of Bekhten, one of the king's vassals. Tall and slender and very shapely, of exquisite form and feature, there was nothing on earth with which to compare her beauty, so men compared it with the beauty of Amen-Ra, the great sun-god, the god of the light of day.

THE PRINCESS AND THE DEMON

Now King Rameses was a great conqueror and a mighty man of valour, who numbered among his vassals princes of no mean degree. These latter came every year to Naharaina, at the mouth of the Euphrates, to do homage to their overlord and to render tribute to him. Rich indeed was the tribute that the king received, for every prince who bowed before him was accompanied by a retinue of slaves bearing treasures of gold and precious stones and sweet-smelling woods, the choicest things that their dominions could afford.

On one such occasion Rameses and his princes were gathered at Naharaina, and the vassals vied with each other in the splendour of their offerings. But the Prince of Bekhten had a treasure which far surpassed that of the others, for he had brought his beautiful daughter, she whose beauty was as that of Amen-Ra. When the king saw her he loved her beyond all else, and wished to make her his wife. For the rest of the tribute he cared nothing, and the homage of the remaining princes was a weariness to him. So he married the princess, and gave to her a name which signifies 'Beauty of Ra.' And when they returned home the queen fulfilled her royal duties as became the Great Royal Wife, and was beloved of her husband and her people.

Now it came about that on the festival of the god Amen, when the sacred barque is born aloft for all to see, the king and queen went up to the temple to do honour to the sun-god. And while they worshipped, attendants sought them with the news that a messenger from the Prince of Bekhten waited without and would have speech with them. The king bade that the messenger be admitted. Rich gifts he bore from the Prince of Bekhten to his daughter, the Great Royal Wife, while to the king he bowed very low, saying :

"Behold, O king, the little sister of the Great Royal

Wife lies ill. I pray thee, therefore, to send a physician to heal her of her malady."

Then the king called his wise men about him and deliberated whom he should send to the succour of his wife's sister. At length the wise men brought before the king one of their number, a scribe named Tehuti-em-heb, who was accordingly appointed to accompany the messenger to Bekhten, there to heal the queen's sister, Bent-reshy.

But, alas! when they reached the domains of the Prince of Bekhten Tehuti-em-heb found that the demon who was the cause of the princess's affliction was far too powerful to be expelled by his skill. When the maid's father heard that the Egyptian scribe was powerless to cast out the demon he fell into despair, thinking his last hope had gone. But Tehuti-em-heb comforted him as best he might, bidding him send once more to Egypt to beseech the intervention of Khonsu, Expeller of Demons, on his daughter's behalf. So the Lord of Bekhten sent yet another messenger to the court of Rameses.

Now the land of Bekhten was far from the land of Egypt, and the journey between them occupied a year and five months. When the messenger of the Prince of Bekhten reached Egypt he found Rameses in Thebes, in the temple of Khonsu, for it was the month which was sacred to that god. And the messenger bowed before Rameses and gave him the message sent by the queen's father. In the temple at Thebes there were two statues of the god Khonsu, one called Khonsu in Thebes Neferhetep, the other Khonsu, Expeller of Demons, both representing the god as a handsome youth. Rameses approached Khonsu in Thebes Neferhetep and prayed that he would permit Khonsu, the Expeller of Demons, to go to the land of Bekhten for the healing of Bent-reshy, the queen's little sister. Khonsu in Thebes Neferhetep bowed his assent, and gave his protection to the Expeller of Demons. When this was done Khonsu, Expeller of Demons, was dispatched to Bekhten, accompanied by a large retinue, and with ceremony befitting a king. They journeyed for a year and five months, and at length reached the land of the queen's father. The prince himself and all his people hastened to greet Khonsu, prostrating themselves and offering rich gifts even as they might have done to the King of Egypt himself. Meanwhile Bent-reshy's illness had continued unabated, for the demon who possessed her was very potent. But when Khonsu was conducted to her chamber, behold! she grew well in a moment, to the joy of her father and his courtiers. The demon who had come out of her acknowledged Khonsu as his superior, and those who stood by heard with awe a conversation pass between them.

"O Khonsu," said the spirit, "I am thy slave. If thou commandest that I go from hence, I will go. But I pray thee ask of the Prince of Bekhten that he will make a holy day for me and a sacrifice. Then shall I go in peace."

"It shall be as thou hast said," replied Khonsu, and he commanded the Prince of Bekhten to make a sacrifice and a holy day for the demon who had possessed Bent-reshy.

First the people made a great sacrifice to Khonsu, the Expeller of Demons; then they made one for the demon, who thereafter departed in peace. But when he had gone the mind of the Prince of Bekhten was grievously troubled, for he thought: "Perchance he will come again unto our land, and torment the people even as he has tormented my daughter, Bent-reshy." So he determined that Khonsu, the Expeller of Demons, must not be allowed to depart from Bekhten, but must be kept there always, lest the demon should return.

For more than three years, therefore, the Prince of Bekhten kept Khonsu within his domains, and would not allow him to depart. But one night he had a dream which altered his determination. In his dream he stood before the shrine of Khonsu, Expeller of Demons. And as he looked, behold! the doors of the shrine were flung wide, and the god himself issued forth, took the form of a hawk with wonderful golden plumage, and flew toward Egypt. When he awoke the Lord of Bekhten knew that the real god had departed to Egypt, and that it was useless to keep any longer his statue. Moreover, he feared the vengeance of Khonsu. So on the morrow he loaded the statue of Khonsu, the Expeller of Demons, with rich and beautiful gifts, and sent him away to Egypt with a princely retinue.

When the return journey was accomplished Khonsu, Expeller of Demons, bestowed all the costly gifts on Khonsu in Thebes Neferhetep, keeping nothing for himself of all he had received.

Minor Deities

There were hundreds of minor gods surrounding the Egyptian pantheon, and the characteristics of only a few of these can be dealt with. Each hour of the day had its representative deity, as had each hour of the night. The four winds were also represented in the Egyptian pantheon, as in the Greek. The north wind was called Qebui, and is pictured as a four-headed ram with wings; the south wind, Shehbui, is represented as a man with a lion's head, and wings; and the west wind, Huzayui, has a serpent's head on the body of a winged man. The east wind, Henkhisesui, sometimes occurs in anthropomorphic shape, and, like the north wind, has a ram's head, but he is occasionally figured as a winged beetle with the head of a ram.

The senses were also symbolized by deities. Saa was the god of the sense of touch or feeling. He is depicted in human shape and wears upon his head a sign composed of parallel lines, which as they rise grow smaller. In the Theban Recension of the *Book of the Dead* he is shown in the judgment scene amongst those gods who watch the weighing of the heart of the deceased. Saa is sometimes shown as sailing with Thoth and other gods in the boat of Ra. In one passage he is alluded to as the son of Geb. He is the personification of intelligence, human and divine.

The god of taste was called Hu. He is also depicted as a man, and is said to have come into existence from a drop of blood which fell from Ra. He became the personification of the divine food upon which the gods and the blessed dead lived.

Maa was the god of sight. He is also drawn as a man having an eye placed over his head, which is also the symbol of his name.

Setem was the god of hearing, and in his case his head is surmounted by an ear.[1]

The planets were also deified. Saturn was called Horus, the bull of heaven; Mars was also identified with Horus under the name of the 'red Horus,' but, strictly speaking, was under the guardianship of Ra; the god of Mercury was Set, and of Venus, Osiris. Some of the constellations were also identified with deities. The Great Bear was known as 'the haunch,' and Draco was identified with the hippopotamus Reret.

The days of the month had also patron gods.

[1] Personifications of the senses with appropriate names.

CHAPTER VI: EGYPTIAN LITERATURE

Egyptian Language and Writing

THE earliest knowledge we have of the Egyptian language is furnished by ancient inscriptions belonging to the First Dynasty, about 3300 B.C. From these onward its rise and its decay may be traced down through the different writings on temples, monuments, and papyri to the fourteenth century A.D.,[1] when Coptic manuscripts end the tale. Of the living tongue, as apart from the purely literary language of the hieroglyphic inscriptions, the truest idea is given by the popular tales, letters, and business documents which have come down to us, wherein the scribes naturally kept close to the current forms of speech, thus revealing the changes the language underwent.

That Egyptian is related to Semitic is practically certain, though here a racial problem intervenes and confuses, for the Egyptian race proper is not and never was, so far as can be ascertained, Semitic in type. Erman tries to explain this by the quite probable theory that in the prehistoric period a horde of warlike Semites conquered a part of Egypt and settled there, like the Arabs of a later period, and imposed their language on the country, but as a distinct race died out, either by reason of the climate or absorption by the native population, who, however, had acquired the strangers' language, though but imperfectly. Under these conditions the language gradually changed. The consonants were mispronounced, strong consonants giving place to weak, and these in turn, disappearing altogether, produced biliterals from the triliteral roots. This tendency, together with periphrastic instead of

[1] Vansleb at the end of the seventeenth century perhaps heard it spoken.

verbal conjugation, continued to the end. Coptic, the latest form, is thus biliteral in character, and tenses of remarkable precision were developed in the verb by means of periphrases; but the great resemblances between Coptic and Semitic must also be traced to the continuous Semitic influences of late periods.

The Egyptian language naturally divides into its progressive stages. These are Old Egyptian, Middle and Late Egyptian, Demotic and Coptic. *Old Egyptian* is the language belonging to the Old Kingdom. It supplied the literary model for the later period, as evidenced by the inscriptions, but that it should be affected by the changing forms of contemporary speech was inevitable, though in the main its chief characteristics were preserved. The earliest specimens we have are inscriptions belonging to the First Dynasty, which, however, are too brief to give much insight into the language and speech of that period. Next come many inscriptions and some few historical texts in the language of the Fourth, Fifth, and Sixth Dynasties. The greatest amount belonging to this phase is the large collection of ritual texts and spells inscribed in the Pyramids belonging to the Sixth Dynasty.

Middle and *Late Egyptian* belong to the Middle and New Kingdoms respectively, and approximate to the common speech of the people. Writings in the former, extant to this day, are tales, letters, and business documents of the Twelfth Dynasty on to the beginning of the New Kingdom, written on papyri in hieratic script. The Eighteenth to the Twenty-first Dynasty furnish us with specimens of Late Egyptian in various hieratic papyri. In regard to these an authority states: "The spelling of Late Egyptian is very extraordinary, full of false etymologies, otiose signs, etc., the old orthography being quite unable to adapt itself neatly to the profoundly modified language. Nevertheless, this clumsy spelling is expressive, and the very mistakes are instructive as to the pronunciation."

Demotic represents the vulgar dialect of the Saïte period, and is really applied to the character in which it is written. It may be traced back to the Twenty-fifth Dynasty, about 900 B.C., and it continued in use until the fourth century A.D. Demotic documents are mostly contracts of sale and legal matters, though some magical texts and a curious tale, the Papyrus of Setna, are also written in this character. *Coptic* is the latest form which the language took, or rather it is a dialect form of Egyptian, of which four or five varieties are known. Coptic is written with the letters of the Greek alphabet, and is really the only stage of the language where the spelling gives a clear idea of the pronunciation. To the Greek characters were added six taken from the Demotic in order to express sounds peculiar to the Egyptian language. This, together with Greek transcriptions of Egyptian names and words, have supplied the only means of arriving at some idea of the accurate vocalization of the Egyptian language. One reason for this ignorance that of necessity prevailed is the fact that the Egyptian system of writing gives merely the consonantal skeletons of words, never recording the internal vowel changes, and often omitting semi-consonants.

The Hieroglyphs

The ancient Egyptian system of writing would seem to be, from all available evidence, of purely native origin. Its rise, development, and final extinction can all be traced within the Nile valley, though it travelled by conquest into Syria under the Eighteenth Dynasty and onward for the engraving of Egyptian inscriptions in that country. Again, it is held by some authorities to be quite possible that the merchants of Phœnicia and the Ægean had evolved from the Egyptian hieratic the cursive form of writing, their 'Phœnician' alphabet, about 1000 B.C. The hieroglyphic character was originally picture-writing in its simplest form, but had become more complex by the time it is met with first, in inscriptions belonging to the First Dynasty. It underwent some changes, but the final mode it assumed persisted practically unaltered from the Fourth Dynasty down to its expiry in the fourth century A.D. By that time all knowledge of the meaning of the characters had died out, and it was not until the discovery of the Rosetta Stone[1] and the decipherment of its lingual inscription in Greek and Egyptian that any progress could be made in the reading of hieroglyphic writing. The signs are of two kinds, one to represent sounds, the phonetic—which is again divided into two varieties, the alphabetic and syllabic—and the other to represent ideas, the ideographic. These latter signs are pictorial representations of the object spoken of, which are placed after the phonetically written words as 'determinatives,' or representative symbols. These again are of two kinds, generic, being determinative of a class, and specific, of a particular object. There is no rule[2] as to the arrangement of the text. It is read either from right to left, left to right, or in columns, its commencement being from that side toward which the bird and animal characters face. About five hundred characters were used. Hieratic writing is to be found

[1] The Rosetta Stone is written in three scripts, hieroglyphic, Demotic, and Greek.

[2] Properly speaking, it should be written from right to left horizontally. Only for decorative purposes is it inscribed from right to left or in columns.

in the First Dynasty, approximating closely to the hieroglyphic, but by the time of the Middle Kingdom this resemblance is lost. The commercial era of the Twenty-sixth Dynasty brought into everyday use the Demotic form, and thenceforth hieratic was used for the copying of religious and traditional texts on papyrus, and in time was understood by the learned only, for in the Ptolemaic period, whenever the text of a royal decree was inscribed upon a stele which was to be set up in a public place, a version of the said decree in the Demotic character was added. Stelæ inscribed in hieroglyphic, Demotic, and Greek have been found, the most famous of these being the Decree of Canopu, belonging to Ptolemy III, 247 B.C., and the Rosetta Stone, set up in the reign of Ptolemy V, Epiphanes, 205 B.C. It was this latter stone and its inscription which gave the key to unravelling the mystery of hieroglyphic writing in the last century, and thus restoring to modern times the knowledge of ancient Egyptian language and literature. As has been shown, the hieroglyphic system of writing had fallen into disuse long before the close of Roman rule in Egypt, and again the widespread use of Greek and Latin among the aristocratic and official classes had caused the disappearance of Egyptian as the language of state. It probably lingered, together with the study of hieroglyphs, among learned men and priests in remote districts, but by the fourth or fifth century A.D. had become a lost art. Then in 1799 came the finding of the Rosetta Stone with its lingual inscription, consisting of fourteen lines of hieroglyphs, thirty-two lines of Demotic, and fifty-four lines of Greek. By the comparison and decipherment of these versions the Egyptian alphabet was discovered, and the clue thus found to the lost language of ancient Egypt. To

Akerblad in 1802, Young in 1818, and Champollion in 1822 must be given the honour for this momentous discovery, restoring to our knowledge the wonderful civilization, art, and literature of a great race.

Literature

If one commences the study of Egyptian texts with an examination of the *Book of the Dead*, and turns from its gloomy, if picturesque, pages to the rest of the national literature, he is perhaps doomed to disappointment, for the field of Egyptian letters, though somewhat widespread, presents a poverty of invention and verbiage exhibited by few literatures, ancient or modern. In the early periods, as might be expected, the style is simple to banality, whilst later a stiff and pompous fashion too often mars what might otherwise have been meritorious work.

Documents of almost every conceivable kind have come down to us—letters of business men, legal scripts, fragments of historical information, magical papyri ; scientific, theological, and popular works, even fiction and poetry, are fairly well represented. Most of the standard works, such as books of proverbs or instructions like those attributed to Ptah-hotep and Kagemni, appear to have been of great age, dating not later than the Middle Kingdom. The style of these was imitated by most writers, just as the shape and colour of the hieroglyphs and wall-paintings were sedulously copied by draughtsmen and scribes. Amenemhat I wrote a work resembling Machiavelli's *The Prince* for the instruction of his son in the principles of good government, and the instructions of Ani to his heir are of similar character. In Egyptian literature we frequently find parallelisms of phrase like those of Hebrew poetry, and repetitions are common.

Philosophical treatises, although rare, appear to have had some vogue, and the great problems of existence seem to have been disputed in their pages in the form of a dialogue. A papyrus of the Middle Kingdom (*c.* 2500 B.C.) now in the Berlin Museum descants upon the justification of suicide. The disputants are a man and his *khu* or other-self. The man in question appears to be weary of existence and has made up his mind to destroy himself. He trembles for the future, and seems afraid that his corpse may be neglected. In this dilemna he turns to his *khu* and entreats it to perform for him the duties of a relative. This request the *khu* refuses point-blank, and urges its possessor to forget his sorrows and to render his life as happy as possible. It indicates that after death the remembrance of the deceased speedily vanishes, and even granite monuments cannot retain it for long. This counsel the man bitterly rejects, exclaiming that his relatives have forsaken him and that his name is utterly condemned; everywhere the proud triumph and the humble are oppressed; the wicked man flourishes and dishonesty is universal; of just and contented men there are none. Death appears to him very pleasing; in his coffin he will be surrounded by the fragrance of myrrh, will repose in the cool shadows and partake of the offerings made to him. After this outburst the *khu* argues no longer and assents to the man's proposals, agreeing that when he is at rest it shall descend to him, and together they will prepare for themselves an abiding-place.

The Cat and the Jackal

Another such discussion, which possesses some rather amusing characteristics, is found in a Late Demotic papyrus, and is perhaps tinged with Greek ideas.

THE CAT AND THE JACKAL

The dialecticians in this instance are a monster cat, who represents the goddess Bast, and a diminutive jackal. The feline adopts orthodox views and gives it as her opinion that the world is directed by the gods, who will see to it that vice is vanquished and that virtue is triumphant in the end. If even a little lamb be injured, the violence offered will rebound upon the man who harms it. The sun may be darkened by clouds for a season, thunderstorms may roll, the sunrise may be veiled by the vapours of morning; but eventually the light of day will break forth through all, and joy will reign supreme. The jackal, on the other hand, is a realist. According to him might is right on earth. The lizard, he remarks, devours the insect, and in its turn becomes the prey of the bat, which is swallowed by the snake, upon which the hawk pounces. Nature is ever at strife. The scheme of the jackal's reasoning reminds one of that advanced by Darwin in his theory of the survival of the fittest: Nature is "careless of the single life." How is the sinner to be punished, and what prayer, however powerful, can deter him? The contest between the animals grows warmer; they adduce many proverbs and fables to illustrate the various points at issue, and occasionally specific complaints are made against the gods themselves. The author has evidently a leaning toward the jackal, whose subtle reasoning occasionally throws the cat into a rage. Most unfortunately the text is badly preserved, and many of its passages are exceedingly obscure; but it stands as an early example of the never-ending war between the optimist and the pessimist.

Travellers' Tales

Some of the most interesting passages in Egyptian literature are those which deal with travel and adventure. The natives of Egypt were by no means travellers, and for the most part confined their journeyings and excursions to the precincts of their own country, and even to their own nomes or provinces. To pass beyond the borders of Khemi appeared to them a formidable undertaking. But it was necessary that ambassadors should be sent to the surrounding states, and that tribute which had been agreed upon should be properly enforced. As the benefits of trade grew apparent Egyptian merchants pushed their way into the surrounding regions, and criminals often saved themselves by flight into foreign countries. Those who had sojourned abroad were wont upon return home to gather their friends and neighbours about them and regale them with an account of their travels. Some of these are in the best style of Sir John Maundeville, while others again are simple and correct narratives of possible events.

The Story of Saneha

One of these, the story of Saneha, dates from the Middle Kingdom, and possessed a great vogue for at least a thousand years. It is unknown whether its central figure is real or fictitious, as the name was a fairly common one at that period. Saneha was an official under the first king of the Twelfth Dynasty, Amenemhat I. When Amenemhat died and his son Senusert I[1] came to the throne, he chanced to be hidden near by where a secret reception of a certain embassy was held, all knowledge of which his royal master

[1] Or Usertsen.

desired should be kept inviolate. In terror lest his presence should have been observed by someone, he fled eastward across the Delta, passed the frontier, and journeyed to the Bitter Lakes, where he became overpowered by thirst. Here he felt that death had come upon him, but, summoning his courage, he pressed forward and, hearing the lowing of cattle, walked in their direction. Tending the cattle was a man of the desert, who provided him with water and boiled milk, and offered him a home with his tribe. But Saneha considered himself unsafe so near the frontier, and proceeded to the Upper Tenu, perhaps the south of Palestine. Here he encountered a tribe, with which he dwelt for some time, marrying the eldest daughter of its chief, and he became wealthy in land and cattle and was regarded with much respect. But as he grew older a great longing came upon him to behold the land of Egypt once more. King Senusert was communicated with, and permission was granted to Saneha to return. The king received him kindly and his bedouin garments were exchanged for costly Egyptian robes. A splendid tomb was built for him, and he was once more received into the royal favour.

The papyrus is valuable as affording vivid descriptions of the life of the tribes of Southern Palestine, the forays of the various clans and the picturesque barbarism of nomadic life. But the narrative is often interrupted by irritating eulogies upon the King of Egypt.

The Shipwrecked Sailor

In sharp contradistinction to this is a tale of the Twelfth Dynasty, known as the Story of the Shipwrecked Sailor, preserved in the Hermitage Collection at Petrograd. A wandering sailor, recounting his adventures to his superior officer, begs of him an introduction to Pharaoh. His master will not credit his story, but the man protests that it is true. He was bound for the mines of the king, he says, and took ship on a vessel 150 cubits long and 40 cubits wide, manned by one hundred of the best sailors of Egypt, whose hearts were stronger than lions, and who were inured to hardship and voyage. They laughed at the thought of tempests, but as they approached land a great wind arose and mighty waves dashed against the vessel. The narrator seized upon a piece of timber, and not too soon, for the ship and all who remained in her were submerged. He floated for three days and then was cast on an island, where he crawled into the shadow of some bushes upon which grew figs and grapes. He also succeeded in finding melons, berries, and grain, and in snaring fishes and birds. Contented to remain there awhile, he dug a pit and lighted a fire, and offered up a sacrifice to the gods.

All at once a terrible uproar like to the rumbling of thunder surprised him out of his equanimity. At first he took it to be the noise of a tempest at sea, but shortly he perceived that the trees shook and that the earth had become violently agitated. Just before him lay a great serpent thirty cubits long, with a beard two cubits in length; its back was covered with scales of gold, and its body was the colour of lapis-lazuli. Terrified, the sailor threw himself on his face before this monster, which regarded him for a moment with its terrible eyes, and then, opening its ponderous jaws, addressed him as follows: "What has brought thee to this island, little one? Speak quickly, and if thou dost not acquaint me with something I have not heard, or knew not before, thou shalt vanish like flame." Without giving the unfortunate mariner time to answer, it raised him in its jaws and carried him to its lair, where it laid him down gently enough, safe and sound. Once more it demanded of him what power had brought him to that island, and the sailor, trembling in every limb, replied that on his way to the mines of Pharaoh he had been wrecked. On hearing his tale the serpent told him to be of good cheer and not to be afraid; that God had brought him to a blessed island where nothing was lacking, and which was filled with all good things; that in four months' time a ship should come for him; that he should return into Egypt; and that he should die in his own town. To cheer him up the benevolent monster described the island to him. Its population consisted of seventy-five serpents, young and old, and there these beings dwelt in harmony and plenty. The sailor on his part was none the less friendly, and in the goodness of his heart offered to recount to Pharaoh the presence and condition of the serpent island, promising to bring to the monster personally sacred oils and perfumes and the incense with which the gods were honoured. He would also slay asses for him in sacrifice, pluck birds for him, and bring him ships full of the treasures of Egypt.

In reply the serpent merely smiled at him indulgently and a little disdainfully. "Tell me not," he said, "that you are rich in perfumes, for I know that all you have is but ordinary incense. I am Prince of the Land of Punt and possess as much perfume as I require, and let me tell you that when you depart from this place you shall never behold it again, for it shall be changed into waves."

In due time the ship approached, as the serpent had prophesied, and in order to observe by what sort of company it was manned the sailor climbed into a high tree. As it neared the shore the serpent bade him farewell, and provided him with gifts of precious perfumes, sweet woods, cassia, kohl, incense, ivory tusks, apes, baboons, and all kinds of precious merchandise. Embarking with these, he was finally told by the genius of the island that in two months he should behold his wife and children. The rescued mariner then sailed through Nubia down the Nile to the residence of the Pharaoh, and the tale ends with the request on the part of its narrator that his captain should provide him with an escort so that he might present himself before the Pharaoh and recount his story. The island upon which he had been wrecked was the island of the Ka—that is, the Soul. Such a story would not by any means seem astounding to the ancient Egyptians, among whom many such romances were current. Indeed, so abundant were these, and so many absurd notions did they propagate, that we find the spirit of satire aroused against them in a London papyrus dating about 1250 B.C., which relates an imaginary journey through Palestine and Phœnicia, the aim of which is not to describe the journey itself, but to laugh to scorn the artificialities and absurdities of the popular romances of the day.

The Fable of the Head and the Stomach

Romances regarding life in Egypt, such as that dealing with King Rhampsinitus given elsewhere, are frequent. A papyrus of about 1250 B.C. has for its background the war against the Hyksos, and describes an encounter between rival princes—Apepi, leader of the Hyksos, and the nationalist prince, Ra-sekenen, who dwelt in Upper Egypt. They propounded riddles to one another, and on their solutions the fate of one of them depended. Fables were extremely popular in the Nile valley from an early period. In the Turin

Museum an example, dating about 1000 B.C., is painted upon two small boards and contains the story of a dispute between the head and the stomach. The Court of the Thirty, the supreme tribunal of Egypt, sits in judgment. The stomach first brings forward its case; but here the document is defective. We have, however, the reply of the head, who at considerable length argues that he is the principal beam, from which all the other beams that support the house radiate. His is the eye that sees, the mouth that speaks, the nose that breathes. The rest of the proceedings and the verdict are unfortunately wanting. It is interesting, however, to know of this early progenitor of the widespread fable of the strife between the stomach and its principals which was adduced by Menenius Agrippa to the Roman plebeians, when, in 492 B.C., they threatened to forsake the city, as a symbol of what might happen if they proceeded to extremities. It contains good proof that the popular story has, as a rule, a lease of life spreading over many centuries, and that, originating in one country, it becomes in time the property of many. It has often been asserted that in all likelihood the fables of Æsop must have originated in Egypt, the land of animal-worship; and it is noteworthy that in the Leyden Demotic papyrus we find the fable of the grateful mouse and the lion which had become entangled in the net. But this dates within the Christian era, and is probably Greek in conception. However, we discover stories of animals acting as human beings, playing games, engaging in war, just as we do in the folklore of other barbarian peoples. Lepsius imagines that the purport of most of these is satirical.

The Rebuking of Amasis

In a papyrus of the Ptolemaic period we find the old expedient of rebuking a king by recounting to him an apposite story. The monarch in question was Amasis (died 526 B.C.), a pleasure-loving ruler, who was wont to imbibe too freely and too often of an Egyptian intoxicating beverage called kelebi. It happened one day that he spake to his nobles, "It is my good pleasure to drink Egyptian kelebi." They spake, "O our mighty lord, it is hard to drink Egyptian kelebi." He said unto them, "Hath that which I say unto you an evil savour?" They said, "O our mighty lord, that which pleaseth the king, let him do." The king commanded, "Let Egyptian kelebi be brought to the lake," and they did according to the word of the king. The king washed himself, with his children, and there was no other wine set before them but Egyptian kelebi. The king feasted with his children, he drank much wine for the love which he bore to Egyptian kelebi; then, on the evening of that day, the king fell asleep by the lake, for he had commanded a couch to be placed in an arbour on the shore of the lake. When the morning dawned the king could not arise because of the heaviness of his carouse. When an hour had passed and he still could not arise, then the courtiers lamented, saying, "Can such things be? Behold, the king drinketh himself drunken like a man of the people.[1] A man of the people cannot come into the presence of the king on matters of business." Therefore the courtiers went to the place where the king was lying, and spake, "O our mighty lord, what wish doth

[1] This expression argues a greater decency in matters convivial in the Egypt of 526 B.C. than obtained in Georgian England.

the king cherish?" The king said, "It is my will and pleasure to make myself drunken. Is there none among you can tell me a story that I may keep myself from sleep?" Now among the courtiers there was a high official named Peun, who knew many tales. He stood before the king, and began: "O our mighty lord, knoweth the king not the story of the young sailor? In the days of King Psammetichus there was a young sailor and he was wedded. Another sailor fell in love with the wife of the first, and she loved him in return. Then it happened one day that the king summoned him to his presence. When the feast was over great desire took hold upon him"—here a hiatus occurs in the text—"and he wished once more to come into the presence of the king. He returned to his home and washed himself, with his wife, but he could not drink as aforetime. When the hour came for bed he could not bring himself to sleep because of the great grief that oppressed him. Then said his wife unto him, 'What hath befallen thee on the river?'" Most unfortunately the remainder of the text is wanting, and exactly in what manner the relation of what happened to King Psammetichus edified King Amasis we cannot tell.

Tales of Magic

As was only to be expected, a goodly number of Egyptian stories abounded in the magical element. Notably is this the case in the Westcar papyrus written about 1800 B.C. and now in the Berlin Museum. Unluckily both the beginning and end of this manuscript are wanting, yet sufficient of it remains to permit us to glean the purport of the whole. It recounts how Khufu, or Kheops, the famous builder of the great pyramid at Gizeh, gathered his sons and his councillors around him and asked if any of them were aware of a man who could recount to him tales of the magicians. His son Khafra, in reply, stated that he was aware of one such tale, which had been handed down from the days of the king's forefather Nebka, and that it dealt with what occurred when he went into the temple of Ptah of Ankhtaui. Whilst proceeding to the temple Nebka turned aside to visit his chief reciter, Uba-aner. He was followed by his retinue, among whom was a certain page, with whom Uba-aner's wife fell in love, and sent her servant to him with a present of a chest full of beautiful raiment. They met clandestinely in a summer-house or pavilion in the garden of Uba-aner, where they quaffed wine and made merry. But the steward of the house considered it his duty to inform his master of these happenings, and Uba-aner, being a man versed in magic, resolved to avenge himself thereby. He called for his casket of ebony and electrum, and when they had brought it he fashioned a crocodile of wax of the length of seven fingers, and he laid a spell upon it; and toward evening the page went to the lake, which was in the garden, to bathe, whereupon, acting on his master's instructions, the steward threw in the waxen crocodile behind him. At once it became a great crocodile, seven cubits in length, and, opening its horrid jaws, seized on the page and dragged him under. During this time the king had been staying with Uba-aner, and at the end of seven days he went forth again. As he was about to leave the house Uba-aner requested him to come and see the marvel which had happened. They went to the lake-side, and the reciter called upon the crocodile, which at once arose from the water holding the page.

"O king," said Uba-aner, "whatever I desire this crocodile to do, he will do." The king requested that the animal should be returned to the water; but Uba-aner lifted the crocodile in his hand, and straightway it turned to wax again. He then acquainted the king with what had passed between the page and his wife, and the monarch indignantly ordered the crocodile once more to seize the page, which it immediately did, plunging into the water with its prey and disappearing for ever. Nebka then commanded that the wife of Uba-aner be brought forth and that she be burned with fire and her ashes cast into the river.

So pleased was Khufu with this story that he ordered that the shade of Nebka should be presented with a thousand loaves, a hundred draughts of beer, an ox, and two jars of incense, and that the *ka* of Uba-aner should receive a loaf, a jar of beer, a jar of incense, and a portion of meat.

The Parting of the Waters

Another of the king's sons then told of a marvellous happening which came to pass in the days of King Seneferu. Seneferu, feeling extremely bored and jaded, sought in every apartment of his palace for something with which to amuse himself, but in vain; so he called for Zazamankh, his chief reciter and scribe of the rolls, to whom he told his predicament. Zazamankh advised that the king should command that a boat be made ready, and that he should go upon the lake of the palace and be rowed to and fro upon its glassy surface by the royal ladies. He asked for twenty oars of ebony inlaid with gold, with blades of light wood inlaid with electrum. These were to be rowed by twenty ladies. The king's heart was gladdened by the exercise; but one of the ladies who was steering lost a jewel of malachite from her hair. Immediately she ceased her singing, and so did her companions, and they ceased to row. Seneferu inquired the reason, and they replied, "The steerswoman rows not." The king then turned to the lady who had lost her jewel and asked her why she did not row. "Alas!" she replied, "my jewel of malachite has fallen in the water, and my heart is sad." The king bade her be of good cheer and said that he would replace it; but she childishly replied that she wanted her own piece of malachite back in its setting. The king then called for Zazamankh and acquainted him with the circumstance which had befallen. Zazamankh then uttered a powerful spell, and behold! one part of the waters of the lake was piled upon the other, so that far below them the king and the rowers could see the jewel lying upon a piece of potsherd. Zazamankh descended from the boat and secured the jewel and brought it back to its owner, after which he once more commanded the waters to return to the place whence they came. This surprising act lightened the hearts of the entire company, so that they spent a joyful afternoon, and Zazamankh was richly rewarded for his magical skill. Pharaoh was so pleased with this tale that he commanded that the shade of Seneferu should receive an offering similar to what had been presented to Nebka, and that the *ka* of Zazamankh should have presented to it a loaf, a jar of beer, and a jar of incense.

The Prophecy of Dedi

But a third son told the king that, so far from recounting tales concerning persons of bygone times, he could tell him a magical story of a man who lived in his own days. His name was Dedi, and he dwelt at Dedsneferu. He was 110 years old, and he ate daily five hundred loaves of bread and a side of beef, and drank a hundred draughts of beer. So great was his magical learning that if the head of a man or an animal were smitten off, Dedi could restore the deceased to life. He could tame wild beasts, and knew the designs of the House of Thoth. This design the king, Khufu, might like to know, and it would perhaps be of use to him in the construction of his pyramid. Khufu at once ordered his son to bring this Dedi before him, and the prince, whose name was Hordedef,[1] took ship up the Nile to where the venerable magician dwelt. He was carried in a litter to the house of Dedi, whom he found lying on a couch at the door of his house in process of being massaged by his servants. Hordedef told him that he had come from afar to bring him before his father, Khufu. Dedi replied with the salutation of praise, and together they went toward the ship which had brought the prince thither. Dedi asked that he might be given a boat and that his youths and his books might be brought to him. He was provided with two boats, in which these were stowed, and Dedi himself sat in the barge of the prince. They duly reached the palace, where Hordedef announced to the king that he had brought the ancient sorcerer. The Pharaoh at once gave orders that he should be led before him, and when he came asked how it was that he had not before heard of him ; and Dedi replied, "He only who is called cometh ; the king calleth me, and behold I come." Khufu said to him, "Is it sooth, as is said of thee, that if the head is smitten off a man or an animal, thou canst restore either to life ?" Dedi replied in the affirmative. The king then requested that a prisoner be brought to him, but Dedi begged that a man should not be used for this purpose, saying, "Behold, we do not even thus to our cattle." A duck was then brought to him and decapitated, and its body was laid on the west side of the hall,

[1] Called Her-tata-f in another part of this manuscript.

and its head on the east side. Dedi then spoke some magic words, and lo! the body and the head of the bird approached each other and joined, and the duck stood up and quacked. He then performed the same feat with a goose and an ox.

Khufu, delighted with the success of these experiments, then asked Dedi if he knew of the designs of the House of Thoth. The magician replied that he did not know their number, but that he knew where they were. Pharaoh then asked him their hiding-place, and was told that in a chamber in Heliopolis, called the Plan-room, was a chest of whetstone in which the plans were concealed, Dedi adding, "O king, it is not I that shall bring them to thee." "Who, then," asked Khufu, "shall bring them to me?" And Dedi replied, "The eldest of the three children of Rud-didet shall bring them to thee." "And who is Rud-didet?" asked Khufu. "She is," replied Dedi, "the wife of a priest of Ra, lord of Sakhebu. But these three sons of hers are the sons of Ra the god, who has promised her that they shall reign over all this land, and that the eldest of them shall be high-priest in Heliopolis." At this the king's heart was much troubled, and Dedi, seeing that he was in fear of the future, said to him, "Be not afraid because of what I have said, O king; for thy son shall reign, and thy son's son, before Rud-didet's sons shall rule the land; and behold! this progeny of Ra is not yet born." Khufu then announced his intention of visiting the temple of Ra when the banks of the canal of Letopolis were cut, and Dedi promised that the banks of the canal should hold at least four cubits of water. The sorcerer was then placed in the palace of Hordedef, and was daily provided with a thousand loaves, a hundred draughts of beer, an ox, and a hundred bunches of onions.

The Visit of the Goddesses

Now when the sons of Ra and Rud-didet were born, that deity requested Isis, Nebhat, Meskhent, Hakt, and Khnumu to go to her, and taking the form of dancing-girls, all except the god Khnumu, who followed them as a porter, they descended to earth and approached the house of the priest Ra-user, Rud-didet's husband, and played before him with their instruments of music. They endowed the children with various attributes, and called them User-ref, Sah-ra, and Kaku. They then quitted the house and bade Ra-user rejoice. In return for their good wishes he bestowed upon them a bushel of barley, which Khnumu placed upon his head; but as they were on the way back to their divine abode Isis said unto the others, "Would it not have been better had we done a marvel for these children?" To this the others assented, and they there and then fashioned a likeness of the crowns of Egypt, of the crown of the Upper Land, and of the crown of the Lower, and hid them in the bushel of barley. They then returned to the house of Ra-user and requested permission to leave the barley in a closed chamber, which they sealed up, and then took their leave. A few weeks afterward Rud-didet asked her handmaid if the house and all that was in it were in good condition, and the handmaid replied that all was satisfactory except that the brewing barley was not yet brought. Her mistress then inquired why that had not been done, and the servant answered that their store had been given to the dancing-girls, who had arrived on the day of the children's birth, and that it now lay in the closed chamber under their seal. Rud-didet then ordered the maid to use it for the present, saying that Ra-user could replace it before their return. The girl opened the chamber and, entering, was surprised to hear people talking and singing, music and the sound of dancing, and such sounds as one hears in the palace of the king. She quickly returned and acquainted her mistress with what she had heard. Rud-didet then entered the room herself and also heard the sounds, but could not locate them. At last she laid her ear to the sack which held the barley, and found that the sounds proceeded from it. She at once placed it in a chest, which she put for security in a greater chest, and this she bound round with leather and laid in a store-room, taking the precaution to seal it, and when Ra-user returned she told him what had occurred.

Some days after, Rud-didet had occasion to rebuke her servant and beat her with stripes, and the maid grumbled and said to her companions, "Why has this been done to me? I will go to King Khufu and tell him that her three sons are destined to become kings." She then betook herself to her uncle; but he would not hearken to her treachery and struck her a violent blow with a bunch of flax which he held. Feeling faint, she went down to the riverside for a draught of water, but was seized upon by a crocodile, who carried her away. Her uncle then presented himself to Rud-didet, whom he found in a most dejected condition. He asked her what made her downcast, and she replied that she feared treachery from the handmaiden. "You need not fear for her," replied the man, "because she has been seized upon by a crocodile." At this point the manuscript fails us. It is indeed unfortunate that such an interesting domestic passage has not been spared. The three kings whose names appear in the story as the triplet sons of Rud-didet reigned during the Fifth Dynasty, so that they could hardly have been

The Goddesses as Dancing-girls
Evelyn Paul

(page 203)

Thoth and the Chief Magician
Evelyn Paul

(page 216)

born in the Fourth. The tale would seem to be based upon the official adoption of the worship of Ra in Egypt. It may be mentioned that the real names of the three children, User-ref, Sah-ra, and Kaku, are intended as a play upon the names of the first three kings of the Fifth Dynasty, User-kaf, Sahu-ra, and Kaka. The story of the fatal children born to usurp a throne is a very common one in all mythologies, and it is inevitable that the monarch whose line is doomed to extinction should make an effort to destroy them while yet they are in the cradle. The Greek myth of Danaë and the old romance of Sir Torrent of Portugal are examples of this. Mediæval romance is, indeed, full of such stories, but this is probably the earliest example on record.

Lyric and Folk Poetry

Egypt was not without its lyric and folk poetry; however, the romantic was not the *forte* of the Egyptians. It is noteworthy at the same time that most Oriental peoples sing while at their work, and it would be strange if the labourer on the banks of the Nile had not done so. The fellah of to-day chants monotonously and endlessly while toiling, repeating the same words and music over and over again; but the scribe of early Egypt regarded the folk-song as unfit for transmission to posterity. Occasionally a song is recaptured from mural inscriptions. The shepherd who wades through the half-submerged fields, driving his sheep before him, sings: "In the water walks the shepherd with the fishes. He talks with the cat-fish; with the fish he exchanges a greeting." We have also a threshing song: "Thresh ye, O oxen; thresh for yourselves. Thresh straw for your fodder and grain for your masters. Rest not, for the air is cool this day."

A few love-songs have also survived. These were probably very numerous. For the most part they are intense and passionate. Three collections of love-songs of about 1200 B.C. have been unearthed, one of which is contained in a papyrus now in the British Museum. On a stele in the Louvre the praise of the wife of a king of about 700 B.C. is sung as follows: "The sweet one, sweet in love; the sweet one, sweet in love in the presence of the king; the sweet one, sweet in love before all men; the beloved before all women; the king's daughter who is sweet in love. The fairest among women, a maid whose like none has seen. Blacker is her hair than the darkness of night, blacker than the berries of the blackberry bush. Harder are her teeth than the flints on the sickle. A wreath of flowers is each of her breasts, close nestling on her arms."

The True History of Setne and his son Se-Osiris [1]

This story was discovered written on some papyrus belonging to the British Museum. An English translation was published in 1900 by Mr. F. Ll. Griffiths, and one in French by Sir G. Maspero in 1901. It is written on the back of some official documents in Greek and dates from the seventh year of the Emperor Claudian. The papyrus is much dilapidated and pasted end to end; it is incomplete, and the beginning of the history has disappeared. By the writing one would judge the copy to belong to the latter half of the second century of our era. The Setne alluded to is the same who figures in the story of Setne and the Mummies related in the chapter on Magic.

Once upon a time there was a king called Ousimares,

[1] The Demotic gives the name (or title) as Setne or Setme, and the name of the miraculous child as Si-Osiris (*i.e.* son of Osiris).

and he had a son called Setne. This son was a scribe; he was clever with his hands, indeed in all things, and he excelled all men of the world learned in the arts or those among the renowned scribes of Egypt. It happened that the chiefs of certain foreign lands sent a message to Pharaoh challenging him to find one who would do such and such a thing under certain conditions. If this were done, then these chiefs would acknowledge the inferiority of their country to Egypt; but if, on the other hand, neither scribe nor wise man could accomplish it, then they would proclaim the inferiority of Egypt. Now Ousimares called his son Setne and repeated these words to him, and immediately Setne gave the answer to that which the chiefs had propounded, so that the latter were forced to carry out the conditions and admit the superiority of Egypt. And thus were they robbed of their triumph, so great was the wisdom of Setne, and none other ever dared to send such messages to Pharaoh.

Now Setne and his wife Mahîtouaskhît were greatly grieved, for they had no son. One day when he was troubled more than usual over this his wife went to the temple of Imhetep, and she prayed before him, saying, "Turn thy face to me, O Imhetep, son of Ptah, thou who workest miracles, who art beneficent in all thy doings. It is thou who canst give a son to those who are sonless. Oh, hear my prayer, and grant that I shall bear a son!" And that night Mahîtouaskhît slept in the temple, and there she dreamed a dream wherein she was directed to prepare a magical remedy, and told that by this means her desire for a son should be fulfilled. On waking she did all according to her dream, and in time it was known that a child was to be born to her and Setne, who told it before Pharaoh with great joy, while to his wife, for her protection, he gave an amulet and put spells about her.

And one night Setne dreamed, and a voice said to him, " Mahîtouaskhît, thy wife, will bring forth a son, and through him many wonders shall be accomplished in the land of Egypt. And the name of thy son shall be Se-Osiris." When Setne awoke and remembered these words he rejoiced and was glad in heart.

Se-Osiris

In due time a son was born, and according to the dream he was called Se-Osiris. And the child developed rapidly beyond all other children, and Setne loved him so greatly that scarce an hour passed without his seeing him. In time he was put to school, but soon showed that he knew more than the tutor could teach him. He began to read the magical papyri with the priestly scribes in the 'Double House of Life' of the temple of Ptah, and all those about him were lost in astonishment. Then was Setne so pleased that he led his son before Pharaoh to the festival that all the magicians of the king might strive against him and have to acknowledge their defeat.

And one day, when Setne, together with the boy Se-Osiris, was preparing for the festival, loud voices of lamentation rose upon the air, and Setne, looking forth from the terrace of his apartments, saw the body of a rich man being carried to the mountains for burial with great honour and loud wailing. Again he looked forth, and this time he saw the body of a peasant borne along wrapped in a mat of straw and without a soul to mourn him. And seeing this Setne exclaimed, " By the life of Osiris, god of Amenti, may it be that I come into Amenti as this rich man comes, honoured and lamented, and not as the peasant, alone and already forgotten ! " Upon hearing this Se-Osiris said, " Nay, my father, rather may the fate of the poor man be thine, and not that of the rich one!" Setne was astonished and hurt at this and cried, "Are they the words of a son who loves his father?" Se-Osiris answered him: "My father, I will show to thee each in his place, the peasant unwept and the rich man so lamented."

A Vision of Amenti

Then Setne demanded of him how he could accomplish this. The child Se-Osiris began to recite words from the magical books, words of power. Next he took his father by the hand and led him to an unknown place in the mountains of Memphis. Here there were seven great halls filled with people of all conditions. They traversed three of these without hindrance. Upon entering the fourth Setne saw a mass of men who rushed hither and thither, writhing as creatures attacked them from behind; others, famished, were springing and jumping in their efforts to reach the food suspended above them, whilst some, again, dug holes at their feet to prevent them attaining their object. In the fifth hall were venerable shades who had each found their proper and fitting place, but those who were accused of crimes lingered kneeling at the door, which pivoted upon the eye of a man who ceaselessly prayed and groaned. In the sixth hall were the gods of Amenti, who sat in council, each in his place, whilst the keepers of the portals called out the causes. In the seventh hall was seated the great god Osiris on a golden throne, crowned with the plumed diadem. On his left was Anubis, and on his right the god Thoth. In the midst were the scales wherein were weighed the faults and virtues of the souls of the dead, while Thoth wrote down the judgment that Anubis pronounced. Then those whose faults outweighed their virtues were delivered to

Amait, the attendant of the Lord of Amenti ; their souls and bodies were destroyed for ever. But those whose virtues were greater than their failings took their place among the gods and shades, and there their souls found a heaven. Those, again, whose merits and faults were equal were put amongst the servitors of Sekerosiris.

Then Setne saw near the place of Osiris one of exalted rank and robed in the finest linen. And while Setne was marvelling at all he had seen in the land of Amenti, Se-Osiris, his little son, said unto him, "My father Setne, seest thou that great personage in fine robes and near to Osiris ? That peasant whom thou didst see carried out of Memphis without a soul to accompany him, and his body wrapped in a mat, dost thou remember, my father ? Well, that peasant is the one beside Osiris ! When he had come to Amenti and they weighed his faults and virtues, lo ! his virtues outweighed all. And by the judgment of the gods all the honours that had been the share of the rich man were given to the peasant, and by the law of Osiris he takes his place midst the honoured and exalted. But the rich man, when he had come to Hades and his merits were weighed, lo ! his faults weighed heavier, and he is that man you have seen upon whose eye pivots the door of the fifth hall, the man who cries and prays aloud with great agony. By the life of Osiris, god of Amenti, if upon earth I said to thee, 'Rather may the fate of the peasant be thine than that of the rich man,' it was because I knew their fates, my father."

And Setne answered and said, "My son Se-Osiris, numberless marvels have I seen in Amenti ; but tell me the meaning of those people we saw rushing before creatures who devoured them, and the others ever trying to reach the food beyond their reach." [1]

[1] The whole of this is very obscure in the original.

Se-Osiris answered him :

"In truth, my father, they are under the curse of the gods ; they are those who upon earth wasted their substance, and the creatures who devour them without ceasing are the women with whom they squandered both life and substance, and now they have naught, though they should work day and night. And so it is with all : as they have been on earth, so it is with them in Amenti, according to their good and bad deeds. That is the immutable law of the gods, the law that knows no change and under which all men must come when they enter Hades."

Then Setne and his son returned hand in hand from the mountains of Memphis. A fear was upon Setne because of Se-Osiris, who answered not, and then he pronounced words that exorcize the ghosts of the dead. Always afterward he remembered all he had seen and marvelled thereat, but spoke of it to no man. And when Se-Osiris was twelve years of age there was no scribe or magician in Memphis who was his equal in the reading of the magical books.

The Reading of the Sealed Letter

After this it happened one day that the Pharaoh Ousimares was seated in the Hall of Audience with the princes, the military chiefs, and the nobles of Egypt, each according to his rank, gathered about him. One said unto Pharaoh, "Here is a rascally Ethiopian who would fain have speech with you and who carries a sealed letter." And Pharaoh commanded that the man be brought before him. And when he was come he made obeisance and said, "Here is a sealed letter which I bear, and I would fain know if amongst your wise men there are any who can read its contents without breaking the seals. If, O king, you have not such a one among your scribes and magicians, I shall take back to my country, the land of the Negro, the story of Egypt's failure and inferiority." Upon hearing these words all were amazed, and those about the king exclaimed loudly, while Pharaoh bade some bring to him his son Setne. When he had come, instantly obeying the royal command and bowing low before him, Pharaoh said, "My son Setne, hast thou heard the words of this insolent Ethiopian?" and then he repeated the challenge. Then was Setne astonished, but he answered immediately, "Great Lord, who can read a letter without its being opened and spread before him? But if you will give me ten days, I will think upon it and do what I can to avoid the report of Egypt's failure being carried to the Negroes, eaters of gum." And Pharaoh said, "Those days are granted, my son." Then were rooms appointed for the Ethiopian, and Pharaoh rose from his palace sad at heart and went fasting to his couch.

And Setne, pondering and much disturbed, threw himself upon his couch, but knew no rest. His wife Mahîtouaskhît came to him and would fain have shared his trouble, but he said that it was not for a woman to share or one that she might help him in. Later, his son Se-Osiris came and begged to know what so sorely troubled his father, and again Setne refused to speak, saying that it was not for a child. But the boy persisted, and at last Setne told him of the challenge of the Ethiopian. The moment he had finished Se-Osiris laughed, and his father asked the reason of his mirth.

"My father," he answered, "I laugh to see you there, so troubled in heart because of such a small affair. I will read that letter of the Ethiopian, read it all without breaking the seals."

Hearing this, Setne rose instantly.

"But what proof can you give me of the truth of what you say, my son?"

Se-Osiris answered, "My father, go thou to the lower floor of this house and take what books you please from their place. As you do so I shall read that which you have taken from its place while I stand before you."

And it happened as Se-Osiris had said. Each book that his father lifted the boy read without its being opened. Upon this Setne lost no time in acquainting Pharaoh with all that Se-Osiris had done, and so lightened was the heart of the king that he made a feast in honour of Setne and his young son.

After this Pharaoh sent for the Ethiopian. And when he entered the Hall of Audience he was placed in the midst of all, and the young Se-Osiris took up his place beside him. But first the boy put a curse upon the man and his gods if he should dare to say falsely that what he read was not true. And seeing the boy, the Ethiopian prostrated himself before him in fear. Then Se-Osiris began to read the letter with its seals still unbroken, and all heard his voice. And the words were:

The Contents of the Letter

"It happened during the reign of the Pharaoh Manakhphrê-Siamon, who was a beneficent ruler and in whose time the land overflowed with all good things, who endowed the temples richly, that when the King of Nubia was taking his rest in the pleasure-kiosk of Amen he overheard the voices of three Ethiopians who were talking behind the house. One of them was speaking in a high voice, saying, among other things, that if the god Amen would preserve him from the enmity of the King of Egypt he could put a spell on the people of that country so that a great darkness should reign and they should not see the moon for three days and three nights. Then the second man said that if Amen would guard him he would cause the Pharaoh to be transported to the land of the Negroes, and there, before the king of that country and in public, he should suffer five hundred blows, and afterward he should be taken back to his country in not more than six hours. After this the third man spoke, saying that if Amen would preserve him he would then send a blight upon the land of Egypt, a blight for the space of three years. When the king heard this he ordered that these three men be brought before him.

"He said unto them, 'Which of you said that he would cause that the people of Egypt should not see the moon for three days and three nights?' And they answered that it was Horus, the son of Tririt (the sow).

"Again the king said, 'Which of you said that he had power to cause the King of Egypt to be brought hither?' And they answered that it was Horus, the son of Tnahsit (the negress).

"Again the king said, 'Which of you said that he would cause a blight to fall upon Egypt?' And they answered that it was Horus, the son of Triphît (the princess).

"Then the king bade Horus, the son of Tnahsit, come near, and he said to him, 'By Amen, the Bull of Meroe, if thou canst accomplish what thou hast said, then rich rewards shall be thine.'

"And Horus, the son of Tnahsit, fashioned a litter and four bearers of wax. Over them he chanted magical words, he breathed upon them and gave them life, and finally he bade them wend their way to Egypt and bring back the king of that land in order that he might suffer five hundred blows from the kourbash before the King of the Negroes."

Here Se-Osiris paused and, turning to the Ethiopian, said, "The curse of Amen fall upon thee! These words that I have said, are they not written in the letter thou holdest in thine hand?" And the rascally Ethiopian bowed low before him, saying, "They are written there, my lord!"

Then Se-Osiris resumed his magical reading:

"And all happened as Horus, the son of Tnahsit, had devised. By the power of sorcery was Pharaoh taken to the land of the Negroes, and there suffered five hundred blows of the kourbash. After that he was carried back to Egypt, as had been said, and, wakening the next morning in the temple of the god Horus, he lay in great pain, his body sorely bruised. Bewildered, he asked his courtiers how such could have happened in Egypt. They, thinking some madness had fallen upon their king, and yet ashamed of their thoughts, spoke soothingly to him, and said that the great gods would heal his afflictions. But still they asked him the meaning of his strange words, and suddenly he remembered all that had happened to him and recounted it to his courtiers.

Magic versus Magic

"When they saw his bruised body they made a great clamour. And then Pharaoh sent for his chief magician, and he at once cried out that the evil and affliction of the king were due to the sorceries of the Ethiopians.

"'By the life of Ptah,' he continued, 'I shall bring them to torture and execution.'

"And Pharaoh bade him make all speed lest he should be carried away the next night. And the chief magician carried his secret books and amulets to the place where Pharaoh lay, and chanted above him magical words and incantations. Then, with many gifts, he embarked in a boat and made haste to reach the temple of Khmounon, and there he prayed to the god Thoth that all evil should be averted from Pharaoh and the land of Egypt. And that night he slept in the temple, and he dreamed a dream in which the god Thoth appeared to him and instructed him in divine magic that would preserve the king from the wiles of the Ethiopians.

"On waking the magician remembered all, and without losing a moment fulfilled all that he had been told in his dream. And then he wrote the charm to preserve Pharaoh from all sorcery. On the second day the Ethiopians endeavoured to renew their enchantments, but all was now unavailing against the person of Pharaoh. The third morning Pharaoh recounted to his chief musicians all that had happened during the night, and how the Ethiopians had failed in their attempts.

"Then the magician fashioned a litter and four bearers of wax. He put a spell upon them and breathed life into them, bidding them go and bring before Pharaoh the King of the Negroes, that he might suffer five hundred blows upon his body and then be carried back to his own land again. And the waxen figures promised to do all as the magician had commanded."

Again Se-Osiris paused, and again he demanded of the Ethiopian if his words were not the words of the sealed letter. And the Ethiopian bowed low to the ground, saying they were the words in very truth.

Se-Osiris began again to read the hidden words:

"And as it happened to Pharaoh, so was the fate of the King of the Negroes, who awoke sorely bruised in the morning following. He called loudly for his courtiers, and when they saw the state of their king they made a great clamour. Again he called and commanded that Horus, the son of Tnahsit, be brought before him. When he had come the king threatened him, and commanded him to go to Egypt and there learn how to save him from the sorceries of Pharaoh's chief magician.

"But no spell devised by the Ethiopian could preserve the king from the magic of the Egyptians, and three times was he carried to that country and humiliated, whilst his body was in great pain, so sorely bruised was it. Then he cursed Horus, the son of Tnahsit, and threatened him with a slow and dreadful death unless he could preserve him from Pharaoh's vengeance.

"Then in fear and trouble Horus went to his mother Tnahsit and told her all, and that he must go to Egypt to see the one who had worked these powerful sorceries and endeavour to inflict upon him a fitting punishment. And his mother, Tnahsit, on hearing this, warned him against coming into the presence of Pharaoh's chief magician, for against him he would never prevail, but know defeat. But he answered that he must go. Then she arranged with him that by signs and signals between them he should let her know how he fared, and if he were in danger, then she should try to save him. And he promised, saying that if he were vanquished, then that which she ate, that which she drank, and the sky above should turn to the colour of blood.

The War of Enchantments

"And after this he journeyed to Egypt, tracking the one whose sorceries had prevailed against his own. He penetrated to the Royal Hall of Audience and came before Pharaoh, crying in a high voice, 'Who is it among you who is putting spells upon me?'

"And Pharaoh's chief magician called out in answer, saying, 'Ha! Ethiopian, is it thou who workedst evil against Pharaoh?' and Horus, the son of Tnahsit, cried out in great anger and by a spell he caused a great flame to rise from the midst of the hall, at which Pharaoh and the Egyptians cried out to the chief of the magicians to succour them. Then by his power he caused a shower of rain to fall so that the flame was extinguished.

"Again the Ethiopian wrought his magic and thereby caused a great darkness to fall upon them all so that the people could not see each other, but this also was dispersed by the magician of the Egyptians. Then followed more machinations by Horus, the son of Tnahsit, but each time was he vanquished. At last he asked for mercy and vowed before the gods that never again would he trouble Egypt or Pharaoh. They gave him a boat and sent him back to his own land. So were the sorceries of the Ethiopians rendered as naught."

With this Se-Osiris finished the reading of the sealed letter. And then he began to reveal to all there, Pharaoh, the princes, and the nobles, that the Ethiopian now before them was none other than that Horus, son of Tnahsit, returned after five hundred years to trouble Egypt and its king again. But against this day he himself, Se-Osiris, had been born again, for he was that former chief magician of the Pharaoh Manakhphrê come back once more to protect Egypt and Pharaoh from the wiles of the Ethiopians.

And with these words he caused a great flame to consume the Ethiopian, there in the midst of the Hall of Audience, so that not a vestige of the creature remained. But afterward when they looked for Se-Osiris he had disappeared as a shadow from before Pharaoh and his father Setne, and never again was he seen of them.

At these happenings everyone marvelled, and Pharaoh said that Se-Osiris was the wisest and most wonderful of all magicians, and that never again would the world see his like.

But the hearts of Setne and his wife were troubled, and they grieved sorely for their son Se-Osiris. Then comfort came to them, and again the wife of Setne bore a son, and they called him Ousimanthor. And so the heart of Setne was glad and he made offerings in the name of Se-Osiris in remembrance.

How Setnau Triumphed over the Assyrians

After the close of the reign of Amysis a priest of 'Vulcan' named Setnau ascended the throne. And this king treated the army with contempt and disdain, thinking he had no need of them. Among other injustices he appropriated the lands which former kings had given to them.

Now it came to pass that when Sennacherib, King of the Arabs and Assyrians, led his hosts against Egypt, the soldiers of the Egyptian army refused to fight and repel them. Setnau, thus reduced to powerlessness, went to the temple and prayed the gods to help him in his dire straits. While thus troubled a sleep fell upon him, and in a dream it seemed that the god himself appeared and exhorted him to courage, saying that all would fall to his advantage in the campaign against the Assyrians.

Greatly cheered by this dream, Setnau called upon those of the army who would follow him, and they camped at Peluce, a main approach into Egypt. Not only soldiers followed him, but merchants, artisans, and men of the street.

Now when the Assyrians besieged the town, as they lay encamped about the field rats during the night gnawed and devoured all the quivers, bows, and fittings of shields of the invaders, so that, on the morrow, when they would have given battle, behold! they were weaponless. Thus disarmed, many of the hosts fled and many perished.

And now in the temple of Vulcan stands a stone image of the god, bearing in his hand the figure of a rat. And the legend inscribed thereon runs, "Who beholds me beholds God."

The Peasant and the Workman

A tale of the Ninth Dynasty, which from the number of copies extant would seem to have been very popular, relates how a peasant succeeded in obtaining justice after he had been robbed. Justice was not very easily obtained in Egypt in those times, for it seems to have been requisite that a peasant should attract the judge's attention by some special means, if his case were to be heard at all. The story runs thus:

In the Salt Country there dwelt a sekhti (peasant) with his family. He made his living by trading with Henenseten in salt, natron, rushes, and the other products of his country, and as he journeyed thither he had to pass through the lands of the house of Fefa. Now there dwelt by the canal a man named Tehuti-nekht, the son of Asri, a serf to the High Steward Meruitensa. Tehuti-nekht had so far encroached on the path—for roads and paths were not protected by law in Egypt as in other countries—that there was but a narrow strip left, with the canal on one side and a cornfield on the other. When Tehuti-nekht saw the sekhti approaching with his burdened asses, his evil heart coveted the beasts and the goods they bore, and he called to the gods to open a way for him to steal the possessions of the sekhti.

This was the plan he conceived. "I will take," said he, "a shawl, and will spread it upon the path. If the sekhti drives his asses over it—and there is no other way—then I shall easily pick a quarrel with him." He had no sooner thought of the project than it was carried into effect. A servant, at Tehuti-nekht's bidding, fetched a shawl and spread it over the path so that one end was in the water, the other among the corn.

When the sekhti drew nigh he drove his asses over the shawl. He had no alternative.

"Hold!" cried Tehuti-nekht with well-simulated wrath, "surely you do not intend to drive your beasts over my clothes!"

"I will try to avoid them," responded the good-natured peasant, and he caused the rest of his asses to pass higher up, among the corn.

"Do you, then, drive your asses through my corn?" said Tehuti-nekht, more wrathfully than ever.

"There is no other way," said the harassed peasant. "You have blocked the path with your shawl, and I must leave the path."

While the two argued upon the matter one of the asses helped itself to a mouthful of corn, whereupon Tehuti-nekht's plaints broke out afresh.

"Behold!" he cried, "your ass is eating my corn. I will take your ass, and he shall pay for the theft."

"Shall I be robbed," cried the sekhti, "in the lands of the Lord Steward Meruitensa, who treateth robbers so hardly? Behold, I will go to him. He will not suffer this misdeed of thine."

"Thinkest thou he will hearken to thy plaint?" sneered Tehuti-nekht. "Poor as thou art, who will concern himself with thy woes? Lo, *I* am the Lord

Steward Meruitensa," and so saying he beat the sekhti sorely, stole all his asses and drove them into pasture.

In vain the sekhti wept and implored him to restore his property. Tehuti-nekht bade him hold his peace, threatening to send him to the Demon of Silence if he continued to complain. Nevertheless, the sekhti petitioned him for a whole day. At length, finding that he was wasting his breath, the peasant betook himself to Henen-ni-sut, there to lay his case before the Lord Steward Meruitensa. On his arrival he found the latter preparing to embark in his boat, which was to carry him to the judgment-hall. The sekhti bowed himself to the ground, and told the Lord Steward that he had a grievance to lay before him, praying him to send one of his followers to hear the tale. The Lord Steward granted the suppliant's request, and sent to him one from among his train. To the messenger the sekhti revealed all that had befallen him on his journey, the manner in which Tehuti-nekht had closed the path so as to force him to trespass on the corn, and the cruelty with which he had beaten him and stolen his property. In due time these matters were told to the Lord Steward, who laid the case before the nobles who were with him in the judgment-hall.

"Let this sekhti bring a witness," they said, "and if he establish his case, it may be necessary to beat Tehuti-nekht, or perchance he will be made to pay a trifle for the salt and natron he has stolen."

The Lord Steward said nothing, and the sekhti himself came unto him and hailed him as the greatest of the great, the orphan's father, the widow's husband, the guide of the needy, and so on.

Very eloquent was the sekhti, and in his florid speech he skilfully combined eulogy with his plea for justice, so that the Lord Steward was interested and flattered in spite of himself.

Now at that time there sat upon the throne of Egypt the King Neb-ka-n-ra, and to him came the Lord Steward Meruitensa, saying:

"Behold, my lord, I have been sought by a sekhti whose goods were stolen. Most eloquent of mortals is he. What would my lord that I do unto him?"

"Do not answer his speeches," said the king, "but put his words in writing and bring them to us. See that he and his wife and children are supplied with meat and drink, but do not let him know who provides it."

The Lord Steward did as the king had commanded him. He gave to the peasant a daily ration of bread and beer, and to his wife sufficient corn to feed herself and her children. But the sekhti knew not whence the provisions came.

A second time the peasant sought the judgment-hall and poured forth his complaint to the Lord Steward; and yet a third time he came, and the Lord Steward commanded that he be beaten with staves, to see whether he would desist. But no, the sekhti came a fourth, a fifth, a sixth time, endeavouring with pleasant speeches to open the ear of the judge. Meruitensa hearkened to him not at all, yet the sekhti did not despair, but came again unto the ninth time. And at the ninth time the Lord Stewerd sent two of his followers to the sekhti, and the peasant trembled exceedingly, for he feared that he was about to be beaten once more because of his importunity. The message, however, was a reassuring one. Meruitensa declared that he had been greatly delighted by the peasant's eloquence and would see that he obtained satisfaction. He then caused the sekhti's petitions to be written on clean papyri and sent to the king, according as the monarch had commanded. Neb-ka-n-ra was also much pleased with the speeches, but the giving of judgment he left entirely in the hands of the Lord Steward.

Meruitensa therefore deprived Tehuti-nekht of all his offices and his property, and gave them to the sekhti, who thenceforth dwelt at the king's palace with all his family. And the sekhti became the chief overseer of Neb-ka-n-ra, and was greatly beloved by him.

Story of the Two Brothers

The manuscript of this tale of the Nineteenth Dynasty was bought in Italy by Mme. Elizabeth d'Orbiney, and is called the d'Orbiney Papyrus. It was acquired by the British Museum in 1857 and copied in facsimile. It has been translated over and over again. The manuscript extends to nineteen pages of ten lines each, the first five pages having been considerably torn. Several gaps have been filled in by the modern possessors of the manuscript, and the restorations are signed. The original manuscript is stamped in two places with the name of its ancient owner, Sety Merenptah, whom we know as Sety II. It was executed by Anena, a scribe who lived during the reigns of Rameses II, Merenptah, and Sety II, and is more than three thousand years old. Bitou, the hero of the story, a herd and husbandman, is perhaps identifiable with the Greek god Bitys.

Anapou and Bitou were two brothers who lived in Egypt a long time ago. To Anapou, as the elder, belonged house, cattle, and fields ; and Bitou, the younger, worked for him. Bitou was marvellously clever in his management of the cattle and in all things relating to agriculture—he could even tell what the cattle said to him and to each other. One day, as the brothers were working in the fields, Anapou sent Bitou home for a large quantity of seed, as he saw the time had come for sowing. Bitou went and got the seed, and after their day's work the two returned, to find Anapou's wife lying moaning, and saying she had been thrashed by Bitou until she was sore because she would not yield him something he had asked of her when he came for the seed. Then Anapou sought to kill Bitou by stealth, but Bitou, warned by the cattle, fled. His brother overtook him, but the god Phra-Harmakhis caused a wide stream full of crocodiles to arise between them, and Bitou asked his brother to wait till break of day, when he would explain all that had happened. When day broke Bitou told Anapou the truth, refusing at the same time ever to return to the house where Anapou's wife was. "I shall go," he said, "to the Vale of the Acacia. Now listen to what will happen. I shall tear out my heart by magic so as to place it on the topmost bough of the acacia, and when the acacia is cut down, and my heart will fall to the ground, you will come to look for it. After you have looked for seven years do not be discouraged, but put it in a vessel of cold water ; that will bring me to life again. I shall certainly live again and be revenged on my enemies. You will know that something of moment is about to happen to me when a jug of beer is given you and the froth shall run over. They will then give you a jug of wine of which the sediment will rise to the top. Rest no more when these things come about."

He went to the valley and his brother returned home, killed his wife, and mourned for Bitou.

Bitou, in the valley, spent his days in hunting, and at night slept under the acacia, on top of which his heart was placed. One day he met the nine gods, who gave him the daughter of the gods for his wife; but the Seven Hathors swore she should die by the sword. He told her about his heart, and that whoever should find the acacia would have to fight with him.

The Treachery of Bitou's Wife

Pharaoh, hearing of this beautiful woman, desired to take possession of her, and sent armed men into the valley, all of whom Bitou killed. Pharaoh at last enticed her away and made her his chief favourite. She told him her husband's secret and bade him cut down the acacia-tree, which was accordingly done, and Bitou fell down dead at the same moment.

Then what Bitou had foretold happened to his brother. Beer that foamed was brought to him, and then wine which became muddy while he held the cup. By these signs he knew that the time had come to act, and taking his clothes and sandals and weapons, he set off for the valley. When he got there he found his brother lying dead on his bed. He went to the acacia to look for the heart, but could find only a berry, which, however, was the heart. He placed it in cold water, and Bitou was restored to life. They embraced each other, and Bitou said to his brother, "I shall now become a sacred bull (Apis). Lead me, then, to Pharaoh, who will reward you with gold and silver for having brought me. I shall then find means to punish my wife for having betrayed me." Anapou did as Bitou directed, and when the sun rose again next day, Bitou having then assumed the form of a bull, he led him to court. There were great rejoicings over the miraculous bull, and Pharaoh rewarded Anapou richly and preferred him before any other man.

Some days after, the bull entered the harem and

addressed his former wife. "You see, I am still alive, after all," he said. "Who are you?" she replied. He said, "I am Bitou. You knew well what you were doing when you got Pharaoh to have the acacia cut down." Then she was very much afraid, and begged Pharaoh to grant her any request she would make. Pharaoh, who loved her so much that he could refuse her nothing, consented. "Then," she said, "give me the liver of the sacred bull to eat, for nothing else will satisfy me." Pharaoh was very much grieved at this, but he had sworn, and one day when the people were offering up sacrifices to the bull he sent his butchers to cut its throat. When the bull was being killed two big drops of blood fell from his neck, and flowing till they were opposite Pharaoh's doorway, they sprang up in the form of two great trees, one at either side of the portal.

At this second miracle all the people rejoiced again and offered sacrifices to the two trees.

A long time after, Pharaoh, in his crown of lapis-lazuli, with a garland of flowers round his neck, got into his electrum chair and was carried out to look at the two trees. His chief favourite—Bitou's wife—was brought after him and they were set down, one under each tree. Then Bitou, the tree under which his wife was seated, whispered to her, "Faithless woman! I am Bitou, and I am still alive in spite of you. You made Pharaoh cut down the acacia, and killed me. Then I became a bull and you had me slain."

Afterward, when she was seated again with Pharaoh at table, she made him swear another oath to do whatever she asked him, and Pharaoh swore again. Then she said, "Cut me down these two trees and make them into two good beams." What she demanded was done, but as the trees were being cut down a chip flew into her mouth. In due time she brought forth a male child, whom Pharaoh loved and made Prince of the Upper Nile, and when Pharaoh died, Bitou, for *he* was this child, succeeded him. Then he summoned all the great officials, had his wife brought before him, and told them all that had happened. So she was put to death. Bitou lived and reigned for twenty years, and then his brother Anapou, whom he had made his successor, reigned in his stead.

The Doomed Prince

This story is to be found in the Harris Papyrus in the British Museum. It was complete when first discovered, but an unfortunate accident partly destroyed it, so that the end of the tale is lost. It is supposed to belong to the end of the Eighteenth Dynasty.

There was once a king who was sore in heart because no son had been born to him. He prayed the gods to grant his desire, and they decreed that as he had prayed, so it should be. And his wife brought forth a son. When the Hathors came to decide his destiny they said, "His death shall be by the crocodile, or by the serpent, or by the dog." And those who stood round, upon hearing this, hurried to tell the king, who was much grieved thereat and feared greatly.

And because of what he had heard he caused a house to be built in the mountains and furnished richly and with all that could be desired, so that the child should not go abroad. When the boy was grown he went one day upon the roof, and from there he saw a dog following a man upon the road. Then he turned to his attendant and said, "What is that which follows the man coming along the road?" And he was told that it was a dog.

And the child at once wished to possess a dog, and

"Who are you?" (page 227)
Evelyn Paul

The Treasure-chamber of Rhampsinites (page 237)
Evelyn Paul

when the king was told of his desire he might not deny him, lest his heart should be sad.

As time went on and the child became a man he grew restive, and, being told of the decree of the Hathors, at once sent a message to his father, saying, "Come, why and wherefore am I kept a prisoner? Though I am fated to three evil fates, let me follow my desires. Let God fulfil His will."

And after this he was free and did as other men. He was given weapons and his dog was allowed to follow him, and they took him to the east country and said to him, "Behold, thou art free to go wheresoever thou wilt."

He set his face to the north, his dog following, and his whim dictated his path. Then he lived on all the choicest of the game of the desert. And then he came to the chief of Nahairana. And this chief had but one child, a daughter. For her had been built a house with seventy windows seventy cubits from the ground. And here the chief had commanded all the sons of the chiefs of the country of Khalu to be brought, and he said to them, "He who climbs and reaches my daughter's windows shall win her for wife."

And some time after this the prince arrived, and the people of the chief of Nahairana took the youth to the house and treated him with the greatest honour and kindness. And as he partook of their food they asked him whence he had come. He answered them, saying, "I come from Egypt; I am the son of an officer of that land. My mother died and my father has taken another wife, who, when she bore my father other children, grew to hate me. Therefore have I fled as a fugitive from her presence." And they were sorry for him and embraced him.

Then one day he asked the climbing youths what it

was they did there. And when they told him that they climbed the height that they might win the chief's daughter for wife, he decided to make the attempt with them, for afar off he beheld the face of the chief's daughter looking forth from her window and turned toward them.

And he climbed the dizzy height and reached her window. So glad was she that she kissed and embraced him.

And thinking to make glad the heart of her father, a messenger went to him, saying, "One of the youths hath reached thy daughter's window." The chief inquired which of the chief's sons had accomplished this, and he was told that it was the fugitive from Egypt.

At this the chief of Nahairana was wroth and vowed that his daughter was not for an Egyptian fugitive. "Let him go back whence he came!" he cried.

An attendant hurried to warn the youth, but the maiden held him fast and would not let him go. She swore by the gods, saying, "By the being of Ra Harakhti, if he is taken from me, I will neither eat nor drink and in that hour I shall die!"

And her father was told of her vow, and hearing it he sent some to slay the youth while he should be in his house. But the daughter of the chief divined this and said again, "By the great god Ra, if he be slain, then I shall die ere the set of sun. If I am parted from him, then I live no longer!"

Again her words were carried to the chief. He caused his daughter and the youth to be brought before him, and at first the young man was afraid, but the chief of Nahairana embraced him affectionately, saying, "Tell me who thou art, for now thou art as a son to me." He answered him, "I come from Egypt;

I am the son of an officer of that land. My mother died and my father has taken another wife, who, when she bore my father children, grew to hate me. Therefore have I fled as a fugitive from her presence!"

Then the chief gave him his daughter to wife; he gave him a house and slaves, he gave him lands and cattle and all manner of good gifts.

The time passed. One day the youth told his wife of his fate, saying to her, "I am doomed to three evil fates—to die by a crocodile, a serpent, or a dog." And her heart was filled with a great dread. She said to him, "Then let one kill the dog which follows thee." But he told her that could not be, for he had brought it up from the time it was small.

At last the youth desired to travel to the land of Egypt, and his wife, fearing for him, would not let him go alone, so one went with him. They came to a town, and the crocodile of the river was there. Now in that town was a great and mighty man, and he bound the crocodile and would not suffer it to escape. When it was bound the mighty man was at peace and walked abroad. When the sun rose the man went back to his house, and this he did every day for two months.

After this as the days passed the youth sat at ease in his house. When the night came he lay on his couch and sleep fell upon him. Then his wife filled a bowl of milk and placed it by his side. Out from a hole came a serpent, and it tried to bite the sleeping man, but his wife sat beside him watching and unsleeping. And the servants, beholding the serpent, gave it milk so that it drank and was drunk and lay helpless on its back. Seeing this, with her dagger the wife dispatched it. Upon this her husband woke and, understanding all, was astonished. "See," she said to him, "thy god hath given one of thy dooms into thy hand. Surely he shall also give thee the others!"

And then the youth made sacrifices to his god and praised him always.

One day after this the youth walked abroad in his fields, his dog following him. And his dog chased after the wild game, and he followed after the dog, who plunged into the river. He also went into the river, and then out came the crocodile, who took him to the place where the mighty man lived. And as he carried him the crocodile said to the youth, "Behold, I am thy doom, following after thee. . . .

At this point the papyrus is so extensively mutilated that in all probability we shall never know what happened to the prince. Was he at last devoured by the crocodile? or perchance did his faithful dog lead him into still graver danger? Let everyone concoct his own ending to the tale!

The Visit of Ounamounou to the Coasts of Egypt

On the sixteenth day of the thirteenth month, the harvest month, Ounamounou, the chief priest of the temple of Amen-Ra, departed on a voyage to procure wood for the fashioning of the sacred barque of the god.

"When I arrived at Tanis," he says, "I gave them the edicts of Amen-Ra, which they read and decided to obey. I stayed at Tanis till the fourteenth month of Shomou, when I embarked to voyage upon the Syrian sea. When the ship arrived at Dora, city of Zakkala, the Prince of the place, Badîl, sent bread, meat, and wine unto me.

"While in this place a man of the vessel deserted, carrying with him much gold and silver. Thereupon I went to the Prince and made my complaint to him, saying that the gold belonged to Amen-Ra. And the

Prince answered and said he knew naught of it, but if the robber were of his country, he would reimburse me out of his own treasury; if, on the other hand, the robber were of my own company, I must stay there for some days and he would search for the thief. I stayed nine days in that port. Then I went again to the Prince, saying, 'You have not yet found the stolen gold. But now I must go. If you should find it in my absence, then keep it against my return.' This was so arranged between us.

"Then I embarked again and reached Tyre, to whose Prince I recounted my loss, and complained that the Prince of Dora had not found my gold, but, being a friend of Badîl, he would not listen—indeed, threatened me. At break of day we set out in the direction of Byblos, and on the way a vessel of Zakkala overtook us with a coffer on board. On opening this coffer I discovered money, and took possession of it. I said to them that I would keep and use it until my stolen gold was restored to me. When they saw I was firm they accepted the situation and left me, and we at last reached Byblos.

"I disembarked, carrying the naos containing the statue of Amen-Ra, having put therein the treasure. But the Prince of Byblos bade me begone. I said to him, 'Is this because the men of Zakkala have told you that I took their money? That money is my own, for in their port the gold of Amen-Ra was stolen. Besides, I come from Herihor to procure wood for the sacred barque of the god Amen-Ra.' I stayed in this port for nineteen days, and each day the Prince sent this message bidding me begone.

"Then one eve when the Prince of Byblos sacrificed to his gods, and one danced before them, he mocked me and bade me bring my god to life. That night I met a man whose vessel was bound for Egypt, and I charged him with all concerning me. I said to him that I would embark and depart unknown to any, and surely the gods I trust would watch over me. While so debating the commander of the port came to me, saying, 'Stay; it is the will of the Prince.' And I answered him, 'Are you not the one who brought me the message each day bidding me begone, and never bade me stay? Now why is it that you bid me rest?'

"He turned and left me and went to the Prince, who this time sent a message to the captain of the vessel bidding him wait till the morrow. The next morning he sent for me to be brought to the palace in which he lived beside the sea. I was taken to his chamber, and there he asked me how long it was I had been on this journey. I answered five months, but he doubted me, asking where were the edicts of Amen-Ra which ought to be in my hands, and where was the letter of the high-priest? I told him that I had given them to other princes. He was angered, and said that I came with no proofs, and what was there to hinder him ordering the captain of the vessel to kill me? Again I answered that I had come from Egypt for wood for the sacred barque. And then he told how formerly those from Egypt had come in state to visit his city. After a long altercation with the Prince, and when I had told him that if he executed the commands of Amen-Ra much good would be his, he still hesitated. Then I asked for a messenger to take a letter from me to the other Princes, Smendes and Tantamounou, and he would see how they would do my bidding and succour me.

"It seemed that the Prince had changed his mind, for after he had given my letter to his messenger he ordered a ship to be loaded with wood, seven pieces in all, and to be taken to Egypt.

"His messenger went to Egypt and returned to me in the first month of the winter. And soon the Princes Smendes and Tantamounou sent me ships laden with many gifts. Seeing this, the Prince was rejoiced, and soon he commanded much wood to be hewn for me. And when it was finished he came saying that he had done as his fathers had done before him, and giving orders that the wood should be loaded on a vessel. He also said that I had not been treated as were the envoys of Khamoîs, who had lived seventeen years in the country and died there. Turning to his courtier, he bade him show me their tomb. But I had no desire to see it, and said so. I also said, 'The envoys of Khamoîs were but men of his household; I came as the messenger of the great god Amen-Ra.'

"Then I bade him erect a stele and this inscription to be engraved thereon:

"'Amen-Ra, the great god of the gods, sent me a divine messenger, together with Ounamounou as his human ambassador, for the wood wherewith his sacred barque should be fashioned. I cut down trees for this and loaded them, furnishing the vessels by which it was carried into Egypt. I did this that I may obtain immortal life from the great god Amen.'

"'And,' I continued, 'a messenger shall come from the land of Egypt who shall read your name upon the stele, and you shall receive the water of Amenti even as the gods.'

"He said, 'This is a wonderful thing you tell me.' Then I told him that when I returned I should acquaint the high-priest of Amen of how he, the Prince, had done all as he was commanded, and that he should assuredly receive the gifts.

"When I went down to the shore where the wood was loaded I beheld eleven vessels sent from Zakkala to seize and imprison and prevent me from reaching Egypt. Then I was distressed and cried out, and a messenger from the Prince approached me, saying, 'What troubles you?'

"I explained to him what menaced me, and he went and told the Prince, who was much distressed. To cheer me he sent gifts of food and wine, and an Egyptian singer, Tantnouit, whose songs he thought might chase away my sorrow. His message was, 'Eat, drink, and be not troubled. You shall hear my plans in the morn.'

"And when the day was come the Prince called his men, and they set out and spoke to the men of Zakkala, asking them the object of their coming. They answered that they had come to seize the vessels and their rascally crews. He answered, 'I have not the power to take prisoner the messenger of Amen-Ra in my country. I shall let him go, and after you can do with him as you please.'

"I embarked and left the port, and the wind drove me into the country of Alasia. There the people of the town came to put me to death, dragging me to the presence of Hatibi, the Princess of the city. I looked at the men around, and asked was there not one who could understand Egyptian? One came forward saying that he understood it. I said that I had heard that if justice was to be found anywhere it was in Alasia, and yet here were they ready to work an injustice. The Princess inquired what I had said.

"Again I spoke, and pleaded that as the storm had driven me into their country they should not slay me, for in truth I was a messenger of the great god Amen-Ra. Then I pointed out that if harm came to me

I would be avenged. In a little while the Princess called her people and caused them to relinquish their evil designs, saying to me, 'Be not troubled. . . .'"

Here the papyrus ends. It is tantalizing not to know how Ounamounou managed to return to Egypt, but we may be sure a person of such infinite resource and determination, not to say doggedness, accomplished all he desired.

The Story of Rhampsinites

The oldest form of this legend has been handed down to us by Herodotus. It occurs in the ancient folklore of both Eastern and Western peoples and its origin has often been debated. If not really of Egyptian origin, it had certainly become Egyptianized when Herodotus found it. It relates how King Rhampsinites possessed so much treasure that none of his successors ever surpassed or even came near to having a like amount.

To ensure its safety he had a seemingly impregnable stone house built, in which he placed all his great wealth. By a clever trick, however, the architect contrived to provide access to the treasure. He made one of the stones in two parts, so that one part could be removed; but so skilfully were the two parts placed together that they presented a perfectly even surface, as of one single stone. Before he died he acquainted his two sons with the secret of the treasure-house, and after his death they did not delay in putting their knowledge into practice. They went by night, found the stone without any difficulty, withdrew it, stole a large sum of money, and replaced it in position.

When the king discovered that thieves were at work he had man-traps placed near the site of the treasure-house. One night the two brothers came as usual, and one of them was caught in a trap. Seeing his danger, he called his brother and said to him, "We shall both perish and the treasure be lost unless you cut off my head and take it away, so that no one will recognize us as the thieves." The brother did as he advised : he moved the stone back into position, cut off his brother's head and carried it home.

When the king found the headless body he was much disturbed, for there were no traces of entrance to or exit from the treasure-house, and he bethought himself of this expedient : he had the dead body exposed on the city wall and placed a guard round it with instructions to watch and report whoever manifested any sign of grief on seeing the body. This act was contrary to the practice of the Egyptians, who had usually too much respect for the dead to indulge in it. Even in the case of an executed criminal the remains were returned to the relatives to be embalmed. Nevertheless Rhampsinites considered himself justified in adopting this measure. The body was exposed, and the mother, although she did not betray any sign of grief, insisted on her other son bringing it to her ; otherwise she threatened to divulge his secret to the king. Seeing that he dared not disobey, the son devised a stratagem. He saddled some asses and loaded them with goatskins full of wine—skins were used in Egypt for water only at most times, wine being held in short narrow vases—he drove the asses past the guard and, when passing, stealthily untied one or two of the skins, and as the wine ran down and flowed on the ground began to beat his head and make a great outcry. The guards ran for vessels to save the precious liquid, and over the catastrophe they became quite friendly with the thief and gave him meat, for which he offered in exchange one of his skins of wine. They all sat down to drink together, and as they became merry over the wine he offered them the remainder of his wine, which they took and drank until they were quite tipsy. The thief, needless to say, had taken care to remain tolerably sober. After the guards were in a drunken sleep, he waited till nightfall and then cut down his brother's body and took it home on the asses to his mother. Before quitting the guards he shaved off all the hair on one side of their faces.

When the king heard of the trick he was furious, and, determined by fair means or foul to discover its author, he hit upon the following plan. He ordered the princess, his daughter, to receive any man in the land, no matter whom, and to grant him whatever favour he might ask of her; but first she must make him tell her what was the cleverest and wickedest thing he had ever done. When the thief told her his trick she was to have him bound before he could escape. The princess was ready to do her father's bidding, but the thief, knowing well what the king had in his mind, resolved to circumvent him a third time. He cut off the arm of a newly dead man and, hiding it under his robe, obtained admission to the princess. On being asked the question that she put to all comers, he told her first about cutting off his brother's head in the trap, and then went on to tell how, having made the guards tipsy, he had cut down his brother's body. She at once called out and tried to seize him, but he placed in her hand that of the dead man, which she grasped firmly, believing it to be the thief's, and he escaped in the darkness of the room.

The king now owned himself beaten, and offered a free pardon and rich rewards to the man who had so boldly outwitted him. Trusting to his word, the thief presented himself before the king, and received not only what Rhampsinites had promised, but also the hand of the princess in marriage, for he held the thief to be the cleverest of men in that he had duped the Egyptians, who prided themselves on their astuteness.

Civil War in Egypt: The Theft of the Cuirass

In the reign of the Pharaoh Petoubastis the Delta and great part of Lower Egypt were divided into two rival factions, one part being headed by the chieftain Kamenophis, Prince of Mendes, and the other ruled by the king-priest of Heliopolis, Ierharerou, and his ally Pakrourou, the great chieftain of the east. Only four nomes in the middle of the Delta were subject to Kamenophis, whilst Ierharerou had succeeded in establishing either his children or relations in most of the other nomes. Ierharerou possessed a cuirass to which he attached great value and which was generally regarded as a talisman. At his death Kamenophis, taking advantage of the mourning and confusion in Heliopolis, seized the cuirass and placed it in one of his own strongholds. Prince Pimonî 'the little'—"Pimonî of the strong fist," as he is sometimes called in the narrative—the successor of Ierharerou, demanded its restoration. Kamenophis refused, and hence arose a quarrel in which all the provinces of Egypt were implicated.

Pimonî and Pakrourou both presented themselves before King Petoubastis, asking his permission to be revenged on Kamenophis; but Pharaoh, who knew that this would entail civil war, endeavoured to dissuade Pimonî from taking steps against Kamenophis and, indeed, forbade him to proceed with his intentions, promising as compensation a splendid funeral for

Ierharerou. Unwillingly Pimonî submitted, but after the funeral ceremonies were over resentment still burned within him, and he and Pakrourou, "the great chieftain of the east," returned again to Petoubastis at his court in Tanis. He received them rather impatiently, asking them why they troubled him again and declaring that he would not allow civil war during his reign. They, however, would not be satisfied and said they could not go on with the celebration of the feast that was to follow the religious rites of Ierharerou's funeral until the shield or cuirass was restored to its rightful owner.

Pharaoh then sent for Kamenophis, and requested him urgently to return the shield, but in vain. Kamenophis declined to do so.

Then said Pimonî, "By Tem, the lord of Heliopolis, the great god, my god, were it not for Pharaoh's decree and that my respect for him protects you, I should kill you this very instant."

Kamenophis replied, "By the life of Mendes, the great god, the war which will break out in the nome, the battle which will break out in the city will stir up clan against clan, and man against man, before the cuirass shall be wrested from the stronghold where I have placed it."

The Horrors of War

Pakrourou then said before the king, "Is it right what Kamenophis has done, and the words he has just spoken are they not said to provoke us to anger that we may measure our strength against his? I will make Kamenophis and the nome of Mendes feel the shame of these words uttered to provoke civil war which Pharaoh has forbidden; I will glut them with war. I said nothing because I knew the king did not want war; but if the king remains neutral I shall be silent no longer, and the king shall see all the horrors of civil war."

Pharaoh said, "Be neither boastful nor timid, Pakrourou, great chieftain of the east, but now go each one of you to your nomes and your towns in peace, and give me but five days, and I swear by Amen-Ra that I shall cause the cuirass to be put back in the place from which it was taken."

Pimonî then said that if the cuirass were replaced nothing more should be said about it, and there should be no war; but if it were withheld, he would fight for it, against the whole of Egypt if necessary.

Kamenophis at this respectfully asked and obtained permission from Pharaoh to order all his men to arm themselves, and to go with him to the Lake of the Gazelle and prepare to fight.

Then Pimonî, encouraged by Pakrourou, sent messages of a similar import to all his nomes and cities. Pakrourou further advised him to hasten to the Lake of the Gazelle and be there before Kamenophis had assembled all his men, and Pimonî, with only one band of men, took his advice and was first in the field, intending to wait there till his brothers, at the head of their respective clans, should join him.

News of this was taken to Kamenophis, and he hastily assembled his four nomes, Tanis, Mendes, Tahait, and Sebennytos. Arrived at the lake, he at once challenged Pimonî, and Pimonî, though his other forces had not yet arrived, accepted the challenge.

Pimonî put on a shirt of byssus embroidered with silver and gold, and over that a second shirt of gold tissue; he also donned his copper corselet and carried two golden swords; he put on his helmet and sallied forth to meet Kamenophis.

While they were fighting, Zinonfi, Pimonî's young servant, ran off to watch for the forces that were to come to Pimonî's aid, and he soon descried a flotilla so large that the river could hardly carry all the barges. They were the people of Heliopolis coming to help their chief. As soon as they came within earshot Zinonfi called out to them to hurry, because Pimonî was being hard pressed by Kamenophis, which, indeed, was true, for his horse was slain under him.

Kamenophis redoubled his efforts when he saw the fresh forces arriving, and Petekhousou, Pimonî's brother, challenged Anoukhoron, the king's son, to single combat. When Pharaoh heard this he was very angry. He went in person to the field of battle and forbade the combatants to proceed, and also commanded a truce until all the forces should be assembled.

Petoubastis and all the chieftains occupied prominent positions so that they could watch what was going on, and the men were as numerous as the sands of the seashore and their rage against each other uncontrollable. The bands of the four nomes were ranged behind Kamenophis, and the bands of the nome of Heliopolis behind Pimonî the Little.

Then Petoubastis gave Pakrourou a signal and he armed himself and went down among the forces, stirring them all to deeds of valour ; he pitted man against man, and great was the ardour he aroused in them.

Succour for Pakrourou

After Pakrourou had left the *mêlée*, he met a mighty man in armour leading forty galleys and eight thousand soldiers. This was Moutoubaal, a prince of Syria, who had been warned in a dream to repair to the Lake of the Gazelle to help to regain the stolen cuirass. Pakrourou gave him a place, though all the forces were now disposed; but he ordered him not to join in the fight until the opposite side—the men of Kamenophis—should attack their vessels. Moutoubaal, therefore, remained in his barque, and Pakrourou went back to his point of vantage to watch the progress of the battle. The two factions fought from four in the morning to nine in the evening. Finally Anoukhoron, the king's son broke under the stress of the bands of Sebennytos and they rushed toward the boats. Then Moutoubaal took his opportunity and went against the bands of Sebennytos and overthrew them. He went on spreading destruction among the forces of Kamenophis till Pharaoh called a halt; then proceeded with Pakrourou to Moutoubaal and besought him to stay his hand, promising that he would see to it that the shield was restored. Moutoubaal accordingly quitted the lists after having wrought great havoc among the men of Kamenophis. Then Pharaoh and Pakrourou went with Moutoubaal to the place where Pimonî was found engaged in mortal combat with Kamenophis. Pimonî had got the upper hand and was about to slay his adversary, but they stopped him, and Pharaoh ordered Kamenophis to quit the lists.

After this Anoukhoron, the royal prince, was overthrown by Petekhousou, the brother of Pimonî, but Pharaoh interposed and persuaded Petekhousou to spare his son, so the young man was allowed to withdraw unhurt.

The king said, "By Amen-Ra, the sceptre has fallen from the hands of Kamenophis, prince of Mendes. Petekhousou has vanquished my son, and the bands of the four strongest nomes in Egypt have been overthrown."

The Shield Regained

Then Minnemai, Prince of the Eupuantine, the son of Ierharerou, the priest-king, to whom the shield had belonged, advanced from Thebes with all his forces. They assigned him a place next the ship of Takhos, the chief soldier of the nome of Mendes, and it happened that in the galley of Takhos lay the cuirass itself. And Minnemai called upon his gods to let him behold his father's cuirass that he might be the instrument of its recapture. He armed himself, went to the galley of Takhos, and met there nine thousand soldiers guarding the cuirass of Ierharerou, son of Osiris. Minnemai placed thirty-four guards on the footbridge of the galley to prevent anyone from getting off, and he fell upon the soldiers guarding the cuirass. Takhos fought well and killed fifty-four men, but finally gave in and retired to his vessel, where Minnemai followed him with his Ethiopian warriors. The children of Ierharerou supported him and they seized the cuirass of Ierharerou.

Thus was the armour recaptured and brought back to its former place. There was great joy among the children of Ierharerou and the troops of Heliopolis. They went before Pharaoh and said to him, "Great master, have the history of the war of the cuirass written, and the names of the warriors who waged it, that posterity may know what a war was made in Egypt on account of the cuirass, in the nomes and in the cities; then cause the history to be engraved on a stone stele in the temple of Heliopolis." And King Petoubastis did as they asked.

The Birth of Hatshepsut

The following story of the birth of Hatshepsut, the great queen, the beloved of the gods, mistress of all lands under the sun, is not a direct translation from the old papyrus which recounts it, but is told in the writer's own words :

In the land of the gods Amen-Ra held court. King of the gods was Amen-Ra, and the maker of men. On his right was Osiris, with the twin goddesses Isis and Nephthys, Hathor the goddess of love, and Horus and Anubis. On his left was Mentu, the god of war, with Geb, the earth-god, and Nut, the sky-goddess, the gods Atmu and Shu, and the goddess Tefnut. And to the assembled gods Amen-Ra spake thus :

"I will make a great queen, who shall rule over Egypt and Syria, Nubia and Punt, so that all lands may be united under her sway. Worthy must the maiden be of her great dominions, for she shall rule the whole world."

As he spoke the god Thoth entered, he who has the form of an ibis, that he may fly more swiftly than the swiftest arrow. In silence he listened to the words of Amen-Ra, the mightiest of the gods, the maker of men. Then he said :

"Behold, O Amen-Ra, there is in the land of Egypt a maiden of wondrous beauty. The sun in his circuit shines not on anything more fair. Surely it is fitting that she be the mother of the great queen of whom thou speakest."

"Thou sayest well," said Amen-Ra. "Where shall we seek this fair princess ? What is her name ?"

"Her name is Aahmes," answered Thoth ; "she is wife to the King of Egypt, and dwelleth in his palace. I will lead thee to her."

"It is well," said Amen-Ra.

Then Thoth, in the shape of an ibis, flew toward the land of Egypt, and with him went Amen-Ra, in the form of the King of Egypt, and all the gods and goddesses, among them Neith, goddess of Sais, and the scorpion goddess, Selk, on whose head was a scorpion bearing in each claw the sign of life.

Silently the gods and goddesses entered the sleeping palace, and were conducted by Thoth to the chamber of Queen Aahmes. The queen lay asleep on a couch shaped like a lion, and as they gazed upon her they saw that Thoth had spoken truly, that she was indeed the fairest of mortal women, and they stood speechless with admiration for her beauty. But the fragrance which they had borne with them from the land of Punt awoke the maiden, who looked with astonishment on her supernatural visitors. Very magnificent was Amen-Ra, the king of the gods, the maker of men, as he stood before the queen. Jewels of gold and precious stones adorned his person, and his beauty was as the beauty of the sun, so that the maiden's heart was filled with delight. Amen-Ra placed in her hand the sign of life and the emblem of power, and the goddesses Neith and Selk raised her couch above the ground, so that she might be above the earth while she conversed with the gods.

At length the gods returned to the land of Punt, and Amen-Ra called for Khnum, the creator, the fashioner of the bodies of men.

"Fashion for me," said Amen-Ra, "the body of my daughter, and the body of her *ka*. A great queen shall I make of her, and honour and power shall be hers all the days of her life."

"O Amen-Ra," answered Khnum, the creator, "it shall be done as thou hast said. The beauty of thy daughter shall surpass that of the gods, and shall be worthy of her dignity and glory."

So Khnum fashioned the body of Amen-Ra's daughter and the body of her *ka*, the two forms exactly alike, and more beautiful than the daughters of men. He fashioned them of clay with the aid of his potter's wheel, and Hekt, goddess of birth, knelt by his side, holding the sign of life toward the clay that the bodies of Hatshepsut and her *ka* might be filled with the breath of life.

Then did the gods bring the bodies to the palace of the King of Egypt. Khnum, the creator, and Hekt, the goddess of birth, Isis, the great mother, and her twin sister Nephthys, Bes, the protector of children, and Meskhent and Ta-urt, all were present to hail the birth of Hatshepsut, the great queen, the daughter of Amen-Ra and Queen Aahmes.

Great were the rejoicings when the child was born, and loud the praises chanted in her honour. And in time she became ruler of all countries, rich and powerful and beloved of Amen-Ra, the great queen for whom she had been designed by the king of the gods.

In the valley of the Nile there was erected a temple to Queen Hatshepsut. The temple stands to this day, and is now known as Deir-el-Bahari, the Northern Convent.

How Thoutii took the Town of Joppa

The fragments of this story are inscribed on the Harris Papyrus. Like the story of the Predestined Prince, they were discovered in 1874 by Goodwin, who recognized in them the remnants of an historical narrative, and who informed the Archæological Society of his find. The beginning is lost. At the point where the narrative commences there are three characters: an Egyptian officer called Thoutii, the prince of a town in Syria, and his equerry. The tale deals with the recapture of Joppa (a town of Palestine mentioned in the Bible) by Thoutii's stratagem. The stratagem employed bears some resemblance to that related in the story of the robber-captain in the *Arabian Nights*.

In the reign of Thothmes III, King of Egypt (Eighteenth Dynasty), the Prince of Joppa rose in rebellion and murdered all the Egyptian soldiers that were quartered in the town. This news naturally excited Pharaoh's wrath, and he called together his nobles and generals and scribes to see what could be done. None of them, however, had any suggestion to make except Thoutii, a brilliant young infantry officer.

"Give me," he begged, "your magic cane, O my king, and a body of infantry and of charioteers, and I undertake to kill the Prince of Joppa and to take the town."

Pharaoh, who esteemed this officer highly and knew his worth, granted all that he asked—not exactly a modest request, for the cane was a talisman supposed to render invisible anyone into whose possession it fell.

Thoutii then marched to Palestine with his men. Having arrived there, he had a large skin bag made, big enough to hold a man, and he had irons made for feet and hands, one pair being especially large and strong; also shackles and yokes of wood, and four hundred jars. Then he sent to the Prince of Joppa the following message: "I am Thoutii, the Egyptian infantry general. King Thothmes was jealous of my bravery and sought to kill me; but I have escaped from him, and I have stolen his magic cane, which is hidden in my baggage; and, if you like, I will give it to you, and I will join forces with you, I and my men, the pick of the Egyptian army."

This message was very pleasant news to the Prince of Joppa, for he knew Thoutii's reputation, and knew that he had no equal in all Egypt. He sent to Thoutii, accepting his offer, and promising him a share of his territory. He then left Joppa, taking with him his equerry and the women and children, to greet the man whom he took to be a new and powerful ally. He welcomed him warmly, and invited him into his camp to dine with him. In course of conversation, as they were eating and drinking together, he asked Thoutii about the magic cane. Thoutii replied that it was concealed in the baggage with which his horses were laden, and requested that his men and horses should be brought into the camp to be refreshed and rested.

This was done: his horses were fed and tied up, the baggage was searched, and the magic cane found.

The Stratagem

Hearing this, the Prince of Joppa expressed his eager wish to behold the magic cane. Thoutii went and fetched it; then suddenly seizing the Prince by his clothes, he said, "Behold here King Thothmes' magic cane," and with that he raised his hand and struck the Prince on the forehead so that the latter fell down unconscious before him. Then he put him into the big leathern sack he had with him and clapped the handcuffs on his wrists and the irons on his feet. The face of the dead man being invisible, Thoutii's stratagem was to pass off the corpse as his own. He had the two hundred soldiers put into an equal number of the four hundred jars he had brought with him and filled the remainder with the ropes and wooden shackles; then he sealed them, corded them, and gave them to as many strong soldiers, saying, "Go quickly and tell the Prince of Joppa's equerry that I am slain. Let him go and tell his mistress, the Princess of Joppa, that Thoutii is conquered, that she may open the city gates to receive the dead body of the vanquished and the jars of booty that have been taken from him." The equerry received this message and ran to tell the joyful news to his mistress. The gates of the town were opened, and Thoutii's men carried the jars containing the other soldiers into the town. Then they released their companions, and the Egyptian force fell upon the inhabitants of the city and took them and bound them.

After he had rested Thoutii sent a message to Pharaoh saying, "I have killed the Prince of Joppa and all the people of Joppa are prisoners. Let them be sent for and brought to Egypt, that your house may be filled with male and female slaves who will be yours for ever. Let Amen-Ra, thy father, the god of gods, be glorified."

CHAPTER VII : MAGIC

TO the peoples of antiquity Egypt appeared as the very mother of magic. In the mysterious Nile country they found a magical system much more highly developed than any within their native knowledge, and the cult of the dead, with which Egyptian religion was so strongly identified, appeared to the foreigner to savour of magical practice. If the materials of the magical papyri be omitted, the accounts which we possess of Egyptian magic are almost wholly foreign, so that it is wiser to derive our data concerning it from the original native sources if we desire to arrive at a proper understanding of Egyptian sorcery.

Most of what has been written by Egyptologists on the subject of Egyptian magic has been penned on the assumption that magic is either merely a degraded form of religion, or its foundation. This is one of the results of the archæologist entering a domain (that of anthropology) where he is usually rather at a loss. For example, we find Sir Gaston Maspero stating that "ancient magic was the very foundation of religion. The faithful who desired to obtain some favour from a god had no chance of succeeding except by laying hands on the deity, and this arrest could only be effected by means of a certain number of rites, sacrifices, prayers, and chants, which the god himself had revealed and which obliged him to do what was demanded of him."[1] Then we find Dr Budge stating that in the religious texts and works we see how magic is made to be the handmaiden of religion, and that whereas non-Egyptian races directed their art against the powers of darkness, and invoked a class of benevolent beings to

[1] *Etudes de Mythologie et d'Archéologie Egyptienne*, Paris, 1893, vol. i, p. 106.

their aid, the Egyptians aimed at complete control over their native deities.

Let us glance for a moment at the question of the origin of magic. Considerable diversity of opinion exists regarding this subject among present-day anthropologists, and the works of Frazer, Marett, Hubert, and Mauss, etc., although differing widely as regards its foundations, have thrown much light upon a hitherto obscure problem. All writers on the subject, however, appear to have ignored one notable circumstance in connexion with it—that is, the element of wonder, which is the true fount and source of veritable magic. According to the warring schools of anthropology, nearly all magic is sympathetic or mimetic in its nature. For example, when the barbarian medicine-man desires rain he climbs a tree and sprinkles water upon the parched earth beneath, in the hope that the deity responsible for the weather will do likewise; when the ignorant sailor desires wind, he imitates the whistling of the gale. This system is universal, but if our conclusions are well founded, the magical element does not reside in such practices as these. It must be obvious, as Frazer has pointed out, that when the savage performs an act of sympathetic magic he does not regard it as magical—that is, to his way of thinking it does not contain any element of wonder at all; he regards his action as a cause which is certain to bring about the desired effect, exactly as the scientific man of to-day believes that if he follows certain formulæ certain results will be achieved. Now the true magic of wonder argues from effect to cause; so it would appear as if sympathetic magic were merely a description of proto-science, due to mental processes entirely similar to those by which scientific laws are produced and scientific acts are performed—that there is a spirit of certainty about it which is not found, for example, in the magic of evocation.

It would, however, be rash to attempt to differentiate sympathetic magic entirely from what I would call the 'magic of wonder' at this juncture; indeed, our knowledge of the basic laws of magic is too slight as yet to permit of such a process. We find considerable overlapping between the systems. For example, one of the ways by which evilly disposed persons could transform themselves into werewolves was by means of buckling on a belt of wolfskin. Thus we see that in this instance the true wonder-magic of animal transformation is in some measure connected with the sympathetic process, the idea being that the donning of wolfskin, or even the binding around one of a strip of the animal's hide, was sufficient to bestow the nature of the beast upon the wearer. In passing, I may say, for the sake of completeness, that I believe the magic of wonder to be almost entirely spiritistic in its nature, and that it consists of evocation and similar processes. Here, of course, it may be quoted against me that certain incenses, planetary signs, and other media known to possess affinities for certain supernatural beings were brought into use at the time of their evocation. Once more I admit that the two systems overlap; but that will not convince me that they are in essence the same.[1]

Antiquity of Egyptian Magic

Like all magic, Egyptian magic was of prehistoric origin. As the savage of to-day employs the sympathetic process, so did the savage of the Egyptian Stone Age make use of it. That he also was fully aware of the spiritistic side of magic is certain. Animism is the

[1] I hope to elaborate this theory more fully in a later work.

mother of spiritism. The concept of the soul was arrived at at a comparatively early period in the history of man. The phenomenon of sleep puzzled him. Whither did the real man betake himself during the hours of slumber? The Palæolithic man watched his sleeping brother, who appeared to him as practically dead—dead, at least, to perception and the realities of life. Something seemed to have escaped the sleeper; the real, vital, and vivifying element had temporarily departed from him. From his own experience the puzzled savage knew that life did not cease with sleep, for in a more shadowy and unsubstantial sphere he re-enacted the scenes of his everyday existence. If the man during sleep had experiences in dreamland or in distant parts, it was only reasonable to suppose that his *ego*, his very self, had temporarily quitted the body. Grant so much, and you have two separate entities, body and soul, similar in appearance because the latter on the dream plane exercised functions identical with those of the former on the corporeal plane.

The Wandering Spirit

But prehistoric logic did not stop here. So much premised, it extended its soul-theory to all animate beings, and even to things inanimate. Where, for example, did the souls of men go after death? Their bodies decayed, so it was only reasonable to suppose that they cast about them for other corporeal media. Failing their ability to enter the body of a new-born infant, they would take up their quarters in a tree, a rock, or any suitable natural object, and the terrified savage could hear their voices crying down the wind and whispering through the leaves of the forest, possibly clamouring or entreating for that food and shelter which they could not obtain in their disembodied condition. All nature, then, we see became animate to early man, and not less so to the early Egyptian than to others. But his hunting life had made prehistoric man exceptionally cunning and resourceful, and it would soon occur to him (in what manner we do not presume to say, as the point greatly requires elucidation) that he might possibly make use of such wandering and masterless spirits as he knew were close to his call. In this desire, it appears to me (if the statement be not a platitude), we have one of the origins of the magic of wonder, and certainly the origin of spiritism. Trading upon the wish of the disembodied spirit to materialize, prehistoric man would construct a fetish [1] either in the human shape or in that of an animal, or in any weird presentment that squared with his ideas of spiritual existence. He usually made it of no great dimensions, as he did not believe that the *alter ego*, or soul, was of any great size. By threats or coaxings he prevailed upon the wandering spirit (whom he conceived as, like all the dead, cold, hungry, and homeless) to enter the little image, which duly became its corporeal abode, where its lips were piously smeared with the blood of animals slain in the chase, and where it was carefully attended. In return it was expected, by dint of its supernatural knowledge, that the soul contained in the fetish should assist its master or coadjutor in every possible way.

Coercing the Gods

Egyptian magic differed from most other systems in the circumstance that the native magician attempted to coerce certain of the gods into action on his behalf.

[1] For a very full account of Fetishism see my article in the *Encyclopedia of Religion and Ethics.*

Instances of this elsewhere are extremely rare, and it would seem as if the deities of Egypt had evolved in many cases from mere animistic conceptions. This is true in effect of all deities, but at a certain point in their history most gods arrive at such a condition of eminence that they soar far above any possibility of being employed by the magician as mere tools for any personal purpose. We often, however, find the broken-down, or deserted, deity coerced by the magician. Of this class Beelzebub might be taken as a good example. A great reputation is a hard thing to lose, and it is possible that the sorcerer may descry in the abandoned, and therefore idle, god a very suitable medium for his purpose. But we find the divinities of Egypt frightened into using their power on behalf of some paltry sorcerer even in the very zenith of their fame. One thing is of course essential to a complete system of sorcery, and that is the existence of a number of spirits, the detritus of a vanished or submerged religion. As we know, there were numerous strata in Egyptian religion—more than one faith had obtained on the banks of the Nile, and it may be that the worshippers of the deities of one system regarded the deities of another as magical on the first introduction of a new system; in fact, these may have been interchangeable, and it is possible that by the time the various gods became common to all the practice had become so universal as to be impossible of abandonment.

If our conclusions are correct, it would seem that Maspero's statement that magic is the foundation of religion is scarcely consonant with fact. We have seen that at least the greater part of barbarian magic so-called (that is, sympathetic magic) is probably not of the nature of magic at all, so that the scope of his contention is considerably lessened. Budge's dictum that the magic of every other nation of the Ancient East but the Egyptian was directed entirely against the powers of darkness, and was invented to frustrate their fell designs by invoking a class of benevolent beings, is so far an error in that the peoples of the Ancient Orient invoked evil beings equally with good. At the same time it must be admitted that Egyptian magic had much more in common with religion than most other magical systems, and this arose from the extraordinary circumstances of the evolution of religion on Egyptian soil.

Names of Power

One of the most striking circumstances in connexion with Egyptian magic was the use of what has come to be known as 'names of power.' The savage fancies that there is a very substantial bond between a man and his name—that, in fact, magic may be wrought on a man just as easily through his name as through the possession of his hair or his nails. Indeed, primitive man regards his name as a vital portion of himself. Sir John Rhys has shown that among the ancient Celts there was a universal belief not only that the name was a part of the man, but that it was that part of him which is termed the 'soul,' and many barbarian races at the present day regard their names as vital parts of themselves and take extraordinary precautions to conceal their *real* names lest these should give to the witch, or shaman, a handle by which to injure their owners. Howitt has shown in a monograph on Australian medicine-men that the Australian aborigine believes that if an enemy has his name he has something which he can use magically to his detriment. The Australian black is always reluctant to reveal his real name to anyone. Thus in many Australian tribes a man gives up his name for ever at the time when he undergoes initiation into the ceremonies which confer upon him the rites of manhood. This results in the use of such titles among the members of the tribe as 'brother,' 'nephew,' or 'cousin,' as the case may be. New names are thus probably given at initiation, and carefully concealed for fear of sorcery. We find the same superstition in Abyssinia, Chile, Senegambia, North America, and a score of other countries. To return to Egypt, we find that many Egyptians received two names—the 'great' name and the 'little' name, or the 'true' name and the 'good' name; the latter was that made public, but the 'true' or 'great' name was most carefully concealed.[1] We find the use of these 'names of power' extremely common all over the East. Even to-day, in reading the sacred name, *Jahveh*, the Jews render it 'Adonai'; but nowhere was its use in such vogue as in Egypt. A good illustration of the power possible to the wielder of a name is found in the legend of the manner in which Isis succeeded in procuring his secret name from Ra. Isis, weary of the world of mortals, determined to enter that of the gods, and to this end made up her mind to worm his secret name from the almighty Ra. This name was known to no mortal, and not even to any god but himself. By this time Ra had grown old, and, like many another venerable person, he often permitted the saliva to flow from the corners of his mouth. Some of this fell to the earth, and Isis, mixing it with the soil, kneaded it into the shape of a serpent, and cunningly laid it in the path traversed by the great god every day. Bursting upon the world in his effulgence, and attended by the entire pantheon, he was astounded when the serpent,

[1] Lefébure, *La Vertu et la Vie du Nom en Egypte.*

rising from its coil, stung him. He cried aloud with pain, and, in answer to the agitated questions of his inferior divinities, was silent. The poison swiftly overcame him, and a great ague seized him. He called all the gods to come that their healing words might make him well, and with them came Isis, who cunningly inquired what ailed him. He related the incident of the serpent to her, and added that he was suffering the greatest agony. "Then," said Isis, "tell me thy name, Divine Father, for the man shall live who is called by his name." Ra attempted a compromise by stating that he was 'Khepera' in the morning, 'Ra' at noon, and 'Atem' in the evening; but the poison worked more fearfully within him than before, and he could no longer walk. Isis conjured him to tell her his name in order that he might live; so, hiding himself from all the other gods, he acquainted her with his hidden title. When this was revealed Isis immediately banished the poison from his veins, and he became whole again. The scribe takes infinite care not to communicate the sacred name to his readers, and the probabilities are that, although he knew the legend, he did not know the name himself, which was possibly 'unknown' to the wizards of Egypt. The speech of Ra, "I consent that Isis shall search into me and that my name shall pass from my breast into hers," would seem to show that not only was the power of the god inextricably bound up with his *real* name, but that it was supposed to be lodged in an almost physical sense, somewhere in his breast, whence it could be extricated and transferred with all its supernatural powers to the breast of another. What Isis was able to do was aspired to by every Egyptian magician, who left no stone unturned to accomplish this end. We find magicians threatening Osiris that if he does not do the

Isis conjured Ra to tell his Name (page 260)
Evelyn Paul

Amulets of Hathor (page 263)

Photo W. A. Mansell & Co.

bidding of the sorcerer, he will be named aloud in the port of Busiris. The practice is by no means extinct in Egypt, for we find in Lane's *Manners and Customs of the Ancient Egyptians* that the man who knows the most great name of God can, by the mere utterance of it, kill the living, raise the dead, and perform most marvellous miracles ; and if this was true of the Egypt of sixty years ago, we may be sure that it is true of the Egypt of to-day.

Occasionally the gods themselves vouchsafed to mankind the secret of their names, and divulged the formulæ by which they might be evoked. We find a parallel in the mythology of certain North American Indian tribes, where the secrets of initiatory ceremonies and 'medicine' in general are divulged by deities to men.

'Right Speaking'

There is no exact evidence that magical force was supposed in Egypt to be drawn from a great central reservoir like the *orenda* of the North American Indians, the *kramat* of the Malays, or the *mana* of the Melanesians. But it is possible that an examination of the texts which had for its end the discovery of the belief in such a force would prove successful. Magic had its recognized representatives ; these were the 'kheri-heb' priests, and in the period of the Old Kingdom the higher offices in this caste were filled by sons of the Pharaohs. Great importance was laid upon the manner in which the spell or magical formula was spoken. When a magician once found that a certain formula was effective at a certain time, he was careful to repeat it, when next he desired to say it, in an exactly similar tone and in similar circumstances. This was called 'right speaking,' [1]

[1] This expression *Maā kheru* etymologically means 'acquitted,' and is a legal term.

and was practised by practically everyone in Egypt, as in the next world a correct knowledge of magic words and formulæ was absolutely essential. The guardians of the various gateways who are pictured in the *Book of the Dead* do not open to those who know not their names and who do not utter them correctly. Unless certain prescribed prayers were uttered with the true intonations food was not forthcoming. The number of these formulæ was great. Each doorway in the otherworld had a title, and would not open to the new-comer unless invoked by him correctly.

A Magical Conspiracy

In these circumstances, then, we see how universal must have been the belief in magic, and, trading upon this, many magical books were written and doubtless sold. One of the most interesting of those that have come down to us is the Harris Papyrus, which contains many spells and charms. Such manuscripts seem to have been housed in the royal libraries, and we read of how a certain official at the court of Rameses III (about 1200 B.C.), holding the office of overseer of the Treasury, conspired with certain of his fellows to dethrone the king. The conspiracy was discovered, and in the official account of it we read that Hui, overseer of the royal cattle, procured a magical book from the king's library by means of which he attempted to injure the king. Betaking himself to a secret place, he moulded figures of men in wax, and these he succeeded in smuggling into the royal palace through another official. The figures were evidently intended to work harm to the king. He was charged with carrying out "all the wickednesses which his heart could imagine," to the horror of the gods; and with making gods of wax and figures of men, which should cause the persons whom they represented to become paralysed and helpless. The conspiracy was carefully investigated by two separate courts of inquiry, and the king ordained that those who were guilty should die by their own hands. He further desired that he should be told nothing whatever about the matter. Hui, amongst others, was doomed to the fate of a suicide. Such wax figures as were employed by him were greatly in use among sorcerers throughout the Middle Ages, and are not yet quite dispensed with. Only a few years ago a clay figure stuck full of pins and placed in a running stream was found in the Highlands of Scotland. It was, of course, modelled to represent the person it was desired to bewitch, and placed in the water in order that it should slowly wear away, the hope of the amateur sorcerer doubtless being that his enemy might, through the powers of sympathetic magic, peak and pine into a mortal illness. The method with the figures of wax was, of course, to place them close by a fire so that they might slowly melt.

Amulets

In no country was the amulet more in use than in ancient Egypt. It was worn both by the dead and the living, and, indeed, every member of the body was under the specific protection of some such talisman. A number of the amulets found upon mummies are inscribed with words of power, or magic formulæ, which would prove of use to them in the otherworld. Some of the more important amulets were those of the Heart, the Scarab, which protected the heart; the Pillow, which was placed under the neck of the mummy with the object of protecting its head; the Collar of Gold, which was intended to give the deceased power to free himself from his swathings; the amulet of the Eye of Horus, the use of which was almost universal, and which brought strength, vigour, protection, and safety.

Spells

The use of spells was universal. In the most primitive times the magician seems to have imagined that all that was necessary for him to do was to inform the evil demon that he intended to exorcize it. To the dead who haunted a certain house and brought illness into it he threatens destruction of their graves and deprivation of food-offerings. To a disease which has attacked a patient he explains that it has fastened upon a most unlikely subject, who would probably do it more harm than good. Later, however, we find the magician requesting the aid of the gods. He invokes Ra, begging that he will keep watch over the evil spirits, and relates to that god their delinquencies. Occasionally he himself takes the name of a divinity, and hurls his thunders at the demon or the malady that threatens his client, saying, for example, "Thou hast not the upper hand over me; I am Amen; I am the Great One, the Lord of Might." The magician was often guided in his choice of a guardian deity by episodes that occurred in the legends connected with him. For example, a god who had once triumphed over serpents would probably be the best protection against them. We find a certain spell which was supposed to cure scorpion stings desiring Ra to remove the poison as the goddess Bast the Cat was cured—an incident in the history of the goddess. But we find that the deities who were nearest humanity, and should typify in their legends the life of a man, were most generally invoked. The crocodile, for example, will hurry off when he is told how the body of Osiris lay in the water and was guarded by the gods. Isis and Horus at one time hid in the swamps of the Delta, and if this be recalled it will act as a safeguard against the sting of a scorpion, an insect which haunts the swamp-lands.

The Gibberish of Magic

All this is, of course, of the nature of sympathetic magic, and we can observe from it how often the spoken word can partake of the character of proto-science. But even in the case of the spoken word we have a cleavage between the two systems, for we find that it may consist, as in these last examples, of sympathetic allusion to an incident in the life of a god, or else of mere gibberish, which certainly constitutes it a part of the magic of wonder. A great many of these seemingly nonsensical spells consist of foreign words and expressions, some of them of Syrian origin. It is well known that the shamanistic class in savage communities is prone to invent a secret language or dialect of its own, and that the vocabulary of such a jargon is usually either archaic or else borrowed from a neighbouring language. For example, we find in one magical formula such a sentence as the following: "I am he that invokes thee in the Syrian tongue, the Great God, Zaalaêr, Iphphon. Do thou not disregard the Hebrew appellation Ablanathanalb, Abrasilôa."

The Tale of Setne

A tale which well instances the high standing of the magician in ancient Egypt and the use of magical models or figures is that related in a papyrus of the Ptolemaic period regarding the prince Setne, who had studied to good purpose the manuscripts in the Double House of Life, or Library of Magical Books. He was conversing on one occasion with one of the king's wise men who appeared sceptical of his powers. In reply to his strictures upon the efficacy of magic Setne offered to take him to a place where he would find a book possessed of magical powers written by Thoth himself, and containing two potent spells, the first of which was capable of enchanting the entire universe, and so powerful that all animals and birds and fishes could be commanded by it. The second enabled a man in the tomb to see Ra rising in heaven with his cycle of gods; the Moon rising with all the stars of heaven; the fishes in the depths of the ocean.

The wise man thereupon very naturally requested Setne to tell him the repository of this marvellous volume, and learned that it was in the tomb of Nefer-ka-Ptah at Memphis. Thence Setne proceeded, accompanied by his brother, and passed three days and nights in seeking for the tomb of Nefer-ka-Ptah, which he eventually discovered. Uttering over it some magical words, the earth opened, and they descended to the chamber where the actual tomb was situated. The book, which lay in the sarcophagus, illuminated the place so brilliantly that they required no torches, and by its light they perceived in the grave not only its original inhabitant, but his wife and son, who, buried at Coptos, had come in their *ka*-shapes to reside with their husband and father. Setne informed them that he desired to remove the book, but Ahura, the wife of Nefer-ka-Ptah, earnestly requested him not to do so, and informed him how its possession had already proved unfortunate to others. Her husband, she said, had given up most of his time to the study of magic, and for the price of a hundred pieces of silver and two elaborate sarcophagi had bought from the priest of Ptah the secret of the hiding-place of the wonderful volume. The book was contained in an iron chest sunk in the middle of the river at Coptos; in the iron box was a bronze box; in the bronze box a box of palm-tree wood, which again contained a box of ebony and ivory, in which was a silver box, which lastly contained a gold box, the true receptacle of the book. Swarms of serpents and noxious reptiles of all kinds guarded the volume, and round it was coiled a serpent which could not die. Nefer-ka-Ptah, his wife and child, set out for Coptos, where he obtained from the high-priest a model of a floating raft and figures of workmen provided with the necessary tools. Over these he recited words of power, so that they became alive. Shortly afterward they located the box, and by further magical formulæ Nefer-ka-Ptah put the reptiles which surrounded it to flight. Twice he slew the great serpent which lay coiled round the chest of iron, but each time it came to life again. The third time, however, he cut it in twain, and laid sand between the two pieces, so that they might not again join together. Opening the various boxes, he took out the mysterious volume which they had contained, and read the first spell upon its pages. This acquainted him with all the secrets of heaven and earth. He perused the second and saw the sun rising in the heavens, with all the accompanying gods. His wife followed his example with similar results. Nefer-ka-Ptah then copied the spells on a piece of papyrus, on which he sprinkled incense, dissolved the whole in water, and drank it, thus making certain that the knowledge of the formulæ would remain with him for ever.

A Game of Draughts with the Dead

But the god Thoth was angry with him for what he had done, and acquainted Ra with the sacrilegious act. Ra at once decided that Nefer-ka-Ptah, his wife and child, should never return to Memphis; and whilst returning to Coptos, Ahura and her son fell into the river and were drowned. Shortly afterward Nefer-ka-Ptah himself met a like fate. All that they could say, however, could not prevail with Setne, who had made up his mind to possess the book. The disembodied Nefer-ka-Ptah proposed, however, that its ownership should be settled by playing a game of draughts, the winner to retain the volume. To this Setne agreed. Nefer-ka-Ptah did his best to win, first honestly, and then by fraud, but in the end he lost the game. Setne requested his brother, who had accompanied him into the mausoleum, to ascend to the place above and bring him his magical writings. This was done, and the spells in question were laid upon Setne, who grasped the wonderful book of Thoth and ascended to heaven with marvellous swiftness. As he departed, however, Nefer-ka-Ptah remarked to his wife that he would soon make him return. The prophecy of Ahura that Setne would be unlucky if he persisted in keeping the volume was fully borne out, for he fell in love with a beautiful woman who worked him much woe, and such were his troubles that the Pharaoh commanded him to return the book to the keeping of Nefer-ka-Ptah.

Medical Magic

Magic very naturally played a large part in the practice of Egyptian medicine. Many illnesses were supposed to be caused by demoniac possession, and the only cure was the expulsion of the evil spirit who had taken up his abode in the body of the afflicted person. The Egyptian physician could not have found the practice of his art very arduous, for he theoretically divided the human body into thirty-six parts, each of which was presided over by a certain demon, and if the demon who attacked a specific part was properly invoked, it was considered that a cure should result. There were gods of healing for each of the bodily divisions. Several medical papyri are in existence which contain formulæ to be employed against the demons of disease, as well as prescriptions for the remedies to be used in specified cases of illness. Prayers were prescribed to be spoken while preparing the drugs. Often the unfortunate patient had to swallow the prescription written upon papyrus. Amulets were regarded as most efficacious in cases of illness. It is said that the peculiar letter which figures before modern medical prescriptions, and which physicians interpret as implying the word 'recipe,' is in reality an invocation to the god Ra, whose symbol it is, and that it signifies "in the name of Ra," or "O Ra, God of Light and Health, inspire me."

Alchemy

It has been averred with much likelihood that the science of alchemy originated in ancient Egypt. The derivation of the word is usually referred to the Arabic *al khemeia*, but it has also been stated[1] that it may be derived from the Egyptian word *kemt*, which means 'black' or 'dusky,' and which was applied to the country on account of the dark colour of the mud which forms the soil on each side of the Nile. The Christian Egyptians or Copts, it is thought, transmitted the word in the form *khême* to the Greeks, Romans, Syrians, and Arabs. At an early period in their history the Egyptians had attained to considerable skill in the working of metals, and according to certain Greek writers they employed quicksilver in the separation of gold and silver from the native ore. The detritus which resulted from these processes formed a

[1] See Budge, *Egyptian Magic*, p. 20.

black powder, which was supposed to contain within itself the individualities of the various metals which had contributed to its composition. In some manner this powder was identified with the body which the god Osiris was known to possess in the underworld, and to both were attributed magical qualities, and both were thought to be sources of light and power. "Thus," says Dr Budge, "side by side with the growth of skill in performing the ordinary processes of metal-working in Egypt, there grew up in that country the belief that magical powers existed in fluxes and alloys; and the art of manipulating the metals, and the knowledge of the chemistry of the metals and of their magical powers, were described by the name *khemeia*—that is to say, 'the preparation of the black ore,' which was regarded as the active principle in the transmutation." If this ingenious theory be correct, we have perhaps here not only the genesis of practical alchemy, but also the origin of a part of alchemistical science, which until recently has been strangely neglected. The allusion is to spiritual alchemy, which employed the same symbols and language as were used in the practical science, and which is credited with containing, in allegory, many a deep psychical and mystical secret.[1]

Animal Transformation

The idea of animal transformation was evidently a very ancient one in Egypt. We find from the texts that it was thought that in the future life both the gods and men were able at will to assume the form of certain animals, birds, and plants. Nearly twelve chapters of the *Book of the Dead* are occupied with spells which provide the deceased with formulæ to enable him to

[1] See A. E. Waite, *Hidden Church of the Holy Grail*, pp. 533 *et seq.*

transform himself into any shape from a bird, a serpent, or a crocodile to a god in the other-world. He was able to assume practically any form, and to swim or fly to any distance in any direction. Strangely enough, no animal is alluded to in the texts as a type of his possible transformation.

In his valuable work upon *Egyptian Magic*, by far the most illuminating text-book on the subject, Dr Budge says: "The Egyptians believed that as the souls of the departed could assume the form of any living thing or plant, so the 'gods,' who in many respects closely resembled them, could and did take upon themselves the forms of birds and beasts. This was the fundamental idea of the so-called 'Egyptian animal-worship,' which provoked the merriment of the cultured Greek, and drew down upon the Egyptians the ridicule and abuse of the early Christian writers." He further states that the Egyptians paid honour to certain animal forms because they considered they possessed the characteristics of the gods, to whom they made them sacred.

In another chapter we have dealt with the question of the totemic origin of certain of the Egyptian deities. There can be little doubt that the origin of the conception whereby the gods took upon themselves the forms of animals was a totemic one, and not magical at all in its basis. Regarding Dr Budge's other statement that it is wrong to say that the Egyptians worshipped animals in the ordinary sense of the word, one must differentiate between the attitude of primitive man toward his personal or tribal totem and toward the full-fledged deity. It is extremely difficult at this time of day, even with the example of living totemic tribes before us, to ascertain the exact status of the totem as regards worship or adoration. The Egyptian god certainly received worship of a very thorough description, and if he received it in his totem form, we may take it that it was on account of his status as a deity, and not as a totem. The contention that the animal form of many of the Egyptian gods is not of totemic origin is a vain one, and cannot be upheld in the light of modern researches. To state that the Egyptian gods were not totemic in their origin simply because they were Egyptian is to take up a totally untenable position—a position which cannot be supported by a single shred of evidence.

We do not hear very much concerning animal transformation on earth—that is, few tales exist which describe the metamorphosis of a sorcerer or witch into an animal form. So far as one can judge, the idea of the werewolf or any similar form was unknown in ancient Egypt. But a kindred type of great antiquity was not wanting—that of the vampire. We do not find the vampire in any concrete form, but figured as a ghost—indeed, as the wicked or spiteful dead so common in Hindu, Burmese, and Malay mythology. The Egyptian ghost slew the sleeping child by sucking its breath, and, strangely enough, the charm employed against such a being was the same as that used to-day in the Balkan peninsula against the attacks of the vampire—to wit, a wreath of garlic, a plant the vampire is known to detest.

The astrological knowledge of the Egyptians appears to have been exercised chiefly in the casting of horoscopes. Certain gods presided over certain periods of time, while others were identified with the heavenly bodies, and all were supposed to have power over the events which occurred in the periods subject to their control. In the later papyri spheres or tables of nativity are found, by means of which the fate of a man could be calculated from such data as the hour of his birth and so forth. As among most Oriental peoples, astrological calendars, stating which days were auspicious or otherwise, were greatly in vogue, and these were to some extent founded on mythological events which had taken place on such and such a date, thus lending to it a certain significance for all time.

Dreams

Dreams were also greatly relied upon in the affairs of life. These were believed to be sent by the gods, and it is probable that the Egyptian who was exercised over his private affairs sought his repose in the hope of being vouchsafed a dream which would guide him in his conduct. Such a practice is in vogue amongst certain North American Indian tribes to-day. Savage man goes to sleep trusting that his totem will grant him a vision for the regulation of his future affairs. If the ancient Egyptian desired such illumination, he considered it wiser to sleep within a temple famous as the seat of an oracle. A class of professional interpreters existed whose business it was to make clear the enigmatic portions of dreams. It was thought that diseases might be cured by nostrums communicated by the gods during sleep.

Mummy Magic

The treatment of the mummy and the various ceremonies in connexion with embalmment were undoubtedly magical in origin. As each bandage was laid in its exact position certain words of power were uttered which were supposed to be efficacious in the preservation of the part swathed. After consecration the priest uttered an invocation to the deceased and then took a vase of liquid containing ten perfumes, with which he smeared the body twice from head to foot, taking especial care to anoint the head thoroughly. The internal organs were at this juncture then placed on the body, and the backbone immersed in holy oil, supposed to be an emanation from the gods Shu and Geb. Certain precious stones were then laid on the mummy, each of which had its magical significance. Thus crystal lightened his face, and carnelian strengthened his steps. A priest who personified the jackal-headed god Anubis then advanced, performed certain symbolical ceremonies on the head of the mummy, and laid certain bandages upon it. After a further anointing with oil the deceased was declared to have "received his head." The mummy's left hand was then filled with thirty-six substances used in embalming, symbolical of the thirty-six forms of the god Osiris. The body was then rubbed with holy oil, the toes wrapped in linen, and after an appropriate address the ceremony was completed.

CHAPTER VIII : FOREIGN AND ANIMAL GODS : THE LATE PERIOD

Foreign Deities

THE attitude of the Egyptians as a nation toward 'other gods' seems to have been singularly free from any bigotry for their native deities, though of course the priesthood, of necessity, were more jealous and conservative in this respect. But the middle and lower classes adopted foreign gods freely, and in time the widespread belief in certain of these compelled official recognition and consequent inclusion in the Egyptian pantheon. Various reasons for this lack of exclusiveness are quite apparent. The state religion was purely a matter of royal and priestly organization, of moment to the attendant court of nobles and officials, but having no permanent or deep-seated effect on the people generally, each district following its local cult. Polytheistic worship was thus a national tendency, and therefore, when the people came into contact with foreign deities who possessed desirable qualities and powers, there was no sufficiently restraining force in their own religion to prevent them from becoming devotees of the strange god. Again, the divinity of another nation's god never seems to have been disputed, for if a nation were powerful, then that itself was sufficient proof of the divine and magical nature of their deity, and by so much, therefore, his power was to be feared and propitiated. That an element of fear was present in much of this god-adoption cannot be doubted. This would hold true especially in the case of the soldiery, who would propitiate gods of war belonging to nations who had shown themselves savage and furious in warfare; also in that of merchants, who, convoying their precious cargoes, would seek the gods who ruled the sea. There was yet another aspect of the question and an important one. According to Egyptian thought, war between peoples was in fact war between their respective deities, a trial of their powers ; and as the vanquished king and people might be taken captive, so might the god. Indeed, it was a necessity, for without the possession of the god it could not be said that the conquest was completed and the kingdom won. We find traces of many of these adoptions, not to be found among the official deities, in the numerous small stelæ belonging to private people and dedicated by them to these strange gods ; in the small images which stood in the people's houses ; while many an inscription carven on the rocks of the desert yields its quota of evidence. Libya, Palestine, Phœnicia, and Syria, each furnished the Egyptians with new gods ; Ethiopia also. It is considered probable by some authorities that the goddesses Bast and Neith were of Libyan origin, though of this no positive statement can be made. The worship of Bast and Neith was prevalent chiefly in the parts where the majority of the population were Libyan, and the latter was almost neglected where the people were of pure Egyptian race.

Asiatic Gods

Semitic Asia supplied the greatest number of gods borrowed by the Egyptians, foremost among them being Baal, Ashtoreth, Anthat, Reshpu, and the goddess Qetesh. The greatest of all is, of course, the Syrian Baal, the terrible god of war, also a personification of those terrors of the desert, the burning heat of the sun and the destroying wind. This god first became known to the Egyptians under the

Eighteenth Dynasty, when they were at war with the Syrians for centuries, and, as they had proved anything but easily vanquished foes, their god must be regarded with due reverence and awe. The Ramessides especially esteemed this deity, and "had a special predilection for calling themselves as brave and mighty as Baal in heaven," and under Rameses II a temple of the god existed at Tanis, where this king carried out his architectural undertakings on such a large scale. To a certain extent Baal was identified with Set, for a figure of the fabulous animal in which the latter became incarnate is placed by the Egyptians after their transliterations of the name Baal, from which it is evident that they believed the two gods to have qualities and attributes in common. Indeed, in one case, that of the texts of Edfû, wherein is related the legend of the Winged Sun Disk, the name of Baal is substituted for that of Set. Unfortunately, of his form and rites nothing is known.

Anthat was a war-goddess whose cult was widespread in Syria, and at the time when the Egyptians were making their Asiatic Empire she naturally became one of the adopted deities. Again, the huge number of Syrian captives brought into Egypt would undoubtedly introduce her worship as well as that of others into the country, and therefore it is no surprise to learn that in the reign of Thothmes III a shrine was built and dedicated to Anthat at Thebes. Rameses II, of the Nineteenth Dynasty, honoured this goddess often in his inscriptions, a custom followed by Rameses III, also a great warrior, and the latter gave to his favourite daughter the name of Banth-Anth, 'daughter of Anth.' Of the form of her worship little is known, but on Egyptian monuments she is called the "lady of heaven and mistress of the gods," and is depicted seated on a throne or standing upright. Seated, she wields a club with her left hand, and with her right holds spear and shield; standing, she is shown wearing a panther-skin, with the emblem of life in her left hand, while in the right she holds a papyrus sceptre. On her head is the White Crown. Her worship was well established in Egypt, and in time she was identified with the native gods, and even said to have been produced by Set.

Ashtoreth

Ashtoreth was called by the Egyptians "mistress of horses, lady of the chariot, dweller in Apollinopolis Magna." She is a Syrian deity, the terrible and destroying goddess of war, and her cult would seem to have been brought into Egypt during the Syrian campaign of Thothmes III. Her worship seems to have been well established in the country by the time of Amen-hetep III, for in a letter from Tushratta, king of the Mitanni, to this Pharaoh, he speaks of "Ishtar of Nineveh, Lady of the World," going down into Egypt in his own reign and that of his father, and seems to infer that her worship there has declined, for he begs Amen-hetep to make it increase tenfold. That it was widespread cannot be doubted. It flourished in the Delta, and was known there down to Christian times. The eastern quarter of Tanis was dedicated to Ashtoreth as was a temple near by on the shores of the Serbonian lake. Mention is made of a priest of Memphis who served Ashtoreth together with the moon-god Ah, for she was also regarded as a moon-goddess, and was identified with one of the forms of Hathor, or Isis-Hathor. In the treaty concluded between the Kheta and the Egyptians she is mentioned as the national goddess of the Syrians, though by this time she was also a familiar deity to the Egyptians, for proper names compounded with hers were current, and Rameses II, who had named his daughter after Anthat, also named one of his sons after Ashtoreth: Mer-Astrot. Her designation 'lady of horses and chariots' shows the comparatively late period at which she entered Egypt, for it was only about 1800 B.C., at the earliest during the Hyksos period, that the Egyptians learned from the Semites of the Eastern Desert how to use horses in war for charging and for drawing war-chariots. Ashtoreth is depicted as lioness-headed, and mounted on a quadriga, she drives her rampant horses over prostrate foes, and thus was the guide of the madly rushing war-chariot on the battlefield.

Qetesh in her native Syria seems to have been worshipped as a nature-goddess with rites that tended to the licentious. In Egypt she came to be identified with one of the forms of Hathor, the goddess of love and beauty, also as a moon-goddess. By some authorities she is considered to have been another form and aspect of Ashtoreth. In Egyptian art she is represented as standing upon a lion, her figure entirely nude; in her right hand she holds lotus blossoms and a mirror, while in her left are two serpents. At a later period she is still depicted in the same attitude, but on her head she wears the headdress of Hathor. On inscriptions of the Eighteenth and Nineteenth Dynasties she is called "lady of heaven, mistress of all the gods, eye of Ra, who has none like unto her." She was prayed to for gifts of life and health, and that after extreme old age her devotees might have a good burial in the west of Thebes, proving that her worship existed in the capital of the country. She sometimes appears with Amsu and the god Reshpu, with whom she seems to be associated as one of a trinity.

Reshpu is another Syrian god whose cult became known in Egypt, the chief centre of his worship being at Het-Reshp, in the Delta. In Syria he was regarded as a god of war, and in Egyptian monuments and temples he is depicted in the form of a warrior with shield and spear in his left hand and a club in his right. Above his forehead projects a gazelle, which would seem to be an ancient symbol of the god denoting his sovereignty over the desert. His titles as given in the Egyptian texts, where he is described as "the great god, the lord of eternity, the prince of everlastingness, the lord of twofold strength among the company of gods," are largely borrowed from the native deities. Reshpu corresponds to the god known to the Phœnicians and worshipped both in Cyprus and Carthage, and is considered by some authorities to be a god of the burning and destructive power of fire, also of the lightning.

Semitic and African Influence

Besides supplying the Egyptians with specific deities, Semitic thought influenced their religious ideas regarding the mythology and nature of their own gods. Certain inanimate objects—especially stones, and in some cases trees—under this influence came to be looked upon as incorporations of deity, as that of the sun-god in Heliopolis, while a sign representing the archaic form of the symbol *Kh* is the usual determinative of the name Set. It is a circumstance of some significance that the Asiatic deities in representation, as regards physical appearance and symbolism, are depicted according to the Egyptian religious convention; but with gods of African origin it is far otherwise. They are figured as hideous, frightful, distorted, and enormously fat creatures, resembling the negro human fetish which may be found to-day among African tribes. Bes is the most important of the African deities, and though he underwent many changes as time went on, which would seem to point to other origins, his original conception is decidedly African, and "his cult in Egypt is coeval with dynastic civilizations." His representations point to a savage origin. He is depicted as a deformed dwarf with large stomach, bowed legs, and a huge, bearded face. From his thick lips hangs a protruding tongue; his nose is flat, while his eyebrows are very shaggy. He wears a tiara of feathers [1] on his head, and round his body a panther-skin, the tail of which hangs down and usually touches the ground behind him. Another distinction is that he is generally drawn in full face, the Egyptian deities being usually presented in profile. Though many names were given to him later, Bes was his usual appellation, which, according to Wiedemann, is derived from *besa*, a word designating one of the great felidæ, the *Cynælurus guttatus*, whose skin formed his clothing. His cult existed over a long period—from the time of the Old Kingdom down to Roman times, in which his oracle at Abydos was consulted down to a late period—and his influence may be traced in Alexandrian, Hellenistic, and Phœnician art. The god Bes had varied characteristics. He was associated with birth, and one of the oldest representations of him is to be found in a relief in the temple of Hatshepsut, where he appears as attendant at the birth of the Great Queen. In this connexion he appears in all the 'Birth Houses' of Egyptian temples, places where the presiding god was supposed to have been born. As the child grew Bes was supposed to provide it with amusement, and in this aspect he is shown as laughing at it, dancing grotesquely

[1] In the earliest representations the feathers do not appear.

and playing on the harp. From this he came to be regarded as god of the dance, of music and joviality, hence of rest, joy, and pleasure; and his quaint figure is to be found carved upon the handles of mirrors, on palettes, and on *kohl* vessels. He was appointed guardian of the young sun-god, and therefore becomes the foe of all serpents, and is shown as gripping and strangling them in his hands, or biting them in pieces. In time he was wholly identified with his ward Horus, and depicted with all the symbols and attributes of that deity, though his peculiar solar province was the east. In the underworld Bes underwent a transformation. He became an avenging deity, carrying a menacing knife with which he essayed to tear out the hearts of the wicked, yet, even thus, to the good and deserving he never failed to be a true friend and cheering companion. In his menacing aspect he was called 'the Warrior,' and sometimes this character was ascribed to him on earth also, where, bearing a shield and wielding a sword, he wages war for those under his protection, and those who wear his image as an amulet.

It is undoubted that many local cults existed in different parts of Egypt and that gods of many and varied origins were the presiding deities, but usually their power remained purely local and never attained to any great influence or fame.

Sacred Animals

From the many sources whence comes our knowledge of ancient Egypt there is to be gathered a most comprehensive survey of the great extent and influence which animal-worship attained to in that country. It prevailed there from the earliest times and was far older than Egyptian civilization. That much of it is of totemic origin cannot be gainsaid, an origin to be

Bes

(page 281)

Photo W. A. Mansell & Co.

Procession of the Sacred Bull
From the picture in the Corcoran Art Gallery, Washington,
by F. A. Bridgman

(page 286)

found among the pre-dynastic tribes whence sprang the Egyptian people.

The inspiring cause of animal-worship was undoubtedly at first nothing more or less than fear, with an admixture of awesome admiration of the creature's excelling power and strength. Later there developed the idea of animals as typifying gods, the actual embodiments of divine and superhuman attributes. Thus the bull and the ram, possessors of exceptional procreative energy, came to represent gods of nature and the phenomena of yearly rejuvenescence, as is stated by Wiedemann: "The generative power in the animal was identical with the force by which life is renewed in nature continually and in man after death." Throughout Egypt the bull and the cow, the latter as typifying fertility, were worshipped as agricultural gods.

Again, to the Egyptian mind, incapable of abstract thought, an immaterial and intangible deity was an impossible conception. A god, and more so by reason of his godhead, must manifest and function in an actual body. The king was believed to be an incarnation of a god, but he was apart and only one, and as the Egyptian everywhere craved the manifestation of and communion with his gods, it thus came about that incarnations of deity and its many attributes were multiplied. Certain animals could represent these to a greater degree than man, though of course to Egyptian thought man was the standard by which all in the universe was to be measured and weighed. The gods were but little greater than men; they were limited, and might know death. Their immortality was only acquired by the power of transmigration from one body to another, escaping human death by transference to successive forms and a renewal of the life force.

The symbolism of the Egyptian religion is mostly

expressed by means of animals. Thus the god of the dead is spoken of as a jackal, the water-god as a crocodile, while the sky is a cow, the sun a falcon, the moon an ibis. Because of this exaltation of certain animals whole species were held as sacred, and this led to the many strange ideas and customs amongst the Egyptians mentioned so often by classic writers, as, for instance, considering a man fortunate who was eaten by a crocodile. When these animals died their owners mourned as for a relative, and the greatest care was taken in the disposal of their remains. Cows were held in such veneration that their bodies were cast into the sacred waters of the Nile, and a bull was buried outside the town, its horns protruding above the ground to mark the place of interment. Other instances might be adduced.

Apis

From the earliest times the bull was worshipped in Egypt as the personification of strength and virility and might in battle. Manetho traces the cult of Apis to Kaiekhos, a king of the Second Dynasty, who appointed a chosen bull, Hap, to be a god; but Ælian ascribes this to Mena, the first historical king of Egypt.

Much of our knowledge concerning this cult is derived from Greek sources. Herodotus gives the following description of Apis: "He is the calf of a cow which is incapable of conceiving another offspring, and the Egyptians say that lightning descends upon the cow from heaven and that from thence it brings forth Apis. This calf has the following marks: it is black and has a square spot of white on the forehead; and on the back the figure of an eagle; and in the tail double hairs, and on the tongue a beetle."

Again, Diodorus gives an account of the finding of the Apis and the method of its installation on the death and funeral of a former incarnation of the god Osiris: "After the splendid funeral of Apis is over those priests who have charge of the business seek out another calf as like the former as they can possibly find, and when they have found one an end is put to all further mourning and lamentation, and such priests as are appointed for that purpose lead the young ox through the city of Nile and feed him forty days. Then they put him into a barge wherein is a golden cabin and so transport him as a god to Memphis and place him in Vulcan's grove. During the forty days before mentioned none but women are admitted to see him, and these, naked, are placed full in his view. Afterward they are forbidden to come into the sight of this new god. For the adoration of this ox they give this reason. They say that the soul of Osiris passed into an ox and therefore whenever the ox is dedicated, to this very day the spirit of Osiris is infused into one ox after another to posterity. But some say that the members of Osiris (who was killed by Typhon) were thrown by Isis into an ox made of wood covered with ox-hides, and from thence the city of Bubastis was called."

Great honour was also paid to the mother of the chosen bull, and apartments in the temple were set apart for her beside the splendid ones occupied by the Apis. This animal was given rich beds to lie upon, its food was of the purest and most delicate, while water from a special well at Memphis was given to it alone, the water of the Nile being considered fattening. A number of carefully selected cows were presented to the Apis, and these again had their attendant priests. Usually the sacred bull was kept in seclusion, but when on certain occasions he appeared in public a crowd of boys marched in procession beside him singing hymns. The birthday of the Apis was celebrated for seven days with great rejoicings, and it was believed that during this period no man was attacked by a crocodile.

The Apis Oracle

Thus in the temple of Ptah were great honours paid to the Apis bull, and the Pharaohs gave lavishly of their wealth to its cult, and foreigners, such as Alexander the Great and Titus, presented it with offerings. Oracles, as usual, were looked for from this god, and the method of obtaining them is thus described by Wiedemann :

"Chiefly it was renowned for its oracles, which were imparted in very various ways. When the bull licked the garments of the celebrated Eudoxus of Cnidus, this signified the astronomer's approaching death ; a like fate was predicted to Germanicus when it refused to eat at his hand ; and the conquest of Egypt by Augustus was announced beforehand by its bellowing. Some inquiries were answered by the animal's passing into one or other of the two rooms placed at its disposition, and others by dreams which were vouchsafed to inquirers who slept in the temple, and which were explained by the sacred interpreters. Other inquiries, again, though presented to the creature itself, found their reply through the voices of children playing before the temple, whose words assumed to the believing inquirer the form of a rhythmic answer to his question. Prophecies of a general kind took place during the procession of the Apis." Of this Pliny says: "Then the youths who accompanied him sang hymns in his honour, while the Apis appeared to understand all, and to desire that he should be worshipped. Suddenly the spirit took possession of the youths and they prophesied."

There were also sacrifices made to the Apis, and these, strangely enough, were oxen, chosen with the greatest care. The head of the slaughtered animal was usually thrown into the Nile with the following words pronounced above it : "If any evil be about to befall either those who now sacrifice or upon the land of Egypt, may it be averted on this head."

Some authorities state that after a certain number of years the Apis was slain and a new one obtained, but it is generally believed that the Apis died a natural death. Its body was embalmed and general mourning was observed. The mummy was buried with all magnificence.[1] In 1851 Mariette discovered the famous Serapeum wherein had been buried the sacred bulls of Memphis from the middle of the Eighteenth Dynasty, 1500 B.C. Here in the gigantic sarcophagi, weighing about fifty-eight tons each, were discovered some of the remains of these animals. The chapels of the Serapeum were evidently places of pilgrimage, for many votive statues and stelæ have been found there dedicated to the dead Apis, "in hopes of thereby gaining his favour and the fulfilment of their various wishes." The Apis, though dead, was even yet more powerful, for his soul became joined to that of Osiris, and thus the dual god Osiris-Apis was formed, a name more familiar in the Grecian form *Serapis*. To this god the Greeks ascribed the attributes of their own deity Hades, convinced of the similarity to Osiris, the great god of the underworld. In both Egypt and Greece Serapis came to be looked upon as the male counterpart of Isis. Under the Romans the cult of Serapis extended in all directions of the Empire, claiming devotees of all classes and races. It reached as far north in Britain as York.

[1] In the earliest sarcophagi in the Serapeum no mummies were found, only a few bones.

At Heliopolis another bull, Mnevis, was worshipped as typifying the sun and its life-giving powers. Manetho ascribes this cult also to Kaiekhos, of the Second Dynasty, as well as the worship of the *Ram of Mendes.*

This obtained chiefly in the Deltaic cities, such as Hermopolis, Lycopolis, and Mendes, the last named being the most famous shrine. The origin of this worship was merely that of a local and tribal animal god, but, persisting through the changing civilization, it became of more than local influence as the city grew in wealth and importance, while the priesthood were among the most wealthy and powerful in Egypt, and the animal god was identified "first with the indigenous god Osiris, secondly with the sun-god Ra, and thirdly with the great Ram-god of the South and Elephantine, *i.e.* Khnemu."

Greek writers furnish us with much graphic material concerning these animal cults, as in some instances they were eye-witnesses of the ritual connected with them. Herodotus states that the god Pan and another goat-like deity were worshipped with a wealth of symbolic display and gorgeous rite as gods of generation and fecundity. As in many countries where animal worship obtained the beast chosen for adoration was picked from a number because of certain distinguishing marks upon its hide, was enthroned with much pomp and received an imposing public funeral on its decease.

On the stele of Mendes deciphered by Mariette was found an inscription stating that Ptolemy II Philadelphus rebuilt the temple of Mendes and assisted in person at the enthronement of two Rams, and in a relief on the upper portion of this stele are to be seen the figures of two royal Ptolemies and an Arsinoë making offerings to the Ram and his female counterpart Hatmehit.

The Crocodile

The crocodile was the incarnation of the god Sebek. It would seem beyond doubt that abject fear was the primal origin of the worship of this repulsive creature, and the idea that its evil and menacing traits might be averted by propitiation, for in the dry season these reptiles wandered over the cultivated lands and devoured all at will. Later, beneficent attributes were ascribed to it, but the dark side always persisted. In the benign aspect he is connected with Ra, and again with Osiris, though in legendary lore he is both the friend and foe of Osiris. One version tells how a crocodile carried the dead body of Osiris safely to land upon its back, whilst another relates that only by Isis placing Horus in a little ark woven of papyrus reeds was she able to protect him against the attacks of the malevolent Sebek. This clearly identifies him with Set, the murderer of Osiris, and in this connexion the powers of darkness are symbolized by four crocodiles, who are shown in the *Book of the Dead* as menacing the deceased. Whilst still living, men sought deliverance from these horrible shapes of the underworld by means of incantations.

But again he is said to be beneficent to the dead, and in the Pyramid Texts it is Sebek who restores sight to the eyes of the deceased, who, indeed, revives all his faculties, is his guide in the untried new life, and helps him to overthrow Set, the evil one who preys upon every 'Osiris.' In this character he is the helper and protector of the child Horus. But his characters are multiple, and he is to be found participating in the rites of all the other gods of the Egyptian pantheon.

Quite in consonance with this is the fact that while in some parts of Egypt the crocodile was held sacred, in other districts it was killed; indeed, the hunting of it was a popular sport with the nobles of the Old Kingdom. By some the crocodile was looked upon as a protector of Egypt, Diodorus stating that "but for them Arabian and African robbers would swim across the Nile and pillage the country in all directions."

Herodotus also states these conflicting views regarding the crocodile, together with many of the fabulous stories of its wisdom and habits. He tells how at Thebes and Lake Moeris they were held sacred, and how when tame the people bedecked them with jewels, placing bracelets on their fore-paws, while they were fed on the most delicate foods. After death the body was embalmed with many rites and buried in the subterranean Labyrinth, a place held so sacred that Herodotus was not allowed to enter it.

The centre of this worship was Krokodilopolis, in the Fayûm, and Strabo, who visited Egypt during the reign of the Emperor Augustus, gives the following account in which he tells that the sacred crocodile "was kept apart by himself in a lake; it is tame and gentle to the priests. It is fed with bread, flesh, and wine, which strangers who come to see it always present. Our host, a distinguished person, who was our guide about the city, accompanied us to the lake, and brought from the supper table a small cake, dressed meat, and a small vessel containing honey and milk. The animal was lying on the edge of the lake. The priests went up to it; some of them opened its mouth, another put the cake into it, then the meat, and afterward poured down the honey and milk. The animal then leaped into the lake and crossed to the other side. When another stranger arrived with his offering, the priests took it and, going round to

Sebek (page 289)

Rameses II accompanied by a Lion (page 292)
Evelyn Paul

the other side, caught the animal and repeated the process in the same manner as before."

This cult lasted far into the Roman period. Sebek also had his oracle, and foretold the demise of King Ptolemæus by refusing to listen to him or obey the attendant priests.

In religious art Sebek is often represented as a crocodile-headed man wearing the solar disk with a uræus, or, again, with a pair of horns and the plumes of Amen.

The Lion

The lion could hardly fail to be the centre of a cult, and there is ample proof that this animal was, from early dynastic times, worshipped for his great strength and courage. He was identified with the solar deities, with the sun-god Horus or Ra. The Delta was the home of the Egyptian lion, and the chief centre of the cult was the city of Leontopolis, in the Northern Delta, where, according to Ælian, the sacred lions were fed upon slaughtered animals, and sometimes a live calf was put in the den that they might have the pleasure of killing it. Whilst the feeding was proceeding the priests chanted and sang. But the same writer also states that lions were kept in the temple at Heliopolis, as well as at many other places throughout Egypt.

The Lion Guardian

The outstanding characteristic of the lion was that of guardianship, and this is to be found in the part played by the ancient lion-god Aker, who guarded the gate of the dawn through which the sun passed each morning. The later idea that the sun-god passed through a dark passage in the earth which hid his light, and so caused the darkness of night, while his emergence therefrom was the signal of day, necessitated the existence of two guardian lions, who were called Sef and Dua—that is, 'Yesterday' and 'Tomorrow.' From this was derived the practice of placing statues of lions at the doors of palaces and tombs as guardians of both living and dead against all evil. These statues were often given the heads of men, and are familiar under the Greek name of 'Sphinxes,' though the characteristics of the Egyptian lion-statue were very different from those of the Grecian 'Sphinx.'

The most famous of all is, of course, the wonderful 'Sphinx' at Gizeh, the symbol of the sun-god Ra, or rather his colossal abode erected there, facing the rising sun that he might protect the dead sleeping in the tombs round about.

There were many lion-headed gods and goddesses, in some cases personifying the destructive power. In the underworld lion-headed deities guarded some of the halls and pylons there, and that the lion was connected in some way with the dead is proved by the fact that the head of the bier was always made in the form of a lion's head, while the foot was not seldom decorated with a lion's tail.

A curious point is that it was evidently permissible to kill the lions of another country, if not those of Egypt, for we find that Amen-hetep III boasted of having shot with his own bow one hundred and two fierce lions. Rameses II and Rameses III both kept a tame lion, which accompanied them into battle and actually attacked the enemy. In this case, however, it is evident that primarily the lion was a symbol of guardianship.

THE CAT

The Cat

The cat was regarded both as an incarnation of Bast, the goddess of Bubastis, and therefore sacred to her, and as a personification of the sun. Throughout Egyptian mythology the cat is to be found, and generally in a beneficent aspect. In the *Book of the Dead* it is a cat who cuts off the head of the serpent of darkness and who assists in the destruction of the foes of Osiris. On every side there is ample evidence that everywhere in Egypt the cat was held in great reverence after the Twenty-second Dynasty. The classical writers are again our authorities. Diodorus relates that the cats were fed on bread and milk and slices of Nile fish, and that the animals came to their meals at certain calls. After death their bodies were carefully embalmed and, with spices and drugs, swathed in linen sheets. The penalty of death was meted out to anyone who killed a cat, be it by accident or of intent, and a case is given in which a Roman who had killed a cat was set upon by the enraged populace and made to pay for the outrage with his life. A passage from Herodotus further illustrates the esteem in which these animals were held : "When a conflagration takes place a supernatural impulse seizes on the cats. For the Egyptians, standing at a distance, take care of the cats and neglect to put out the fire ; but the cats, making their escape, and leaping over the men, throw themselves into the fire ; and when this happens great lamentations are made among the Egyptians. In whatsoever house a cat dies a natural death all the family shave their eyebrows only, but if a dog die they shave their whole body and the head. All cats that die are carried to certain sacred houses, where, being first embalmed, they are buried in the city of Bubastis."

The Dog

Dogs were held in great honour by the Egyptians, as in the city of Cynopolis, yet strangely enough, they were never looked upon as a possible incarnation of a god, though there seems to have been some confusion of the dog with the jackal, sacred to Anubis, who ministered to Osiris and acted as guide to the souls of the dead. Another animal so confounded was the wolf, which was specially venerated at Lycopolis. The fact that the jackal was to be found chiefly in the deserts and mountains where tombs were usually located led to its early association with the dead and the underworld in Egyptian mythology, the character ascribed to it being beneficent and that of a guide.

The Hippopotamus

Another cult probably founded on fear was that of the hippopotamus. Ta-urt, the hippopotamus-goddess, came in time to be identified with nearly every goddess in the Egyptian pantheon, and though her attributes are those of benevolence and protectiveness, the original traits of ferocious destructiveness were not wholly obliterated, for we find these personified in the monster, half-hippopotamus, called Amemt, who attends the Judgment Scene. In this same scene is the dog-headed ape, who sits and watches the pointer of the scales and reports the results to Thoth. This animal was greatly revered by the Egyptians. The cult is probably extremely ancient. Apes were kept in many temples, mostly those of the lunar deities, as that of Khensu at Thebes.

Other Animals

Two animals, the ass and the pig, attained a peculiar reputation for evil, though in some aspects looked upon as sacrosanct. They were always connected with the powers of darkness and evil. In the case of the ass opinion seems to have fluctuated, for in some instances this animal figures as a personification of the sun-god Ra. Many smaller animals are to be found in the mythology of Egypt, among which may be mentioned the hare, which was worshipped as a deity, the shrew-mouse, sacred to the goddess Buto, the ichneumon, and the bat, whilst reptiles were represented by the tortoise, associated with night, therefore with darkness and evil ; and the serpent, clearly propitiated through fear at first, though afterward credited with beneficent motives. The uræus became the symbol of divinity and royalty, a symbol worn by the gods and the kings. But the evil side was undoubtedly prominent in the mind of the Egyptian, for all the terrors of death and the Unknown were personified in the monster serpent Apep, who led his broods of serpents against both gods and men in the gloom of the underworld. Others were the scorpion, associated sometimes with evil, but also sacred to Isis; and the frog, worshipped in pre-dynastic times as the symbol of generation, birth, and fecundity. This cult was the most ancient in Egypt and is connected with the creation myth. The goddess Heqt, identified with Hathor, is depicted with the head of a frog.

The Ibis

Amongst birds worshipped by the Egyptians, one of the most important was the ibis. It was associated with Thoth and the moon, and in the earliest period the city of Hermopolis was the centre of this cult. A passage in Herodotus gives many interesting details concerning the ideas held regarding the bird. He tells us that he went to a certain place in Arabia, near the city of Buto, to learn about the winged serpents, brought into Egypt by the west wind, which the ibis was believed to destroy along with the ordinary reptiles common to the country. Arriving there, he "saw the backbones and ribs of serpents in such numbers as it was impossible to describe; of the ribs there were a multitude of heaps, some great, some small, some of medium size. The place where the bones lie is at the entrance of a narrow gorge between steep mountains, which there opens upon a wide plain communicating with the great plain of Egypt. The story goes that, with the spring, the winged snakes come flying from Arabia toward Egypt, but are met in this gorge by the birds called ibises, who bar their entrance and destroy them. The Arabians assert, and the Egyptians admit, that it is on account of this service that the Egyptians hold the ibis in so much reverence. The ibis is a bird of a deep black colour, with legs like a crane; its beak is strongly hooked, and its size that of the landrail. This is a description of the black ibis which contends with the serpents."

Another bird held in great reverence was the bennu, a bird of the heron species which gave rise to the mythical bird, the phœnix. It is identified with the sun, a symbol of the rising and the setting sun. Many fables arose concerning this bird, and are recounted by Herodotus and Pliny. Another sun-bird was the falcon, sacred to Horus, Ra, and Osiris, and this was worshipped throughout Egypt in the predynastic period. In another form, represented with a human head, it was symbolic of the human soul, a distinction it shared with the heron and swallow, in both of which it was believed the human soul might reincarnate itself. Plutarch says that it was in the form of a swallow that Isis lamented the death of Osiris. Also sacred to Isis was the goose, though one species of it was devoted to Amen-Ra ; while the vulture was the symbol of the goddesses Nekhebet and Mut. There is some evidence to prove that certain fish were held as sacred, and worshipped because of their mythological connexion with divers gods and goddesses.

Sacred Trees

Though as a country Egypt was not rich in trees, yet certain of the family played a not unimportant part in the religious cult, so much so that tree-worship has been accepted as a fact by most Egyptologists. That these trees were held in special veneration would support that belief, though recorded instances of actual tree-worship are rare. This Wiedemann attributes to the same reason that accounts for the scant notice taken in Egyptian texts of animal-worship, though we know from other sources that it formed the most considerable part in popular religion. And the reason is that official religion took but little notice of the 'minor' divinities to whom the people turned rather than to the greater gods ; that the priestly class hardly admitted to their pantheon the 'rustic and plebeian' deities of the lower classes. He goes on to say that "so far as we can judge, the reception of tree-worship into temple-service and mythology was always the result of a compromise ; the priests were compelled to make concessions to the faith of the masses and admit into the temples the worship of the people's divinities ; but they did so grudgingly, and this explains the apparent insignificance of the official cult of vegetation in Egypt as compared with the worship of the great gods and their cycles."

In their religious symbolism we find the ancient sacred tree which grew in the 'Great Hall' of Heliopolis on the place where the solar cat slew that great serpent of evil, Apep, the place, too, from which the Phœnix rose. The leaves of this tree possessed magical powers, for when Thoth or the goddess Safekht wrote thereon the name of the monarch, then was he endowed with immortality. Again, there was the wonderful tree, a tamarisk, which wound its stem and branches about the chest that held the dead Osiris. An olive-tree is mentioned, too, the habitation of a nameless demon.

The sycamore, whose shade was so welcome in the brazen glare of Egypt, had its counterpart in the Land of the Dead, and from its midst leaned out a Hathor, Lady of the Underworld, offering sustenance and water to the passing souls. Sometimes it is a palm-tree from which she ministers to the dead, and perhaps it is a leaf from this tree circled by inverted horns which stands for the peculiar symbol of Safekht, the goddess of learning. But the sycamore seems to have been first favourite, and on some monuments it is represented with peasants gathered round fervently paying their devotions to it and making offerings of fruit and vegetables and jars of water. It was always held as sacred to Nut and Hathor, and their doubles were believed to inhabit it, a certain species being regarded as "the living body of Hathor on earth"; indeed, the Memphite Hathor was called the 'Lady of the Sycamore.'

As to the later development of this belief Wiedemann states: "In Ptolemaic times a systematic attempt was made to introduce this form of cult into the temple of every nome; according to the contemporary lists relating to the subject, twenty-four nomes worshipped the Nile acacia, seventeen the *Corda myxa*, sixteen the *Zizyphus Spina Christi*, while other trees, such as the sycamore, the *Juniperus Phœnica*, and the *Tamarisk Nilotica*, are named but once or twice. Ten kinds of sacred trees are here mentioned, in all of which as many as three were sometimes worshipped in the same nome." Again, there is evidence to prove that every temple had its sacred tree and sacred groves, whilst it is recorded that rare trees were brought as precious spoil from conquered countries, their roots carefully encased in great chests of earth that they might be planted about temples and palaces.

The Lotus

Amongst flora the only kind which may be said to be sacred is the lotus. In Egyptian symbolism and decoration it is to be found everywhere. From the cup of a lotus blossom issues the boy Horus, the 'rising sun,' and again it is the symbol of resurrection, when Nefer-tem, crowned with the flowers, grants continuance of life in the world to come. On the altars of offering the blossoms were laid in profusion.

Religion of the Late Period

The conclusion of the New Empire and the succession of political chaos during what is known as the Libyan period witnessed what was really, so far as Egyptian religion is concerned, the beginning of the end. Thenceforward a gradual decline is apparent in the ancient faith of the Pharaohs, a subtle decay which the great revival of the eighth century and onward was powerless to arrest. The ever-increasing introduction into it of foreign elements, Greek and Persian and Semitic, and the treasuring of the dry husks of ancient things, from which the soul had long since departed—

these sapped the strength and virility of the Egyptian religion, hampered true progress, and contributed to its downfall, till it was finally vanquished and thrown into obscurity by the devotees of Christianity.

At the beginning of the Libyan period, then, there were a number of petty rulers in the land of Egypt—a monarch held court at Tanis, in the Delta ; at Thebes the priesthood of Amen's cult were the rulers ; other districts were governed by the chief men among the Libyan soldiery. One of these latter, Sheshonk by name, attained supremacy about the middle of the tenth century B.C., and as his capital was at Bubastis, Bast, the cat-headed goddess of that locality, became for a time supreme deity of Egypt, while other Delta divinities also came into vogue. A share of the worship also fell to Amen. It is remarkable that this deity was himself the ruler of Thebes, being represented by a *Divine Wife*, always the eldest princess of the ruling family. So firm was the belief in the divine government of Thebes that no human monarch of the Late period, however powerful, made any attempt to take the city. Meanwhile a revulsion of feeling occurred against Set, the dark brother of Isis and Osiris. Hitherto his position among the gods of the Egyptian pantheon had been unquestioned, but now he was thrown from his high estate and confused or identified with the dragon Apep ; he was no longer a god, but a devil.

The cult of the oracle flourished greatly during the decadent period, and afforded, as we may conjecture, considerable scope for priestly ingenuity. The usual method of consulting the oracle was to write on papyrus certain words, whether of advice or judgment, which it was proposed to put into the mouth of the deity, and to which he might assent by nodding.

A Religious Reaction

Toward the end of the eighth century B.C. a great religious reaction set in. Hitherto the brilliant opening of the New Empire, particularly the time of Rameses II, had set a model for the pious of the Late period; now the Old Kingdom, its monuments, rites, and customs, its fervent piety and its proud conservatism, was become the model epoch for the whole nation. It was, however, less a faithful copy than a caricature of the Old Kingdom which the Decadent period provided. All that was most strange and *outré* in the ancient religion was sought out and emulated. Old monuments and religious literature were studied; the language and orthography of long-past centuries were revived and adopted; and if much of this was incomprehensible to the bulk of the people, its very mystery but made it the more sacred. In the funerary practices of the time the antiquarian spirit is very evident. Ancient funerary literature was held in high esteem; the Pyramid Texts were revived; old coffins, and even fragments of such, were utilized in the burying of the dead. The tomb furniture was elaborate and magnificent—in the case of rich persons, at least—while even the poorest had some such furnishings provided for them. Ushabti figures of blue faience were buried with the deceased, to accomplish for him any compulsory labour he might be called upon to do in the domain of Osiris, and scarabs also were placed in his coffin. The rites and ceremonies of mummification followed those of the Old Kingdom, and were religiously carried out. The graves of even the royal Thebans were not so magnificent as those of private persons of this era. Yet because their inscriptions were almost invariably borrowed from the Old Kingdom, it is hard to guess what their ideas really were on the subjects of death and the underworld. It may be that these also were borrowed. From the tombs of foreigners—of Syrians belonging to the fifth century B.C.—some little information may be gathered relative to the status of the dead in the underworld which probably represents the popular view of the time. Herodotus asserts that the Egyptians of this epoch believed in the transmigration of souls, and it is possible that they did hold this belief in some form. It may well have been a development of the still more ancient idea that the soul was capable or appearing in a variety of shapes—as a bird, an animal, and so on.

The Worship of Animals

A very prominent feature of the religion of the Late period, and one which well illustrates the note of exaggeration already mentioned, was the worship of animals, carried by the pious Egyptian to a point little short of ludicrous. Cats and crocodiles, birds, beetles, rams, snakes, and countless other creatures were reverenced with a lavishness of ceremony and ritual which the Egyptian knew well how to bestow. Especially to Apis, the bull of the temple of Ptah in Memphis, was worship accorded. The Saïte king Amasis, who did a great deal in connexion with the restoration of ancient monuments, is mentioned as having been especially devoted to the sacred bull, in whose honour he raised the first of the colossal sarcophagi at Saqqara. But these elaborate burial rites were not reserved for individual sacred animals; they were accorded to entire classes. It was a work of piety, for instance, to mummify a dead cat, convey the remains to Bubastis, where reigned the cat-headed Bast, and

Mummied Cats

In the British Museum

(page 302)

Horus the Child (page 308)

there inter the animal in a vault provided with suitable furnishings. Dead mice and sparrowhawks were taken to Buto; the ibis found his last resting-place at Eshmunên; while the cow, the most sacred of Egyptian animals, was thrown at death into the Nile.

It is notable that, despite the exclusiveness which characterized this phase of the Egyptian religion and the contempt with which the Egyptians regarded everything that was not of their land, several foreign elements crept into their faith and were incorporated with it during the Saïtic and Persian supremacies. The oracles, which played a conspicuous part in the religious government of the country, were probably not of Egyptian origin; the burning of sacrifices was a Semitic custom which the people of the Nile valley had adopted. Already there was a considerable Greek element in Egypt, and in the time of Amasis a Greek town—Naukratis—had been founded there. It is therefore not improbable that Greek ideas also entered into the national faith, colouring the ancient gods, and perhaps suggesting to Herodotus that resemblance which caused him to identify the divinities of Egypt with those of Greece—Osiris with Dionysos, Isis with Demeter, Horus with Apollo, Set with Typhon, and so on. Naturally this identification became much more general and complete in later years, when the Hellenes were masters in Egypt.

Besides these foreign ideas grafted on the Egyptian religion, there were innovations suggested by the native priests themselves, such as the deification of certain national heroes admired by the populace for their skill in learning and magic. Such hero-gods were Imhotep, a distinguished author and architect under King Zoser at an early period of dynastic history, and Amenhetep, son of Hāpu, who was thought to have seen and conversed with the gods. Both heroes were adored with the gods at Thebes and Karnak.

Religion under Persian Rule

If the Saïte rulers endeavoured to keep on good terms with the priesthood, the Persian monarchs who succeeded them were no whit behind in this matter. Even the boldest of them found it to his advantage to bow before the native deities, and to give to these his protection. Meanwhile the Egyptian dynasts, who ruled contemporaneously with the Persians, were allowed to proceed unmolested with the building of temples and monuments. Strangely enough, in view of the nearness of the Greek conquest and the consequent amalgamation of the religions of Greece and Egypt, this period was characterized by a hatred and contempt on the part of the Egyptians for all foreigners dwelling in their cities. Kambyses, who heaped indignity upon the Apis bull and finally slew the animal, was afterward persuaded by his physician, Usa-hor-res-net, to recant his heresy, and was further induced to banish foreigners out of the temple area and to destroy their houses. Other rulers levied taxes on Greek imports, devoting the revenue thus obtained to the goddess Neith.

The Ptolemaic Period

As has been said, Greek ideas had already found their way into the religion of Egypt when the Alexandrine conquest in the fourth century B.C. made the Greeks dominant. Yet the ancient religion held its ground and maintained its established character in all essential respects. The Hellenic monarchs vied with their predecessors in the tolerance and respect which they accorded to the native religion. It was they who maintained the Egyptian deities in splendid state; restored statues, books, and so on which the Persians had taken from the country; even they themselves worshipped the absurd animal deities of the Egyptians.

This was the great epoch of temple-building in Egypt. The temples of Dendereh, Edfû, Kom Ombo, Philæ, and many other famous structures were raised under Ptolemaic and Roman rulers. For the favours shown them by the conquerors the priests were duly grateful, even to the extent of deifying their rulers while they were yet alive. It was said of Ptolemy and his consort that "the beneficent gods have benefited the temples in the land and greatly increased the dignity of the gods. They have provided in every way for Apis, Mnevis, and the other esteemed sacred animals with great sumptuousness and cost." There was even a new order[1] of priesthood instituted, known as the "priesthood of the beneficent gods."

During the period of Roman ascendancy the high-priest was the most important religious official within a considerable area, acting as the representative of a still higher Roman official, the high-priest of Alexander and of all Egypt. The priests of the larger temples, on which grants of money and land had been lavishly bestowed, were doubtless sufficiently well provided for, but in the smaller temples things were far otherwise, if we are to judge from the evidence at our disposal. The Theban priests especially were regarded as sages well versed in the lore of antiquity, and as such were much sought after by travellers from Rome. In Thebes also were priestesses, consecrated to the service of Amen, the god of that district, to whom the Greeks as well as the Egyptians rendered homage, identifying him with Zeus.

[1] *Cf.* the priests of the kings of the Old Kingdom.

The worship of animals continued unabated during the Hellenic period; it is even probable that this phase of the Egyptian religion had become more pronounced under the Greek rule, for Strabo, writing in the time of Augustus, asserts that statues of sacred animals had practically displaced those of the gods. The sacred Ram (Khnemu) of Mendes was worshipped both by conquered and conquerors, as was the Apis bull and the sacred crocodile, and it would seem that the temple revenues were at times increased by the displaying of these animals to the curious gaze of strangers.

Fusion of Greek and Egyptian Ideas

Meanwhile Greek and Egyptian ideas were becoming more and more completely fused. As already mentioned, Amen was identified with Zeus, Isis with Demeter, Hathor with Aphrodite, Osiris with Pluto, Set with Typhon, Bast with Artemis, and Horus with Apollo. This feature was very strikingly exemplified in the god Sarapis,[1] a deity equally reverenced by the Greeks and the Egyptians. Sarapis, as the former called him, or Asar-Hapi, as he was known to the latter, was a name compounded from Osiris and Apis. So early as the beginning of the New Empire these two deities—Apis, the sacred bull of Mendes, and Osiris, the 'Bull of the West'—had been to some extent identified, and finally the Apis had been given the attributes of a god of the underworld. To the Greeks, it would appear, Sarapis was the form taken by the *deceased* Apis bull. Tradition assigns the identification of Sarapis with Pluto to the reign of Ptolemy Soter. Plutarch gives the following version of the legend.

[1] Or Serapis.

The Legend of Sarapis

"Ptolemy, surnamed the Saviour, had a dream wherein a certain colossean statue, such as he had never seen before, appeared unto him, commanding him to remove it as soon as possible from the place where it then stood to Alexandria. Upon this the king was in great perplexity, as he knew neither to whom the statue belonged nor where to look for it. Upon his relating the vision to his friends, a certain person named Sosibius, who had been a great traveller, declared that he had seen just such a statue as the king described at Sinope. Soteles and Dionysius were hereupon immediately dispatched in order to bring it away with them, which they at length accomplished, though not without much difficulty and the manifest interposition of providence. Timotheus the Interpreter and Manetho, as soon as the statue was shown to them, from the Cerberus and Dragon that accompanied it concluded that it was designed to represent Pluto, and persuaded the king that it was in reality none other than the Egyptian *Sarapis*; for it must be observed that the statue had not this name before it was brought to Alexandria, it being given to it afterward by the Egyptians, as the equivalent, in their opinion, to its old one of Pluto."

Another version of the tale asserts that the people of Sinope would not consent to part with the statue of their god, whereupon the statue of its own accord set sail for Alexandria, which it reached at the end of three days. But whatever the means by which Ptolemy contrived to bring the statue to Egypt, there is no doubt that his provision of a god which could be worshipped both by Greeks and Egyptians, without violation of the principles of either, was a diplomatic move which was justified in its results. In the temples

Sarapis was figured as a mummy with a high crown and plaited beard ; or, as Asar-Hapi, he was represented as a bull, with the solar disk and uræus between his horns. In the small figures which were worshipped privately, however, he is shown in human shape, bearded and curly-haired after the Greek fashion.

If Sarapis was one of the most important of Egyptian deities of this period, Horus the Child (the Greek Harpocrates) was one of the best-loved. In the early centuries of the Christian era he is shown as a child, sometimes seated in a lotus-blossom, sometimes in a ship, or again enthroned as a follower of the sun-god ; frequently he carries a cornucopia or a jar. It is as a child that he was loved and worshipped by the people, with whom he seems to have been a universal favourite. Another popular deity was Isis, some of whose forms were decidedly Grecian. She was the goddess of Alexandria and patron of sea-faring, the Aphrodite of the Greeks and the Isis of the Egyptians, and at times she is confused with Hathor. She and Osiris are also figured as serpents, though the god of the dead is more often represented in his Sarapis form, ruling in the underworld and accompanied by Cerberus. Another deity who became popular during the Hellenic period, though formerly occupying a very obscure position in the Pantheon, was the god Bes, figured as an armed warrior, still, however, retaining his grotesque character. A figure borrowed, doubtless, from Christianity represents Isis and Horus in a posture strongly reminiscent of the Madonna and Child.

An Architectural Renaissance

The cult of the Old Kingdom persisted through the early, and perhaps even into the later, Hellenic period. Those temples raised in the time of the Ptolemies exhibit strong resemblances to those of the Old Kingdom. Dendereh, for example, was built to a design of the time of Kheops, and Imhotep, the hero-god, was the architect of Edfû. The walls of these Ptolemaic temples were covered with inscriptions dealing with the rites and customs used therein. Temple ceremonials and festivals, such as that of Horus of Edfû, were held as in ancient times. The ancient written language was studied by the priests, who thus had at their command a tongue unknown to the laity. A reversion to ancient things was evident in every phase of the Egyptian religion, and the Greeks, far from dispelling the dust of long-past centuries, entered partly into the spirit of the time, gave their protection to the old customs and cults, and themselves worshipped at the shrines of sacred cats, cows, and crocodiles. Truly a strange position for the fathers of classicism!

During the early centuries of the Christian era foreign religions began to penetrate the land of the Pharaohs and to mingle with the Græco-Egyptian compound in a manner most perplexing to the student of the period. The predominant alien faith, and the one which finally triumphed, was Christianity. Osiris, the Greek gods, and the archangel Sabaoth are mentioned in the same breath. In the magical texts especially this confusion is noticeable, for they frequently contain Christian, Jewish, Greek, and Egyptian allusions. Doubtless the magicians reasoned that if the deities of one faith failed them those of another might prove more successful, and so, to make assurance doubly sure, they included all the gods they knew in their formulæ.

Change in the Conception of the Underworld

Meanwhile a change took place in the popular conception of the underworld. It was still the Duat, governed by Osiris or Sarapis; but now it tended to be a place of punishment for the wicked, where the future of the deceased was influenced less by his tomb-furnishings and inscriptions than by the conduct of his life while on earth. Nevertheless, the burial rites continued to be elaborate and costly. Mummification was extensively practised even among Christians, and amulets were buried in their coffins. In the fourth and fifth centuries there was still a considerable proportion of pagans in the country: in Alexandria Sarapis was the principal deity; in Memphis Imhotep was worshipped under the name of Asklepios; Zeus, Apollo, and Rhea were favourite divinities, while at Abydos the oracle of Bes was worshipped.

Twilight of the Gods

At length, however, Christian fanaticism blotted out the ancient religion of the Pharaohs, as well as many of its priests and adherents. The temple of Sarapis was stormed amid scenes of riot and turbulence, and the last refuge of the Egyptian faith was gone. Henceforth the names and myths of the ancient deities survived only in the spells and formulæ of the magicians, while their dreary ghosts haunted the ruined temples wherein they were nevermore to reign.

CHAPTER IX: EGYPTIAN ART

THE output of the great Egyptian masters of the graphic arts has virtually no counterpart, and, bold as this statement may appear at first sight, it will be found to withstand tolerably close scrutiny. Looking at some of the incomparable embroideries of bygone Persia, studying the divine porcelain of mediæval China, or turning over woodcuts by the great Japanese artists of the Ukiyoé school—men like Hokusai and Utamaro, Hiroshige, Yeizan and Toyokuni—we no doubt feel ourselves in touch with something different from European art, yet only partly different. Strange as these Eastern objects are, we find in them a certain familiarity, we find them expressive of emotions and sentiments not altogether unknown to us; and herein Egyptian things are different, for these seem to us entirely novel, they suggest some weird, enchanted world untrodden by the foot of man, perhaps a supernatural world. Nor is their strangeness, their almost sinister unfamiliarity so very hard to explain, it being due not only to the curious conventions which the Egyptian masters obeyed so implicitly century after century, but to the fact that the arts were indigenous to ancient Egypt. Japan derived her painting from China about the fourteenth century A.D.; Chinese work, in turn, frequently discloses affinities with that of ancient Greece; and the great Italian masters of the Renaissance owed much to the Græco-Roman school; while the old Spanish artists, again, were under obligations to the Moors and Arabs, and in England and in Scotland, in Germany and in France, painting did not grow up like a flower, but was rather an exotic imported chiefly from the Low Countries. In short, throughout bygone times, no less essentially than in modern periods, the arts in nearly every country owed something to those of other countries, a great interchange going forward perpetually; but the mighty works of Egypt were mostly wrought long before the advent of this interchange, and painting and sculpture, architecture and other domestic arts, would seem to have arisen of their own accord in the land of Isis, there to thrive and develop throughout æons of years a pure African product, uninfluenced in any way by the handiwork of other races.

It is always difficult to speak of the origin of anything, for even the oldest thing has its ancestry. And while it is possible to treat with some definiteness of the first great period of Egyptian art, the Thinite, which commenced about 5000 B.C., we have to remember that the output of this period was no exception to the rule aforesaid, but had its ancestry, this consisting in the work of the shadowy pre-dynastic time. Even at that far-off era crude images of living animals were made in Egypt, mud, of course, being the material commonly used; while a great deal of pottery, some of it incised with quaint patterns, was also produced; and if many of these vases and the like are no better than those of most primitive artists, others, again, manifest a distinct feeling for shapeliness and proportion. Nor did the Egyptians of this period eschew that immemorial practice, the decoration of themselves; for among the oldest relics of the country's art are numerous personal ornaments, some made of bone or of shell, some of stone or ivory, and some even of precious metals. Moreover, rude forms of architecture were early essayed, this in its turn begetting pristine efforts at mural embellishment.

In pre-dynastic Egypt the dead were usually interred in shallow graves with no embellishment, only one painted tomb of that early period being known. When, however, we pass to the study of the period which succeeded, it is the art of sepulchral decoration which first claims attention. Not even in Roman Catholic countries, not even in China, has the welfare of the dead ever been thought of so lovingly, so constantly and zealously, as in ancient Egypt. A very solid affair was the Egyptian tomb of this era, built commonly of limestone or sandstone, but occasionally of granite, or of breccia from the Arabian mountains ; and in the case of a notable person the sides of his tomb were duly carved with pictures of his deeds while on earth, and more especially with pictures illustrating his prospective passage through the underworld. Generally, too, a statue glorified the outside of his tomb, this statue being wrought of alabaster, schist or serpentine, diorite or limestone, granite or sandstone ; and the sculptor, be it noted, never aimed primarily at decoration, but invariably at a portrait of the defunct. Moreover, he would seem to have pondered very deeply on the question of durability, attaching his work firmly to its *repoussoir*, or, more often, making it a very part thereof ; and to illustrate the Egyptian's predilection in this respect we may mention two works, both in the Cairo Museum, the one showing the Pharaoh Mycerinus seated, the other depicting a group of three people, likewise seated. In both cases the statuary have been hewn out of the great pieces of rock supporting them, and could not possibly be removed therefrom save by elaborate cutting with mallet and chisel.

A wealth of other statues belonging to the early dynastic era are still extant, many of them possessing rare artistic value. And if the same can hardly be said with reference to existing specimens of the relief-cutting of this period, when turning from these to early domestic art we are struck repeatedly by its infinite loveliness. Prominent among such things as merit this praise are numerous bracelets, while the Cairo Museum contains two fine carved ivory feet of a stool which express great vigour of artistic conception, and the same collection includes sundry tiny figures of monkeys, lions, and dogs, all of them manifestly the work of a master who had a keen sense for the curious beauty which lurks in the grotesque.

To an early period also, that of the Pyramid Kings, should be assigned those amazing monuments of the industry and ingenuity of bygone Egypt, the Pyramids and the Sphinx—works which have evoked nearly as much eloquence, alike in prose and verse, as the *Monna Lisa* of Leonardo da Vinci and the Elgin Marbles of Phidias. Usually supposed to have been wrought early in the era in question, their inception is, however, wrapped in mystery; but whatever the true solution of that enigma, this Memphite period was certainly one which witnessed considerable developments in Egyptian art. True, there is little opportunity of studying the architecture of the time, such relics as exist consisting in little more than heaps of stone or masses of sun-dried brick; yet in the field of sculpture, on the contrary, we are enabled to note and scrutinize progress. Heretofore sepulchral statues had been virtually a preserve of the rich and great, but now all sorts and conditions of tombs—or, at least, the tombs of many comparatively poor people—were garnished in this way; and as the defunct was often portrayed in an attitude indicating his career on earth, this statuary offers a valuable sidelight on Memphite Egyptian life. Thus we find, here a man engaged in brewing, there another seated at secretarial work, his posture practically that of the modern tailor; while we

Hauling Blocks of Stone for the Pyramids (page 314)
Evelyn Paul

A Head-rest
British Museum

(page 318)

observe also that care for the welfare of a deceased magnate of any kind was being manifested on a more intricate scale than hitherto. That is to say, suppose his friends and relations should be anxious that he should be well fed in the hereafter, they would embellish his resting-place with statuary delineating a kitchen in being ; while sometimes, with an analogous end in view, they would represent in the tomb-chapel a group of musicians, each depicted with his instrument in his hands.[1] And in all these works, as also in divers others of a different nature, we notice a more fluent handling than that characterizing the generality of those of pre-dynastic days, as witness what is possibly the very crown of the Pyramid age (Fourth Dynasty) sculpture, the full-length at Cairo of the 'Sheikh-el-Beled' (whose real name was Ka-aper), a figure wrought in a fashion vigorous and confident as anything from the hand of Rodin or Mestrovic. Furthermore, we mark again and again that artists were now beginning to express their respective individualities, they were showing themselves less prone to conform slavishly to a given *régime* ; and it is significant that one of the Pyramid age sculptors, Ptah-Ankh, far from hiding his identity like all his predecessors, saw fit on one occasion to model a stone relief in which he himself figured as sitting in a boat.

The Materials of Painting

It should be noted at this juncture that these Egyptian bas-reliefs were not usually left in a monochromatic state as is customary in modern Europe ; for the painter, on the contrary, was generally called to the sculptor's aid, while even portrait statues were

[1] Single statues in the Old Kingdom, figures in groups in Middle Kingdom.

frequently coloured also. And apart from work of this order, the craft of painting on sun-dried clay was carried to no mean height of excellence during Pyramid days, as also was that of painting on papyrus, while mummy cases were often decked with multitudinous hues. The colours in many of these old Egyptian works still possess great depth and brilliance, while, indeed, some of them have lasted far better than those in divers Italian frescoes of the Renaissance, and infinitely better than those in numerous pictures by Reynolds and Turner; and thus we naturally pause to ask the questions: What manner of pigments were commonly used in Egypt? and what, exactly, was the *modus operandi* of the country's painters? Well, an Egyptian artist usually kept his paints in the condition of powder, and on starting work he liquefied them with a mixture of water and gum tragacanth; while he next proceeded to apply this solution with a reed pen, or with brushes made of soft hair, few men being in the habit of using more than two brushes, a thick one and a thin. Then as to the colours themselves, the gold we sometimes see is, of course, easily accounted for; while black, it would seem, was obtained by burning the bones of animals, and white was made of gypsum mixed with honey or albumen. Red and yellow, again, were procured by more familiar processes, the former being derived from sulphuret of mercury, the latter simply from clay; while blue, a comparatively rare shade in natural objects other than the sea and sky, and therefore hard to obtain, was evolved from lapis-lazuli. The picture duly finished, some painters would cover it with a coat of transparent varnish, made from the gum of the acacia; but the men who did this were really few in number, and the colours in their works have not lasted well—not nearly so well as those in paintings by masters who left varnish severely alone.

Leaving these technical details and returning to the actual history of the arts in Egypt, we must speak now of the Middle Kingdom, which commenced with the Ninth Dynasty (*c.* 2445) and lasted to the Seventeenth Dynasty. During this time the craft of building developed apace, among the results being the obelisk of Heliopolis. And if these are works reflecting thaumaturgic mechanical ingenuity rather than great artistic taste, the latter is certainly manifest in two other vast structures of early Theban days, the temple of Kom-es-Sagha and the portico of Sa Renput I. Much fine domestic art was also made at this time, as witness the diadem and crown of Khnemit, both of which are now at Cairo. A more natural style became discernible, both as regards bas-reliefs and paintings. Indeed, many sketches and paintings of this period, especially those which delineate scenes of sport, war, and athletics, possess a spirit and dash which show that the race of Egyptian artists was becoming more skilled in the free use of the brush. One of the most remarkable paintings of this period is a picture at Beni Hassan, the subject of which is a series of wrestling bouts.

New Empire Art

In the period of the New Empire (Eighteenth to Thirty-first Dynasties) the student of Egyptian art is confronted with a veritable embarrassment of riches, chiefly architectural. It was this period which witnessed the completion of such imposing structures as the hypostyle hall at Karnak, the temple of Rameses III at Medinet-habû, and the great assemblage of ecclesiastical edifices at Dêr-el-Bahari. The finest and most imposing buildings at Luxor likewise belong to this era, as do the rock-cut temples at Bêt-el-Wálî and Abu-Simbel. The sculptors of the period also achieved lasting triumphs, especially in the two colossal figures of Memnon at Thebes, and the famous Avenue of Sphinxes at Karnak. The statue of Thothmes III, Amenophis, the son of Hapu, and Queen Tyi are also of great æsthetic interest. Turning to bas-relief, the likenesses of Seti I (Abydos), Septah Meneptah, and Queen Aahmes (a plaster cast in the temple at Dêr-el-Bahari) claim our attention, the last-named being among the loveliest of all Egyptian works of the kind. The delicacy and refinement of this masterpiece surpasses almost any relief executed in Egypt before it. In fact, a greater refinement begins to be apparent in the Egyptian art work of this period, even the domestic arts showing greater attention to delicacy. Lines of great subtlety appear chased on table utensils, while equal skill is apparent in numerous amulets and much of the jewellery of the period. Little boxes, handles of mirrors and spoons designed to hold cosmetics are in many cases the result of craftsmanship of a very high order. One of the spoons depicts a woman swimming behind a swan, and inevitably recalls the myth of Leda. Finally, much beautiful furniture was made during this period, perhaps the best existing specimen being a chair in the Cairo Museum, its arms adroitly carved in the form of stealthy-looking panthers.

During this period the use of wood as a medium for artistic representation seems to have been on the increase. Contemporaneously the craft of casting in metal was improved and then virtually perfected, a consummation which had an important influence upon sculpture. This, too, was the epoch at which the Egyptian artists in colour revolted against the conventionality which had in ancient times beset their craft. Until this time they had not attempted to colour realistically. Certain objects were tinted according to tradition as taught in their schools. Thus the flesh of a man was painted a reddish brown, that of a woman yellow, that of a priest blue, and so forth. And it was not until the period of the New Empire that artists began to revolt seriously against this system. One unknown master went so far as to indulge in rosy flesh-tints, and it is natural to inquire whether it was foreign influence which aroused this iconoclastic act. Be that as it may, there can be no doubt that Egyptian artists began to learn from those of other lands—the Assyrians, for instance—and this circumstance renders the study of Egyptian art during this period somewhat difficult and complex.

The last period of Egyptian art, the Saïte, commenced about 721 B.C. During this epoch the incursions of the Persians, Greeks, and finally of the Romans are seen acting materially on the country's productions, often to their detriment, for instead of working naturally, instead of employing their own national style, the Egyptian artists of the Saïte period were prone to imitate, uttering themselves haltingly in fashions borrowed from other races.

But it is a mistake to maintain, as is occasionally done, that this waning of lofty traditions began with the very advent of the Saïte age. It is a mistake to contend that no vital art was executed by the Egyptians thenceforward. Not till the eve of the advent of Christ did Egyptian jewellery and craftsmanship in general begin to decline; while as to architecture, Herodotus speaks in the most eulogistic terms of the great buildings at Saïs. Unfortunately most of these are demolished, and we have no chance of studying them at first hand. The Pharaohs of the Saïtic period lost the vast command of labour of their Theban and

Memphite predecessors; nevertheless the dawn of the last period in Egyptian art saw the completion of many noble edifices. The pronaos of Komombos, the temple of Isis at Philæ, and the kiosk of Nectanebu at the same place, deserve citation, as also do the Mammisi and temple of Horus at Edfû. Yet everywhere are to be seen structures of this period influenced by Greek or Roman ideas, and others which are clearly the work of Egyptian masons acting under the instructions of alien masters.

The painting of this period embraces numerous works equal to any product of earlier times—for example, the vignette of the Judgment before Osiris contained in the papyrus of Queen Mat-ka-ré. But we also observe Egyptian artists forsaking their time-honoured colour-schemes and using such tints as green and mauve, probably copied from Hellenic decorations. In the bas-reliefs of the time, moreover, we find much which is sadly mechanical—so mechanical that we are persuaded that it was done to order from drawing supplied by foreigners. Nor is the history of Saïte statuary greatly different from that of those arts mentioned above, for while at first a wealth of splendid things were achieved—notably a study of Osiris recumbent and a portrait of Petubastis—the mechanical element crept into this domain as it had done into the others. Sculptors became mere artisans, slaving at the reproduction of prescribed patterns. Some actually kept in stock ready-made statues of the human body, the heads to be added as clients presented themselves.

Egyptian Art Influences

Still, the expression of a nation's soul does not entirely vanish, and if Egyptian artists were ultimately influenced by the conquering Romans, the Italian

Temple of Isis at Philæ

Photo Bonfils

(page 320)

Temple of Horus at Edfû

(page 320)

craftsmen came no less surely under the sway of the great Egyptian schools, and, as noted at the outset of this chapter, the Romans inspired much of the work of the Italian masters of the Renaissance, whose output was long regarded as the flower of European art. We find Egyptian influences strong in Spain, for the art of the Nile had cast its potent spell over the Arabs, who at a later date became almost the fathers of the domestic arts in the Iberian peninsula; and so it is with no surprise that, when looking at old Spanish ornaments, we frequently find them bearing a close resemblance to analogous articles made for the belles of Memphis and of Thebes. Nor was France without some more direct Egyptian influence than that which reached her indirectly through Italy. The characteristic art of the French Empire was directly descended from Egyptian art. Under Louis XIV French painting and craftsmanship were ornate and pompous in the extreme, but in the following reign luxury in all departments of life was at a discount. A new simplicity was demanded, and while craftsmen were casting about for patterns suited to this taste, the Comte de Caylus published his monumental work on the antiquities of Greece, Rome, and Egypt, its pages embellished throughout with illustrations from the author's own hand.[1] It speedily kindled inspiration in the minds of numerous artists, and we may place to its credit some of the most tasteful and beautiful furniture ever designed. The Egyptian expedition of Napoleon, too, led to the importation of Egyptian articles, and thenceforth until the eve of Waterloo scarcely a table, chair, or mirror of French manufacture with any claims to artistry but disclosed the influence of the Egyptian schools. Not only were actual shapes

[1] *Recueil d'antiquités égyptiennes, étrusques, grecques, romaines et gauloises.* Six vols. Paris, 1752–1755.

borrowed, but it was quite common to decorate furniture with pseudo-Egyptian statuettes and reliefs, or with brass plaques chased in imitation of parts of Egyptian pictures.

The pseudo-Egyptian craftsmanship of the Empire—so apt an expression of the temper of French thought at that time—may be studied well at Fontainebleau or at Marlborough House in London, while of course it is in evidence in the backgrounds of many Empire pictures, in particular those of Louis David. Indeed, that master himself, the most influential French painter of his day, owed something to the Egyptian school, while a similar debt is suggested by sundry works of the sculptors Chinard and Houdon ; and a study of Empire buildings reveals that the architects of the period, mainly devoted though they were to ancient Greece and Rome, were not uninfluenced by the art of the land of the Pharaohs. Nor was this true only of the French architects, for that great Scottish artist in stone, Robert Adam, who died the year the French Republic was established, would seem to have shared the attraction. He often introduced Egyptian objects into his decorative schemes, while the large, imposing simplicity he frequently attained is rich in suggestion of notable Egyptian edifices. The same massive 'Egyptian' simplicity is to be seen in the statuary of the mighty Serb, Ivan Mestrovic, as also in that of the Swede, David Edström. Indeed, it would be wearisome to enumerate all the artists of different nationalities who have clearly been indebted to the genius of Egypt, but we must not conclude without some reference to the influence of the school on the Post-Impressionist painters.

The Post-Impressionists were not, as is commonly said, direct descendants of the Impressionist group, but rather seceders therefrom. Their watchword was simplicity, and in pursuance of this ideal they turned lovingly to study primitive art, especially that of the Egyptians, finding therein that simple element which they desired.

Artistic Remains

Returning to our main subject, we may ask, What is the actual æsthetic value of Egyptian art to our own generation?

Imagine a museum, some thousands of years hence, ostensibly representing the art of France from the beginning of the fifteenth century to the end of the nineteenth; and suppose this crammed with the off-scourings of the Salon school and the autotypes and *bric-à-brac* of the Rue de Rivoli, with only here and there a Clouet, a Boucher, or a Lancret, only here and there a Clodion, a Dalou, or a Rodin. Would not visitors to such a collection be certain to conclude that the French were anything but artistic? Conditions such as those indicated above obtain in nearly every Egyptian collection of the present day. The point of view of those in charge of museums and exhibits seems to be that anything of Egyptian origin should be treasured, however lacking it may be in artistic merit, and small wonder if the average visitor of taste has not the patience to search through such heterogeneous collections in which the few vital articles are buried. The great mass of Egyptian remains are far inferior to those of Greek origin, wrought in the time of Phidias and Apelles; the master works of Egypt, on the other hand, are equal to the artistic products of any age, and it is with these master works, and only with these, that we must concern ourselves here.

Egyptian Colour-harmonies

The Egyptian painter seldom or never sought to blend his different shades into each other, he seldom or never dealt in gradations ; instead he painted in large patches, each patch clearly demarked from its neighbour. But with this system he achieved some of the grandest colour-harmonies, as witness the papyrus of Ani,[1] wherein the prominent notes are brown and yellow, green, white and black. Even more beautiful is the papyrus of Queen Mat-ka-ré, slightly higher in pitch than the last-named, and dominated by an exquisite reddish yellow ; while, turning to polychromatic sculpture, surely there was never a lovelier piece of colouring than the statue of Princess Neferet, with its rich greens and reds, its browns and whites. Scarcely inferior to this is the coffin of Khnumu-Hotep, painted with gold, black, and brown, and with stripes of peacock-blue decorated with patterns in gold.

If the Egyptian was a divine colourist, he was still more surely a master of composition. The artist striving after harmony in design may arrange a host of figures upon a canvas, or he may take for his purpose only a very few objects. The former, the usual practice of the European school, is infinitely the easier of the two ; but the Egyptian commonly chose the latter, and on his piece of papyrus or on his plaque of stone he placed his few objects so happily and in such perfect æsthetic relationship to each other that the whole space used appears to be decorated. His draughtsmanship, besides, is usually of high excellence ; here, too, he faces a difficulty, giving a bold impression rather than a detailed drawing, yet so expressive are his lines that the work possesses abundantly the illusion of life.

[1] See Frontispiece and illustration facing p. 120 [reproduced in black and white in the present edition].

The Great Simplicity of Egyptian Art

We have spoken of sundry Egyptian works as subtle, delicate, and refined; but these are not characteristic examples, they are not those which chiefly command homage. Subtlety, an exquisite quality, one of the ultimate qualities, is nevertheless closely allied to weakness, and the sustained effort to express it is apt to prove injurious to the artist. Whistler, for one, striving after the delicate, the refined and subtle, too often approximated effeminacy; and some of the greater Japanese painters, preoccupied with dreamy half-tints and febrile lines, came dangerously near producing the merely pretty. In the characteristic work of the Egyptians, however, we never detect a hint of this failing; for theirs is before all else a powerful, bold, simple art, often reflecting a grand, ruthless brutality like that in the great English dramatists. We have seen that it was their simplicity which engaged the Frenchmen of the Empire, eager to make something of a strenuous temper; we have seen that it was this element, too, which commanded homage from the Post-Impressionists, so intensely serious and aspirational a group. And may we not add that this simplicity is the loftiest factor discernible in Egyptian art? May we not add that the Egyptians achieved this merit with a triumph almost unrivalled by other races? And may we not say, finally, that simplicity is the noblest of all artistic qualities? The great poems, those which live from generation unto generation, are most assuredly those in which the subject is expressed with divine simplicity, the poet attaining the maximum of expression with the minimum of means, which is exactly what the great painters and sculptors of Egypt compassed.

But simplicity, like subtlety, has its concomitant danger, for what is very simple is apt to be deficient in mystery, so essential an item in a vital work of art. Yet here, again, we find the Egyptian victorious; he has adroitly evaded the peril of baldness. The Egyptian sculptor, producing a portrait, always adumbrates the character of his sitter, itself a mysterious quality, and there is in a host of Egyptian works of art a curious sense of infinity, a suggestion of the eternal riddle of the universe. They are the most mysterious works ever wrought by man, some seeming verily eloquent of silence; we feel in their presence a strange mood of awe, a feeling which has been thus happily expressed:

> Tread lightly, O my dancing feet,
>   Lest your untimely murmurs stir
> Dust of forgotten men who find death sweet,
>   At rest within their sepulchre.

These lines, written by Lady Margaret Sackville while tarrying at Assouan, crystallize the reverential mood which often possesses us in the presence of Egyptian art; and yet, are these entombed men of whom the writer sings really forgotten?

> Past ruined Ilion Helen lives,

eternal life vouchsafed to her by the song of Homer; surely bygone Egyptians have, in like fashion, won immortality through the genius of their mighty artists.

GLOSSARY AND INDEX

THE PRONUNCIATION OF EGYPTIAN

The correct pronunciation of Old, Middle, and Late Egyptian can only be gleaned by analogy from that of Coptic, which represents the popular language of Egypt from the third to the ninth century A.D. But this tongue was strongly reinforced by Greek loan-words, and as it was rendered in writing by the Greek alphabet it is difficult to say how much of the native linguistic element it really represents. But its orthography gives a clear idea of its pronunciation, and it is the mainstay of Egyptian philologists in restoring the word-forms of the ancient language, or at least Late Egyptian, between which and the Middle and Old dialects there is a wide linguistic gap. Indeed, the pronunciation of these archaic forms is probably for ever lost to modern scholarship. Speaking generally, Egyptian words and names are usually pronounced by scholars as they are spelt.

GLOSSARY AND INDEX

A

AAH'MES, QUEEN. Wife of King of Egypt, 246; visited by Amen-Ra, 247; raised above the earth by Neith and Selk 247; the mother of Queen Hatshepsut, 248; likeness, of, 318
AAH-TE-HU'TI, or TE-HU'TI. Equivalent, Thoth, 106, 107
AA-RU. Underworld known as, 64
AAT-AB. Shrine of Heru-Behudeti at, 86
AB'TU. A pilot fish to Ra's barque, 131
ABU. Alternative, Elephantine, 152
ABU RO'ASH. Second pyramid built at, 25
AB-Y'DOS. Five priests comprised the staff at, 54; centre of worship of Osiris, 63; oracle of Bes at, 281, 310; likeness of Seti I at, 318
AB-YSS-IN'IA, 259
AB-YSS-IN'IANS, 34
ADAM, ROBERT, 322
AD-O'NIS. Similarity of myth to that of Osiris, 70; reference to, 160
Æ-GE'AN. Merchants of the, evolved their alphabet from Egyptian hieratic, 185
Æ'LI-AN, 284, 291
ÆSOP'S FABLES, 195
AF'A. Beings in heaven; characteristics of, unknown, 126
AF'RA. Variant of Ra-Osiris, 78; boat of, meets boats of Osiris in underworld, 117; as Afra, Osiris continues his journey through the Duat, 118; passes through body of monstrous serpent, and emerges as Khepera, 118
AFRICA-N. Origin of older religion of Egypt certainly, 3; Osiris, god of North-east, 64; origin, Osiris of, 64; origin, Anqet of, 156
AFRICA-N INFLUENCE. Semitic and, on Egyptian religious ideas, 280–282; deities, Bes the most important of, 281
AH. The moon-god; Ashtoreth and, 278
AH-U'RA. Wife of Neper-ka-Ptah, 268; her prophecy regarding Setne, 268; requests Setne not to remove her husband's book, 266
AÏ. The palace of, 42; hymn to Aten found in tomb of, 161
AI'NU OF JAPAN. God of the, 146
AK'ER. The lion-god; guarded the gate of the dawn, 291
AK'ER-BLAD. One who helped decipher Rosetta Stone, 187
AK'ER-TET. Celebration of mysteries of, 57
AK'HEN-AT-EN. *See* Amen-hetep IV. 1. King; Amen-hetep changes his name to, 158; religion of, 158; introduced cult of Aten into Egypt, 159; his reign, 160; reference to, 161. 2. Palace of, 42; new capital built by Amen-hetep, 158; social life in, 159
AL-AS'IA. Ounamounou drives into the country of, 236; Hatibi, the Princess of, 236
AL'CHE-MY, 269
ALEXANDER THE GREAT, 142
ALEXANDRIA. Wine made in Mareotis, 46; writings of Greeks of, 108; statue of Sarapis at, 307; Sarapis, principal deity in, 310
ALEXANDRINE-CONQUEST. The religion of Egypt and, 304
AL KHE-MEI'A, 269
AM-A'IT. The attendant of the Lord of Amenti, 209, 210
AM-AS'IS. An Egyptian monarch who died 526 B.C., 196, 197; Saïte King, 302; raised sarcophagi to the sacred bull, 302; Naukratis founded in time of, 303

GLOSSARY AND INDEX

GLOSSARY AND INDEX

E

F

GLOSSARY AND INDEX

I

J

GLOSSARY AND INDEX

GLOSSARY AND INDEX

M

MAA. God of sight, 181
MAĀ KHER'U (' Right speaking '). Etymological meaning, 261
MAĀT. Signifies law, &c., 53; goddess of justice, identified with Isis, 82; closely resembles Thoth; one of the original goddesses; symbolized by ostrich feather, 108; appellations, 109; path of Ra across the sky planned by, 131
MAC'BETH. Reference to, 143
MACH-I-A-VEL'LI. Reference to, 187
MAF'TET. Reference to the goddess, 16
MAGIC-AL. Chapter on, in tale of the Magicians, 132, 206; force in Egypt, 261; formulæ (' right speaking ') in Egypt, 261; *versus* Magic; tale of, 215–219; cane, King Thothmes', 249, 250; Egypt the mother of 252; Egyptian, is assumed to be a degraded form of religion, 252; Professor Maspero's statement *re*, 252; Dr. Budge's statement *re*, 252; the antiquity of Egyptian, 254, 255; Frazer, Marrett, Hubert and Mauss, on origin of, 253, 256; the savage of the Egyptian Stone Age and, 254; difference between other systems and Egyptian, 256; statement of Professor Maspero *re*, 257; names of power in connexion with Egyptian, 258; force, in Egypt, 261; its recognized representatives, 261; formulæ, *Book of the Dead* and, 262; conspiracy, of Hui, 262, 263; words of power, inscribed on amulets, 263; the gibberish of, 265; Books—the Double House of Life, or Library of, 265; medical, 268; powers, belief *re*, in Egypt, 270; mummy, 273, 274; Amenophis author of a book on, 303
MAGICIAN-S. Tale of the, 132, 152; none in Memphis equal to Se-Osiris, 211; Pharaoh Ousimares' chief, 215; war of enchantments between Horus and Pharaoh's chief, 217–219; coercion of the gods by, 256
MAH-Î-TOU'AS-KHÎT. Wife of Setne; prays to Imhetep for a son, 207, 212; her prayer is answered, 208
MALAY-S. Depict the soul in bird-shape, 32; magical force in Egypt and the *kramat* of the, 261
MALAYSIA. Belief occurring in, 6
MA'NA. Of the Melanesians, 261
MAN-AKH'PHRÊ - SI - AM'ON. *See* Pharaoh Manakhphrê-Siamon
MAN-E'THO. Divided Egyptian history into dynasties, 35; chronology of, 35; cult of Apis traced by, to Kaiekhos, 284; the *Sarapis* statue and, 307
MANHOOD. Superstition regarding new name given at initiation rites conferring, 259
MAN'U. The mountain of sunset, 125
MAN'ZET. The barque, 131; model of the, in temple at Heliopolis, 134
MAR'DUK. Slew Assyrian monster Tiamat, 132
MAR-E-O'TIS. District of, 46
MA-RI-ETTE. Reference to, 38, 169, 287, 288
MARETT. The works of, and the origin of magic, 253
MARS. A war-god, 19; reference to, 102; identified with Horus, 181
MAS-A'I. Reference to, 34
MAS-PE'RO, SIR GASTON. Reference to companies of gods, 16; contributions to Egyptian archæology, 38; reference to, 41, 42, 64, 112, 113, 257; translated "True History of Setne and his Son, Se-Osiris," 206; his statement *re* Egyptian magic, 252
MĀ'TER. Governor of King Tcheser, 154, 155
MAT-KA-RÉ, QUEEN. Papyrus of, 320

O

GLOSSARY AND INDEX

crocodile, a serpent, and a dog, 231
PRO-CON-NES'US. Aristeas of, 6
PROPHECIES. The Apis Oracle, and, 286
PRUSSIA. Reference to expedition sent by, into Egypt, Nubia, Syria, and Palestine, 38
PSAM-MET'ICH-US I. Founded town of Naucratis, 46; story of the days of, 197
PTAH. A form of the sun-god, 21; temple of, 53; *Book of the Dead*, and, 119; greatest of the gods at Memphis; derivation of name, uncertain, 144; alluded to in Pyramid Texts, 144; a master architect and framer of everything in the universe, 144; partakes of the nature of Thoth, and also of Shu, 145; as Ptah-Seker represents union of creative power with that of chaos or darkness, 145; absorbs attributes of Seker; also connected with Tenen, 146; had variants which took attributes of Min, Amsu, and Khepera; described as, triune god of the resurrection, 146; centre of worship at Memphis, 147; female counterpart, Sekhmet, 147; Seven Wise Ones, and, 147; reference to, 150, 154, 171, 207; Pharaoh Manakhphrê-Siamon swears by, 215; the Apis oracle in temple of, 286; Apis, the bull of the temple of, 302
PTAH-ANKH. One of the Pyramid Age sculptors, 315
PTAH-HOT'EP. Books of proverbs or instructions attributed to, 187
PTAH OF ANKH'TAUI. Temple of, 198
PTAH-SEK'ER. One of the gods alluded to in *Book of the Dead*, 119; represents union of creative power with that of chaos or darkness 145
PTAH-SEK'ER-AS'AR. Equivalent, Ptah-Seker-Osiris, 146
PTAH-SEK'ER-O-SIR'IS. *See* Ptah-Seker-Asar.
PTOL-EM-Æ'US. Demise of King of foretold by oracle of Sebek, 291
PTOL-E-MA'IC. Period; travelling courts instituted in, 47; Saïte Recension employed to the end of the, period, 114; forms small figures of Amen-Ra made in, 141; period; references to, 152, 186, 196
PTOL'EM-IES. Reference to text of the, 151
PTOL'EM-Y II, PHIL-A-DEL'PHUS. Temple of Mendes rebuilt by, 288; Apis and Mnevis provided for, by, 305
PTOLEMY III. Decree of Canopu, belonging to, 186
PTOLEMY SO'TER. Identification of Sarapis with Pluto, assigned by tradition to reign of, 306
PUNT. Queen Hatshepsut designed to reign over, 246
PYRAMID AGE. Equivalent to the Old Kingdom, 22
PYRAMIDION, HOUSE OF THE. Temple built to his god by Amen-hetep, 159
PYRAMID-S. Ritual texts and spells inscribed in the, 183; the Sphinx and the; monuments of bygone Egypt, 314; the *Monna Lisa* of Leonardo da Vinci and the Elgin Marbles of Phidias, evoked by the, 314; age sculptors; Ptah-Ankh, one of the, 315; days; craft of painting on sun-dried clay, during, 316
PYRAMID TEXTS. Allusion to the, 12; mention of deities in the, 15, 19–21; a double group of eighteen gods mentioned in the, 16; inscriptions antedating the, 18; material for study of Egyptian pantheon found in the, 19; origin of, 24; Set alluded to in the, 99; reference to, 63, 110; Ptah alluded to in the, 144; Bast mentioned in, 148; Sebek referred to in the, 289; revival of the, 301
PYTHAGOREANS. Typho and the, 102

GLOSSARY AND INDEX

S

GLOSSARY AND INDEX

T

GLOSSARY AND INDEX

A CATALOG OF SELECTED

DOVER BOOKS

IN ALL FIELDS OF INTEREST

A CATALOG OF SELECTED DOVER BOOKS IN ALL FIELDS OF INTEREST

CONCERNING THE SPIRITUAL IN ART, Wassily Kandinsky. Pioneering work by father of abstract art. Thoughts on color theory, nature of art. Analysis of earlier masters. 12 illustrations. 80pp. of text. 5⅜ x 8½. 23411-8

ANIMALS: 1,419 Copyright-Free Illustrations of Mammals, Birds, Fish, Insects, etc., Jim Harter (ed.). Clear wood engravings present, in extremely lifelike poses, over 1,000 species of animals. One of the most extensive pictorial sourcebooks of its kind. Captions. Index. 284pp. 9 x 12. 23766-4

CELTIC ART: The Methods of Construction, George Bain. Simple geometric techniques for making Celtic interlacements, spirals, Kells-type initials, animals, humans, etc. Over 500 illustrations. 160pp. 9 x 12. (Available in U.S. only.) 22923-8

AN ATLAS OF ANATOMY FOR ARTISTS, Fritz Schider. Most thorough reference work on art anatomy in the world. Hundreds of illustrations, including selections from works by Vesalius, Leonardo, Goya, Ingres, Michelangelo, others. 593 illustrations. 192pp. 7⅛ x 10¼. 20241-0

CELTIC HAND STROKE-BY-STROKE (Irish Half-Uncial from "The Book of Kells"): An Arthur Baker Calligraphy Manual, Arthur Baker. Complete guide to creating each letter of the alphabet in distinctive Celtic manner. Covers hand position, strokes, pens, inks, paper, more. Illustrated. 48pp. 8¼ x 11. 24336-2

EASY ORIGAMI, John Montroll. Charming collection of 32 projects (hat, cup, pelican, piano, swan, many more) specially designed for the novice origami hobbyist. Clearly illustrated easy-to-follow instructions insure that even beginning papercrafters will achieve successful results. 48pp. 8¼ x 11. 27298-2

THE COMPLETE BOOK OF BIRDHOUSE CONSTRUCTION FOR WOODWORKERS, Scott D. Campbell. Detailed instructions, illustrations, tables. Also data on bird habitat and instinct patterns. Bibliography. 3 tables. 63 illustrations in 15 figures. 48pp. 5¼ x 8½. 24407-5

BLOOMINGDALE'S ILLUSTRATED 1886 CATALOG: Fashions, Dry Goods and Housewares, Bloomingdale Brothers. Famed merchants' extremely rare catalog depicting about 1,700 products: clothing, housewares, firearms, dry goods, jewelry, more. Invaluable for dating, identifying vintage items. Also, copyright-free graphics for artists, designers. Co-published with Henry Ford Museum & Greenfield Village. 160pp. 8¼ x 11. 25780-0

HISTORIC COSTUME IN PICTURES, Braun & Schneider. Over 1,450 costumed figures in clearly detailed engravings–from dawn of civilization to end of 19th century. Captions. Many folk costumes. 256pp. 8⅝ x 11¾. 23150-X

FRANK LLOYD WRIGHT'S DANA HOUSE, Donald Hoffmann. Pictorial essay of residential masterpiece with over 160 interior and exterior photos, plans, elevations, sketches and studies. 128pp. 9¼ x 10¾. 29120-0

THE MALE AND FEMALE FIGURE IN MOTION: 60 Classic Photographic Sequences, Eadweard Muybridge. 60 true-action photographs of men and women walking, running, climbing, bending, turning, etc., reproduced from rare 19th-century masterpiece. vi + 121pp. 9 x 12. 24745-7

1001 QUESTIONS ANSWERED ABOUT THE SEASHORE, N. J. Berrill and Jacquelyn Berrill. Queries answered about dolphins, sea snails, sponges, starfish, fishes, shore birds, many others. Covers appearance, breeding, growth, feeding, much more. 305pp. 5¼ x 8¼. 23366-9

ATTRACTING BIRDS TO YOUR YARD, William J. Weber. Easy-to-follow guide offers advice on how to attract the greatest diversity of birds: birdhouses, feeders, water and waterers, much more. 96pp. 5³⁄₁₆ x 8¼. 28927-3

MEDICINAL AND OTHER USES OF NORTH AMERICAN PLANTS: A Historical Survey with Special Reference to the Eastern Indian Tribes, Charlotte Erichsen-Brown. Chronological historical citations document 500 years of usage of plants, trees, shrubs native to eastern Canada, northeastern U.S. Also complete identifying information. 343 illustrations. 544pp. 6½ x 9¼. 25951-X

STORYBOOK MAZES, Dave Phillips. 23 stories and mazes on two-page spreads: Wizard of Oz, Treasure Island, Robin Hood, etc. Solutions. 64pp. 8¼ x 11. 23628-5

AMERICAN NEGRO SONGS: 230 Folk Songs and Spirituals, Religious and Secular, John W. Work. This authoritative study traces the African influences of songs sung and played by black Americans at work, in church, and as entertainment. The author discusses the lyric significance of such songs as "Swing Low, Sweet Chariot," "John Henry," and others and offers the words and music for 230 songs. Bibliography. Index of Song Titles. 272pp. 6½ x 9¼. 40271-1

MOVIE-STAR PORTRAITS OF THE FORTIES, John Kobal (ed.). 163 glamor, studio photos of 106 stars of the 1940s: Rita Hayworth, Ava Gardner, Marlon Brando, Clark Gable, many more. 176pp. 8⅜ x 11¼. 23546-7

BENCHLEY LOST AND FOUND, Robert Benchley. Finest humor from early 30s, about pet peeves, child psychologists, post office and others. Mostly unavailable elsewhere. 73 illustrations by Peter Arno and others. 183pp. 5⅜ x 8½. 22410-4

YEKL and THE IMPORTED BRIDEGROOM AND OTHER STORIES OF YIDDISH NEW YORK, Abraham Cahan. Film Hester Street based on *Yekl* (1896). Novel, other stories among first about Jewish immigrants on N.Y.'s East Side. 240pp. 5⅜ x 8½. 22427-9

SELECTED POEMS, Walt Whitman. Generous sampling from *Leaves of Grass*. Twenty-four poems include "I Hear America Singing," "Song of the Open Road," "I Sing the Body Electric," "When Lilacs Last in the Dooryard Bloom'd," "O Captain! My Captain!"–all reprinted from an authoritative edition. Lists of titles and first lines. 128pp. 5³⁄₁₆ x 8¼. 26878-0

THE BEST TALES OF HOFFMANN, E. T. A. Hoffmann. 10 of Hoffmann's most important stories: "Nutcracker and the King of Mice," "The Golden Flowerpot," etc. 458pp. 5⅜ x 8½. 21793-0

FROM FETISH TO GOD IN ANCIENT EGYPT, E. A. Wallis Budge. Rich detailed survey of Egyptian conception of "God" and gods, magic, cult of animals, Osiris, more. Also, superb English translations of hymns and legends. 240 illustrations. 545pp. 5⅜ x 8½. 25803-3

FRENCH STORIES/CONTES FRANÇAIS: A Dual-Language Book, Wallace Fowlie. Ten stories by French masters, Voltaire to Camus: "Micromegas" by Voltaire; "The Atheist's Mass" by Balzac; "Minuet" by de Maupassant; "The Guest" by Camus, six more. Excellent English translations on facing pages. Also French-English vocabulary list, exercises, more. 352pp. 5⅜ x 8½. 26443-2

CHICAGO AT THE TURN OF THE CENTURY IN PHOTOGRAPHS: 122 Historic Views from the Collections of the Chicago Historical Society, Larry A. Viskochil. Rare large-format prints offer detailed views of City Hall, State Street, the Loop, Hull House, Union Station, many other landmarks, circa 1904-1913. Introduction. Captions. Maps. 144pp. 9⅜ x 12¼. 24656-6

OLD BROOKLYN IN EARLY PHOTOGRAPHS, 1865-1929, William Lee Younger. Luna Park, Gravesend race track, construction of Grand Army Plaza, moving of Hotel Brighton, etc. 157 previously unpublished photographs. 165pp. 8⅞ x 11¾. 23587-4

THE MYTHS OF THE NORTH AMERICAN INDIANS, Lewis Spence. Rich anthology of the myths and legends of the Algonquins, Iroquois, Pawnees and Sioux, prefaced by an extensive historical and ethnological commentary. 36 illustrations. 480pp. 5⅜ x 8½. 25967-6

AN ENCYCLOPEDIA OF BATTLES: Accounts of Over 1,560 Battles from 1479 B.C. to the Present, David Eggenberger. Essential details of every major battle in recorded history from the first battle of Megiddo in 1479 B.C. to Grenada in 1984. List of Battle Maps. New Appendix covering the years 1967-1984. Index. 99 illustrations. 544pp. 6½ x 9¼. 24913-1

SAILING ALONE AROUND THE WORLD, Captain Joshua Slocum. First man to sail around the world, alone, in small boat. One of great feats of seamanship told in delightful manner. 67 illustrations. 294pp. 5⅜ x 8½. 20326-3

ANARCHISM AND OTHER ESSAYS, Emma Goldman. Powerful, penetrating, prophetic essays on direct action, role of minorities, prison reform, puritan hypocrisy, violence, etc. 271pp. 5⅜ x 8½. 22484-8

MYTHS OF THE HINDUS AND BUDDHISTS, Ananda K. Coomaraswamy and Sister Nivedita. Great stories of the epics; deeds of Krishna, Shiva, taken from puranas, Vedas, folk tales; etc. 32 illustrations. 400pp. 5⅜ x 8½. 21759-0

THE TRAUMA OF BIRTH, Otto Rank. Rank's controversial thesis that anxiety neurosis is caused by profound psychological trauma which occurs at birth. 256pp. 5⅜ x 8½. 27974-X

A THEOLOGICO-POLITICAL TREATISE, Benedict Spinoza. Also contains unfinished Political Treatise. Great classic on religious liberty, theory of government on common consent. R. Elwes translation. Total of 421pp. 5⅜ x 8½. 20249-6

MY BONDAGE AND MY FREEDOM, Frederick Douglass. Born a slave, Douglass became outspoken force in antislavery movement. The best of Douglass' autobiographies. Graphic description of slave life. 464pp. 5⅜ x 8½. 22457-0

FOLLOWING THE EQUATOR: A Journey Around the World, Mark Twain. Fascinating humorous account of 1897 voyage to Hawaii, Australia, India, New Zealand, etc. Ironic, bemused reports on peoples, customs, climate, flora and fauna, politics, much more. 197 illustrations. 720pp. 5⅜ x 8½. 26113-1

THE PEOPLE CALLED SHAKERS, Edward D. Andrews. Definitive study of Shakers: origins, beliefs, practices, dances, social organization, furniture and crafts, etc. 33 illustrations. 351pp. 5⅜ x 8½. 21081-2

THE MYTHS OF GREECE AND ROME, H. A. Guerber. A classic of mythology, generously illustrated, long prized for its simple, graphic, accurate retelling of the principal myths of Greece and Rome, and for its commentary on their origins and significance. With 64 illustrations by Michelangelo, Raphael, Titian, Rubens, Canova, Bernini and others. 480pp. 5⅜ x 8½. 27584-1

PSYCHOLOGY OF MUSIC, Carl E. Seashore. Classic work discusses music as a medium from psychological viewpoint. Clear treatment of physical acoustics, auditory apparatus, sound perception, development of musical skills, nature of musical feeling, host of other topics. 88 figures. 408pp. 5⅜ x 8½. 21851-1

THE PHILOSOPHY OF HISTORY, Georg W. Hegel. Great classic of Western thought develops concept that history is not chance but rational process, the evolution of freedom. 457pp. 5⅜ x 8½. 20112-0

THE BOOK OF TEA, Kakuzo Okakura. Minor classic of the Orient: entertaining, charming explanation, interpretation of traditional Japanese culture in terms of tea ceremony. 94pp. 5⅜ x 8½. 20070-1

LIFE IN ANCIENT EGYPT, Adolf Erman. Fullest, most thorough, detailed older account with much not in more recent books, domestic life, religion, magic, medicine, commerce, much more. Many illustrations reproduce tomb paintings, carvings, hieroglyphs, etc. 597pp. 5⅜ x 8½. 22632-8

SUNDIALS, Their Theory and Construction, Albert Waugh. Far and away the best, most thorough coverage of ideas, mathematics concerned, types, construction, adjusting anywhere. Simple, nontechnical treatment allows even children to build several of these dials. Over 100 illustrations. 230pp. 5⅜ x 8½. 22947-5

THEORETICAL HYDRODYNAMICS, L. M. Milne-Thomson. Classic exposition of the mathematical theory of fluid motion, applicable to both hydrodynamics and aerodynamics. Over 600 exercises. 768pp. 6⅛ x 9¼. 68970-0

SONGS OF EXPERIENCE: Facsimile Reproduction with 26 Plates in Full Color, William Blake. 26 full-color plates from a rare 1826 edition. Includes "The Tyger," "London," "Holy Thursday," and other poems. Printed text of poems. 48pp. 5¼ x 7. 24636-1

OLD-TIME VIGNETTES IN FULL COLOR, Carol Belanger Grafton (ed.). Over 390 charming, often sentimental illustrations, selected from archives of Victorian graphics–pretty women posing, children playing, food, flowers, kittens and puppies, smiling cherubs, birds and butterflies, much more. All copyright-free. 48pp. 9¼ x 12¼. 27269-9

PIANO TUNING, J. Cree Fischer. Clearest, best book for beginner, amateur. Simple repairs, raising dropped notes, tuning by easy method of flattened fifths. No previous skills needed. 4 illustrations. 201pp. 5⅜ x 8½. 23267-0

HINTS TO SINGERS, Lillian Nordica. Selecting the right teacher, developing confidence, overcoming stage fright, and many other important skills receive thoughtful discussion in this indispensible guide, written by a world-famous diva of four decades' experience. 96pp. 5⅜ x 8½. 40094-8

THE COMPLETE NONSENSE OF EDWARD LEAR, Edward Lear. All nonsense limericks, zany alphabets, Owl and Pussycat, songs, nonsense botany, etc., illustrated by Lear. Total of 320pp. 5⅜ x 8½. (Available in U.S. only.) 20167-8

VICTORIAN PARLOUR POETRY: An Annotated Anthology, Michael R. Turner. 117 gems by Longfellow, Tennyson, Browning, many lesser-known poets. "The Village Blacksmith," "Curfew Must Not Ring Tonight," "Only a Baby Small," dozens more, often difficult to find elsewhere. Index of poets, titles, first lines. xxiii + 325pp. 5⅝ x 8¼. 27044-0

DUBLINERS, James Joyce. Fifteen stories offer vivid, tightly focused observations of the lives of Dublin's poorer classes. At least one, "The Dead," is considered a masterpiece. Reprinted complete and unabridged from standard edition. 160pp. 5$\frac{3}{16}$ x 8¼. 26870-5

GREAT WEIRD TALES: 14 Stories by Lovecraft, Blackwood, Machen and Others, S. T. Joshi (ed.). 14 spellbinding tales, including "The Sin Eater," by Fiona McLeod, "The Eye Above the Mantel," by Frank Belknap Long, as well as renowned works by R. H. Barlow, Lord Dunsany, Arthur Machen, W. C. Morrow and eight other masters of the genre. 256pp. 5⅜ x 8½. (Available in U.S. only.) 40436-6

THE BOOK OF THE SACRED MAGIC OF ABRAMELIN THE MAGE, translated by S. MacGregor Mathers. Medieval manuscript of ceremonial magic. Basic document in Aleister Crowley, Golden Dawn groups. 268pp. 5⅜ x 8½. 23211-5

NEW RUSSIAN-ENGLISH AND ENGLISH-RUSSIAN DICTIONARY, M. A. O'Brien. This is a remarkably handy Russian dictionary, containing a surprising amount of information, including over 70,000 entries. 366pp. 4½ x 6⅛. 20208-9

HISTORIC HOMES OF THE AMERICAN PRESIDENTS, Second, Revised Edition, Irvin Haas. A traveler's guide to American Presidential homes, most open to the public, depicting and describing homes occupied by every American President from George Washington to George Bush. With visiting hours, admission charges, travel routes. 175 photographs. Index. 160pp. 8¼ x 11. 26751-2

NEW YORK IN THE FORTIES, Andreas Feininger. 162 brilliant photographs by the well-known photographer, formerly with *Life* magazine. Commuters, shoppers, Times Square at night, much else from city at its peak. Captions by John von Hartz. 181pp. 9¼ x 10¾. 23585-8

INDIAN SIGN LANGUAGE, William Tomkins. Over 525 signs developed by Sioux and other tribes. Written instructions and diagrams. Also 290 pictographs. 111pp. 6⅛ x 9¼. 22029-X

PHOTOGRAPHIC SKETCHBOOK OF THE CIVIL WAR, Alexander Gardner. 100 photos taken on field during the Civil War. Famous shots of Manassas Harper's Ferry, Lincoln, Richmond, slave pens, etc. 244pp. 10⅝ x 8¼. 22731-6

FIVE ACRES AND INDEPENDENCE, Maurice G. Kains. Great back-to-the-land classic explains basics of self-sufficient farming. The one book to get. 95 illustrations. 397pp. 5⅜ x 8½. 20974-1

SONGS OF EASTERN BIRDS, Dr. Donald J. Borror. Songs and calls of 60 species most common to eastern U.S.: warblers, woodpeckers, flycatchers, thrushes, larks, many more in high-quality recording. Cassette and manual 99912-2

A MODERN HERBAL, Margaret Grieve. Much the fullest, most exact, most useful compilation of herbal material. Gigantic alphabetical encyclopedia, from aconite to zedoary, gives botanical information, medical properties, folklore, economic uses, much else. Indispensable to serious reader. 161 illustrations. 888pp. 6½ x 9¼. 2-vol. set. (Available in U.S. only.) Vol. I: 22798-7
Vol. II: 22799-5

HIDDEN TREASURE MAZE BOOK, Dave Phillips. Solve 34 challenging mazes accompanied by heroic tales of adventure. Evil dragons, people-eating plants, bloodthirsty giants, many more dangerous adversaries lurk at every twist and turn. 34 mazes, stories, solutions. 48pp. 8¼ x 11. 24566-7

LETTERS OF W. A. MOZART, Wolfgang A. Mozart. Remarkable letters show bawdy wit, humor, imagination, musical insights, contemporary musical world; includes some letters from Leopold Mozart. 276pp. 5⅜ x 8½. 22859-2

BASIC PRINCIPLES OF CLASSICAL BALLET, Agrippina Vaganova. Great Russian theoretician, teacher explains methods for teaching classical ballet. 118 illustrations. 175pp. 5⅜ x 8½. 22036-2

THE JUMPING FROG, Mark Twain. Revenge edition. The original story of The Celebrated Jumping Frog of Calaveras County, a hapless French translation, and Twain's hilarious "retranslation" from the French. 12 illustrations. 66pp. 5⅜ x 8½. 22686-7

BEST REMEMBERED POEMS, Martin Gardner (ed.). The 126 poems in this superb collection of 19th- and 20th-century British and American verse range from Shelley's "To a Skylark" to the impassioned "Renascence" of Edna St. Vincent Millay and to Edward Lear's whimsical "The Owl and the Pussycat." 224pp. 5⅜ x 8½. 27165-X

COMPLETE SONNETS, William Shakespeare. Over 150 exquisite poems deal with love, friendship, the tyranny of time, beauty's evanescence, death and other themes in language of remarkable power, precision and beauty. Glossary of archaic terms. 80pp. 5 3/16 x 8¼. 26686-9

THE BATTLES THAT CHANGED HISTORY, Fletcher Pratt. Eminent historian profiles 16 crucial conflicts, ancient to modern, that changed the course of civilization. 352pp. 5⅜ x 8½. 41129-X

THE WIT AND HUMOR OF OSCAR WILDE, Alvin Redman (ed.). More than 1,000 ripostes, paradoxes, wisecracks: Work is the curse of the drinking classes; I can resist everything except temptation; etc. 258pp. 5⅜ x 8½. 20602-5

SHAKESPEARE LEXICON AND QUOTATION DICTIONARY, Alexander Schmidt. Full definitions, locations, shades of meaning in every word in plays and poems. More than 50,000 exact quotations. 1,485pp. 6½ x 9¼. 2-vol. set.
Vol. 1: 22726-X
Vol. 2: 22727-8

SELECTED POEMS, Emily Dickinson. Over 100 best-known, best-loved poems by one of America's foremost poets, reprinted from authoritative early editions. No comparable edition at this price. Index of first lines. 64pp. 5$\frac{3}{16}$ x 8¼. 26466-1

THE INSIDIOUS DR. FU-MANCHU, Sax Rohmer. The first of the popular mystery series introduces a pair of English detectives to their archnemesis, the diabolical Dr. Fu-Manchu. Flavorful atmosphere, fast-paced action, and colorful characters enliven this classic of the genre. 208pp. 5$\frac{3}{16}$ x 8¼. 29898-1

THE MALLEUS MALEFICARUM OF KRAMER AND SPRENGER, translated by Montague Summers. Full text of most important witchhunter's "bible," used by both Catholics and Protestants. 278pp. 6⅝ x 10. 22802-9

SPANISH STORIES/CUENTOS ESPAÑOLES: A Dual-Language Book, Angel Flores (ed.). Unique format offers 13 great stories in Spanish by Cervantes, Borges, others. Faithful English translations on facing pages. 352pp. 5⅜ x 8½. 25399-6

GARDEN CITY, LONG ISLAND, IN EARLY PHOTOGRAPHS, 1869–1919, Mildred H. Smith. Handsome treasury of 118 vintage pictures, accompanied by carefully researched captions, document the Garden City Hotel fire (1899), the Vanderbilt Cup Race (1908), the first airmail flight departing from the Nassau Boulevard Aerodrome (1911), and much more. 96pp. 8⅞ x 11¾. 40669-5

OLD QUEENS, N.Y., IN EARLY PHOTOGRAPHS, Vincent F. Seyfried and William Asadorian. Over 160 rare photographs of Maspeth, Jamaica, Jackson Heights, and other areas. Vintage views of DeWitt Clinton mansion, 1939 World's Fair and more. Captions. 192pp. 8⅞ x 11. 26358-4

CAPTURED BY THE INDIANS: 15 Firsthand Accounts, 1750-1870, Frederick Drimmer. Astounding true historical accounts of grisly torture, bloody conflicts, relentless pursuits, miraculous escapes and more, by people who lived to tell the tale. 384pp. 5⅜ x 8½. 24901-8

THE WORLD'S GREAT SPEECHES (Fourth Enlarged Edition), Lewis Copeland, Lawrence W. Lamm, and Stephen J. McKenna. Nearly 300 speeches provide public speakers with a wealth of updated quotes and inspiration–from Pericles' funeral oration and William Jennings Bryan's "Cross of Gold Speech" to Malcolm X's powerful words on the Black Revolution and Earl of Spenser's tribute to his sister, Diana, Princess of Wales. 944pp. 5⅜ x 8⅜. 40903-1

THE BOOK OF THE SWORD, Sir Richard F. Burton. Great Victorian scholar/adventurer's eloquent, erudite history of the "queen of weapons"–from prehistory to early Roman Empire. Evolution and development of early swords, variations (sabre, broadsword, cutlass, scimitar, etc.), much more. 336pp. 6⅛ x 9¼. 25434-8

AUTOBIOGRAPHY: The Story of My Experiments with Truth, Mohandas K. Gandhi. Boyhood, legal studies, purification, the growth of the Satyagraha (nonviolent protest) movement. Critical, inspiring work of the man responsible for the freedom of India. 480pp. 5⅜ x 8½. (Available in U.S. only.) 24593-4

CELTIC MYTHS AND LEGENDS, T. W. Rolleston. Masterful retelling of Irish and Welsh stories and tales. Cuchulain, King Arthur, Deirdre, the Grail, many more. First paperback edition. 58 full-page illustrations. 512pp. 5⅜ x 8½. 26507-2

THE PRINCIPLES OF PSYCHOLOGY, William James. Famous long course complete, unabridged. Stream of thought, time perception, memory, experimental methods; great work decades ahead of its time. 94 figures. 1,391pp. 5⅜ x 8½. 2-vol. set. Vol. I: 20381-6 Vol. II: 20382-4

THE WORLD AS WILL AND REPRESENTATION, Arthur Schopenhauer. Definitive English translation of Schopenhauer's life work, correcting more than 1,000 errors, omissions in earlier translations. Translated by E. F. J. Payne. Total of 1,269pp. 5⅜ x 8½. 2-vol. set. Vol. 1: 21761-2 Vol. 2: 21762-0

MAGIC AND MYSTERY IN TIBET, Madame Alexandra David-Neel. Experiences among lamas, magicians, sages, sorcerers, Bonpa wizards. A true psychic discovery. 32 illustrations. 321pp. 5⅜ x 8½. (Available in U.S. only.) 22682-4

THE EGYPTIAN BOOK OF THE DEAD, E. A. Wallis Budge. Complete reproduction of Ani's papyrus, finest ever found. Full hieroglyphic text, interlinear transliteration, word-for-word translation, smooth translation. 533pp. 6½ x 9¼. 21866-X

MATHEMATICS FOR THE NONMATHEMATICIAN, Morris Kline. Detailed, college-level treatment of mathematics in cultural and historical context, with numerous exercises. Recommended Reading Lists. Tables. Numerous figures. 641pp. 5⅜ x 8½. 24823-2

PROBABILISTIC METHODS IN THE THEORY OF STRUCTURES, Isaac Elishakoff. Well-written introduction covers the elements of the theory of probability from two or more random variables, the reliability of such multivariable structures, the theory of random function, Monte Carlo methods of treating problems incapable of exact solution, and more. Examples. 502pp. 5⅜ x 8½. 40691-1

THE RIME OF THE ANCIENT MARINER, Gustave Doré, S. T. Coleridge. Doré's finest work; 34 plates capture moods, subtleties of poem. Flawless full-size reproductions printed on facing pages with authoritative text of poem. "Beautiful. Simply beautiful."–*Publisher's Weekly.* 77pp. 9¼ x 12. 22305-1

NORTH AMERICAN INDIAN DESIGNS FOR ARTISTS AND CRAFTSPEOPLE, Eva Wilson. Over 360 authentic copyright-free designs adapted from Navajo blankets, Hopi pottery, Sioux buffalo hides, more. Geometrics, symbolic figures, plant and animal motifs, etc. 128pp. 8⅜ x 11. (Not for sale in the United Kingdom.) 25341-4

SCULPTURE: Principles and Practice, Louis Slobodkin. Step-by-step approach to clay, plaster, metals, stone; classical and modern. 253 drawings, photos. 255pp. 8⅛ x 11. 22960-2

THE INFLUENCE OF SEA POWER UPON HISTORY, 1660–1783, A. T. Mahan. Influential classic of naval history and tactics still used as text in war colleges. First paperback edition. 4 maps. 24 battle plans. 640pp. 5⅜ x 8½. 25509-3